Dacha Idylls

Dacha Idylls

Living Organically in Russia's Countryside

Melissa L. Caldwell

UNIVERSITY OF CALIFORNIA PRESS

Berkeley · Los Angeles · London

University of California Press, one of the most distinguished university presses in the United States,
enriches lives around the world by advancing scholarship in the humanities, social sciences, and natural
sciences. Its activities are supported by the UC Press
Foundation and by philanthropic contributions from
individuals and institutions. For more information,
visit www.ucpress.edu.

University of California Press
Berkeley and Los Angeles, California

University of California Press, Ltd.
London, England

© 2011 by The Regents of the University of California

Library of Congress Cataloging-in-Publication Data

Caldwell, Melissa L., 1969–.
    Dacha idylls : living organically in Russia's countryside /
Melissa L. Caldwell.
        p.   cm.
    Includes bibliographical references and index.
    ISBN 978-0-520-26284-3 (cloth : alk. paper)
    ISBN 978-0-520-26285-0 (pbk. : alk. paper)
    1. Country homes—Russia (Federation).   2. Vacation
homes—Russia (Federation).   3. Organic living—Russia
(Federation).   4. Gardening—Russia (Federation).
5. Russia (Federation)—Social life and customs.   I. Title.
    DK32.C27 2011
    643'.250947—dc22   2010003233

Manufactured in the United States of America

19   18   17   16   15   14   13   12   11
10   9   8   7   6   5   4   3   2   1

This book is printed on Cascades Enviro 100, a 100%
post consumer waste, recycled, de-inked fiber. FSC
recycled certified and processed chlorine free. It is
acid free, Ecologo certified, and manufactured by
BioGas energy.

For my parents, Bill and Sandy Caldwell,
mushroom hunters extraordinaire

Contents

Illustrations

Note on Transliteration
and Pronunciation

I have followed the U.S. Library of Congress system of transliteration in this book, except in cases where alternate spellings have become more familiar to North American readers (for instance, *Anya* instead of *Ania* and *banya* instead of *bania*). The word *dacha* is pronounced with a soft /ch/ sound, as in *church,* and the stress is on the first syllable. The words *dachnik* and *dachniki* are similarly pronounced with the stress on the first syllable.

Preface

Finally we tired [of walking along the river], and we decided to
depart from the river along the path to the right. Near to the
right on a rounded hillock, thicketed with oaks, led a little path.
We walked along it and in half an hour we were surrounded by
an old-growth pine forest. It was silent and quiet in the forest.
There, so very high, where the bright green of the pine crowns
were stretching out to the bright whiteness of the clouds, perhaps, and where the breezes roamed, it was absolutely quiet.

—Vladimir Soloukhin, "Vladimirovskii By-Ways" (Soloukhin 2006:15)

In fall 1998, as I was concluding a year of fieldwork in Moscow, my parents
came for a visit. My apartment was located in a small Khrushchev-era
apartment block in Fili, a leafy and quiet residential district on the western
edge of the city center. Just a few minutes' walk from my apartment was
Filevskii Park, one of the largest forested parks in Moscow. During my
parents' visit we often spent our afternoons and evenings walking through
the peaceful park, joined by many other residents from the neighborhood.
Despite its location near the center of a sprawling postindustrial megalopo-
lis of approximately twelve million residents, Filevskii Park is a surprisingly quiet and cool oasis. Like many of the forested parks and nature
reserves in the Moscow area, Filevskii Park is heavily wooded with thick
vegetation covering the ground. Visibility is so limited on the narrow paths
that twist and turn through the trees that it is frequently impossible to see
more than twenty feet ahead. Even on the sunniest and hottest days, the
forest is dark and cool.

There is a peculiar Brigadoon-like quality to Filevskii Park, as people,
dogs, sounds, and smells suddenly appear and disappear out of the leafy
thickets, even in winter. Pedestrians stroll through the serpentine maze
of the forest, confronted at random turns by the emergence out of noth-

ingness of the unexpected: a bus depot, slides and swings at a children's playground, a Ferris wheel and merry-go-round in a small carnival venue, a bandstand, picnic tables, summer cafés, people sprawled on blankets and benches to take a nap or read, small groups of families and friends gathered around a campfire and singing to the accompaniment of a guitar, and mothers and grandmothers aimlessly pushing baby strollers through the woods. As soon as one turns another corner or goes behind another tree, the signs of human habitation and entertainment quickly disappear into the greenness of the forest. Above all, the forest of Filevskii Park is marked by a feeling of aloneness among the trees. The sounds of the nearby streets and apartment blocks fade away, and a profound stillness emerges. All that can be heard are twittering birds, an occasional dog bark, and, once in a while, disembodied laughter floating through the trees.

On this particular occasion, a late Sunday afternoon in early September, my parents and I were strolling slowly and enjoying the calm. Suddenly we emerged in a small clearing in the woods, and, without any warning, we found ourselves face to face with three other forest wanderers: an elderly man playing an accordion and two elderly women dancing merrily on either side of him. The musicians greeted us, laughing, and then continued past us, dancing down the path until they were swallowed up by the forest and disappeared from view. My parents and I continued our meandering walk and eventually returned to the park's main entrance, where we discovered that the accordion player and his companions had attracted a small crowd. Both the young and the old had gathered to listen to the music and to dance, singly, in couples, and in small groups. Men with women, women with women, grandparents with grandchildren—all were singing, dancing, talking, and laughing in this festive, seemingly spontaneous social gathering. Young adults hovered on the fringes, enjoying a beer or ice cream while they watched and participated in their own way. Small children chased each other around the baby carriages and their elders. Other individuals wandered through, stopping for a few moments to enjoy the festivities before continuing on their way.

We, too, were drawn into the magic of the moment, taking pleasure in the music and one another's company and delighting in the festive warmth of the early autumn evening. We stayed there for a while—how long, I no longer remember, although I do remember feeling as if time had somehow receded into the background—before continuing our wanders. As we followed the path back into the trees, the music and laughter disappeared behind us. After a few steps it was not clear who had been swallowed up by the forest: the dancers and musicians or us.

Fast-forward seven years to a Saturday evening in September 2005. I was back in Moscow on my way home from fieldwork and had met up with one of my students from California, newly arrived in Russia for a study-abroad program. My student had not yet experienced a Russian forest, so I took him to Filevskii Park for *shashlyk* (shish kebabs). As we ventured into the greenery, at first it seemed as if the park were unchanged, although further inside along the main path we discovered two new outdoor cafés serving beer and *shashlyk*. We strolled leisurely through the park, making our way past in-line skaters and stroller-pushers down the steep hill to walk along the riverbank and join the sunbathers and swimmers who were enjoying the refreshing water and sunset. When we eventually returned to the park's entrance, we discovered an accordion player and two dancers on the main path, surrounded by a crowd of people of all ages. There was no way of knowing if this was the same trio that my parents and I had encountered seven years previously, but the setting was identical: a large crowd of people gathered to dance, talk, laugh, and socialize.

Once again, the forest had provided the setting for a magical evening of pleasure.

. . .

Such experiences are no doubt recognizable to anyone who has spent time in Russia, particularly during the summer and autumn. Even for those who have never visited Russia, these experiences come powerfully to life in Russian literature from the past several centuries. Thus, if an ethnographer could risk making a generalization about Russia, it would be that nature is an essential part of Russian life and perhaps that a deep, abiding, even spiritual appreciation of nature is a fundamental quality of Russianness itself. My objective with this book is to capture the magical, mystical, and pleasurable qualities that constitute Russians' engagement with nature. In particular, I am interested in how these engagements with nature generate a particular philosophy about meaningful living and where a meaningful life can best be found. To that end, we will journey into what is perhaps the heart of this natural world—the *dacha*, or summer cottage.

Before beginning this inquiry into Russians' relationships with dachas and nature, I first offer a disclaimer about my own interest in this subject. From an academic perspective, it is a topic I have been cultivating since I began fieldwork in Russia in 1995. Even while working on other projects, I have continued to conduct participant observation (even if inadvertently at times) on dachas and natural spaces. This is also a topic that is very meaningful to me on a personal level. Every time that I have sat down to write about Russian dachas and nature or talked about them with informants, colleagues, students, and family members, I have felt a rush of excitement and satisfaction that is matched only by the excitement of my interlocutors. It has been a deeply satisfying and pleasurable experience to work through these materials. Every time that I have visited someone's dacha—whether during the actual moment of the encounter or later, as I worked through my field notes and memories—I have experienced a sense of joy and relaxation. It is a magical experience, but it is also a fleeting one, much like the mythical Brigadoon that appears for a moment in all its glory and then disappears. It is my hope that I can convey just a small part of this enchantment in the pages that follow.

My first dachalike experience was not, in fact, in Russia, but in Finnish Karelia during the mid-1980s. The occasion was a visit with my Girl Scout pen pal, who came from a Karelian family that had been displaced westward into Finland during Finland's 1939–40 Winter War with the Soviet Union. My pen pal's family owned a summer cottage, and they took me there several times during my short stay to enjoy the *sauna* (it was actually a Russian-style *banya* and not a Finnish-style dry sauna, although I did not realize that until much later) and the fresh air. Those trips to their cottage were marked by lazy afternoons in the shade, long picnics and baths in the sauna, and swimming in the coldest water I have ever felt. Although I was an avid camper and had spent a considerable amount of time in the woods, I was unprepared for the experience of life at the cottage. In short, there was something not only refreshing but also deeply sensuous about sitting in the shade under the trees, napping on cots in the cottage's loft, snacking on fresh fruits and vegetables, and talking with my new family. The summer seemed endless, and my life as a high school student seemed a world apart. After I returned to the United States, that experience stayed with me—or perhaps it would be more accurate to say that it haunted me. Hints of life at the cottage teased me, waiting at the edges of my memories. Even hikes and camping trips in the beautiful Smoky Mountains of my childhood could not elicit the feelings of deep joy and satisfaction that I remembered from my Finnish cottage experience.

My second summer cottage experience was in the early 1990s, in Wisconsin, where I worked as a camp counselor. Despite the romantic notions many of us have about summer camp based our own experiences as campers, the reality of being a counselor is quite different. In short, living in the woods and arranging an authentically natural experience for adolescents is exhausting. To recuperate, I spent my twenty-four-hour weekend leaves with my aunt, uncle, and two cousins in a nearby city in central Wisconsin.

One weekend, the family of my aunt's sister-in-law invited us to their cottage on a lake in northern Wisconsin. I did not know anybody there except for my four relatives; my uncle and cousins knew only a few other people as well. Yet as soon as we arrived, it was just like Finland: we were all "family" as we ate and drank around the table, played cards, talked, and frolicked in the frigid lake. My exhaustion was gone, replaced by the magic of the moment and the feeling of being part of something larger than myself. Then, all too quickly, the weekend ended, and I was back to the drudgery of everyday life and summer employment. Even today, however, I can still conjure up visceral memories of that weekend.

The magic reemerged several years later, when I made my first trip to Russia in 1995. In two short months my landlady managed to provide me with three dacha experiences. The first was a weeklong trip to stay with her best friend at the friend's dacha several hours outside Moscow. We spent long hours picking raspberries in the forests, and even longer nights processing them into preserves to take back home with us on the train. In the afternoons we went mushroom picking and lounged in the backyard, reading. Evenings were spent lingering over simple meals made with fresh herbs, boiled potatoes, and pots of fresh raspberry jam. One night we went to visit some friends of my hostess at their dacha on the other side of the forest. We stayed until early in the morning, eating, drinking, singing, and laughing. Despite the long hours and the hard work, I felt exhilarated. This feeling was repeated during our two subsequent dacha trips to visit other family members and to attend a birthday party.

Although I was not able to articulate it at the time, it was clear to me that there was something fascinating and compelling about cottage life. It was time out of time, a world apart from ordinary life. It was a place of hard work, but also a place of refreshment and recuperation. It was natural. When my parents visited me in Russia and went on a mushroom hunt with some friends, they, too, were captivated, as were other relatives who sat through the many stories and pictures that I brought home with me. Among the many avid North American and Western European cottagers, gardeners, and nature enthusiasts I have met over the years, there is an instant sense of familiarity with Russians' dacha culture, signaling a universal appeal and recognition.

But perhaps more important is the fact that it is not only non-Russians like my American relatives and friends who find Russia's dacha life so thrilling, enticing, and fascinating. As will become clear in what follows, conversations with Russian colleagues, friends, and complete strangers reveal that same sense of excitement associated with the mystical specialness of a natural life. All it takes is a single question or comment about dacha life to spark a lively and passionate discussion, as I have verified during many a taxi ride upon my arrival at one of Moscow's airports.

Although these experiences planted the seeds of this book, it was not until I was back in the United States that I began to consider that the dacha experience could be treated as a serious topic and to think about how it could be linked to social analysis outside the postsocialist framework. This realization came about through conversations with my family back home. My husband's family, for example, owns a summer cottage on a lake in New Hampshire. As people who had built their cottage themselves and had always planted a summer garden (fresh peas and New Englanders seem to go hand in hand), they had questions for me about what dacha life was like. Through my summer weekends at our family cottage, and my in-laws' belief that their cottage and plot of land in the woods was sacred, I came to see that there was something to the dacha project. And, with their encouragement, I continued the project that culminated in this book.

This research has benefited from the assistance and support of many people in both the United States and Russia. It could not, in fact, have been written without their help and encouragement. Given the enormous number of people who have contributed to this project, both directly and indirectly, I cannot thank each of them individually, although they know who they are. But I would like to recognize those whose assistance went above and beyond the call of duty.

For taking me on dacha trips and forest frolics, and for feeding me vast quantities of ecologically clean foods, I thank Oktiabrina Cheremovskaia, Valentina and Iura Gribov, Valentina Osipova, Lena, Sergei, Zoia, Vera, and Elena and her family. This book could not have been written without the help of the glorious Tver dachniki who have for several years welcomed me into their homes and their dachas. I am especially grateful to the residents of Nadezhda, as well as their visiting friends and relatives, who eagerly discussed dacha life with me and allowed me to live in their midst for a summer. I hope that this book is capable of expressing some small bit of the tremendous joy and delight that they so obviously experience at their dachas.

In summer 2005 my fieldwork was greatly enhanced by Valentina Uspenskaia and her husband Grigorii, who listened to me ramble about this project for many years and then opened doors to the local Tver dachniki community. Lena has also been an inspiration for this project, both for her knowledge about dachas, forests, and the natural life, but even more so for her passion for it all. I could not ask for three better colleagues and friends.

Lastly, this book would not exist were it not for the generosity of one amazing family: Anna and Dima Borodin, Anna's parents Tamara and Vladimir Cherkassov, Anna's aunt Liudmila Cherkassova, and my god-cats. They took me in not as a visiting anthropologist and friend, but as family. Their encouragement, suggestions, generosity in locating inter-viewees, and willingness to turn their dacha into "command central" for my research allowed me to develop the larger project in ways that I never anticipated. Perhaps more importantly, by taking me in as family, they gave me the gift of experiencing dacha life as an insider. I can never thank them enough or repay them for their many, many kindnesses.

Anna also performed heroic feats by helping as a research assistant. She set up appointments, handled navigation duties on our dacha visits, and even transcribed all of my interview tapes. She and Dima also talked through many ideas with me and helped me formulate questions and tenta-tive conclusions. I am blessed to have such great colleagues as friends.

Other colleagues have contributed in myriad ways to this project. Rubie Watson was perhaps the first person to recognize that this dacha project had merit, and she has been pushing me to complete it for many years. I am grateful for her support and her ability always to zero in on the most important issues. I would especially like to thank Don Brenneis and Andrew Mathews, who read a draft of the manuscript almost in its entirety, and Heath Cabot and Jarrett Zigon, who read the final draft. Many other friends and colleagues read and discussed parts of the manu-script at various stages of development. I would like to thank Michael Herzfeld and Woody Watson, who read an early version of this work and made suggestions for developing the fieldwork and analysis. Other friends and colleagues who have generously offered helpful comments on more recent incarnations of this project include Alie Alkon, Danielle Berman, Charlotte Biltekoff, Zach Bowden, Nancy Chen, Jim Clifford, Carolyn de la Peña, Melanie DuPuis, Shelly Errington, Bill Friedland, Susan Gillman, Julie Guthman, Otto Habeck, Donna Haraway, Gail Hershatter, Yuson Jung, Tobias Köllner, Dan Linger, Fuji Lozada, Carolyn Martin Shaw, Kimberly Nettles, Triloki Pandey, Vanita Seth, Bettina Stoetzer, Anna Tsing, Megan Thomas, Mike Urban, and Michael Ziser. I have also ben-efited from the comments and suggestions of participants in numerous forums where I have presented this work, and I would like to thank the stu-dents and faculty at Davidson College, my fellow foodies in the University of California Food and the Body Multicampus Research Group, the mem-bers of the UCSC Agroecology Working Group, and participants in the UCSC Cultural Studies colloquia series. I am grateful to Carol Vesecky and her agricultural colleagues in Russia for their time and for allowing me to tag along on a biointensive farming tour.

Several sections of this book were written during research visits to the Max Planck Institute for Social Anthropology in Halle, Germany. I owe a special debt of gratitude to the institute's director, Chris Hann, for hosting me as a visiting scholar at the MPI and for introducing me to the institute's tremendous resources, most notably a wonderful community of scholars in the Socialist and Postsocialist Eurasia Research Group and the Siberian Studies Centre. Friends and colleagues at the MPI contributed immensely to the development of this project by kindly talking through many ideas with me and by sharing their own experiences. Additional thanks to Bettina Mann, Anke Meyer, Berit Westwood, Ingrid Schüller, and Manuela Pusch for their behind-the-scenes work to arrange my visits, and to librarian Anja Neuner for guiding me through the MPI's extensive library collections.

An earlier version of chapter 4 appeared as "Feeding the Body and Nourishing the Soul: Natural Foods in Postsocialist Russia" in *Food, Culture & Society* (Spring 2007, vol. 10, no. 1, pp. 43–71), published by Berg Publishers, an imprint of A&C Black Publishers Ltd. I am grateful to *FCS* and Berg Publishers for allowing me to reprint this material. I also thank *FCS* editor Warren Belasco, Jane Zavisca, and an anonymous reviewer for their excellent feedback, much of which made its way beyond that chapter and into other sections of this book.

I am always humbled by the superhuman abilities of librarians who can, seemingly effortlessly, pull rabbits out of hats. That professional trait was exceedingly valuable in the later stages of this book as I attempted to track down Russian- and English-language versions of several short stories and plays by Anton Chekhov and Maxim Gorky. Despite the fact that these writings are frequently discussed in the literature on dachas and nature, and that my informants frequently discussed them and encouraged me to read them for myself, these texts are exceptionally difficult to find. A dedicated group of librarians worked their magic to locate copies for me. For their assistance, I am especially grateful to Laura McClanathan and Sheri Kurisu of the McHenry Library at UCSC, to Jan Adamczyk of the University of Illinois Library's Slavic Reference Service, and to Kristin Caldwell Peto at the Scarborough Public Library in Scarborough, Maine. I would also like to express my special gratitude to Stanford University, which made available to me an extremely old and rare copy of Gorky's *Dachniki* in the original Russian.

Because this project spans more than ten years, funding for it has come from a variety of sources: the U.S. Department of Education (Title VI); the Mellon Foundation; and the Kathryn W. and Shelby Cullom Davis Center for Russian States, the Department of Anthropology, and the Committee on Degrees in Social Studies, all at Harvard University. The University of California, Santa Cruz provided additional financial and administrative support, including a Social Sciences Divisional Summer Research Grant. I am especially grateful to my chair, Judith Habicht-Mauche, for arranging a course relief so that I could write a first draft of this manuscript.

I have been privileged to work yet again with the University of California Press. Stan Holwitz first recognized and encouraged this project. I am grateful to him for his support and for bringing this book to the press, and I am honored that I was able to work with him again before his much-deserved retirement. I have been delighted to work with Sheila Levine as this project has gone into its final stages of publication and am looking forward to future projects with her. Special thanks to Nick Arrivo, Kate Marshall, and Kalicia Pivirotto, who have shepherded this book at various stages of the process. I am especially grateful to Marilyn Schwartz, who has overseen the production process and responded to my many queries, and to Sharron Wood, who did a terrific job with the copyediting. Reviewers Cathy Wanner, Pam Ballinger, and Caroline Ford offered helpful suggestions for tightening the analysis and enhancing the ethnography. Any remaining shortcomings in this book are mine. All photographs in this book are mine.

Lastly, none of this would have been possible, or perhaps even necessary, without the encouragement, curiosity, love, and support of friends and family. They have been with me every step of the way and have consistently asked the right questions to jog my tired brain or let me know that this project was worthwhile. Thanks to Kristin, Joe, and Arwen Peto; Pat and Cliff Baker; Jan and Bob Trevor; and Fran Teeter. Andy, Pico, and Duke, my partners in crime, deserve special recognition for their endless good humor while enduring the encroachment of this project in our home. Andy has also endured more than his fair share of chapter drafts, photo-editing sessions, and being the stay-at-home partner during my frequent fieldwork absences. Finally, I am grateful to my parents, Bill and Sandy Caldwell, who have perhaps been even keener than I have to see how this project turns out. My hope is that this book reminds them of their trip to Russia and the wonderful times we spent walking in the woods, eating *shashlyk,* and picking mushrooms.

CHAPTER I

Dacha Enchantments

The city is always a stress . . . But with nature, it is like you have
gone to another planet.

—Irina, sixties, Berezka (Birch Tree) dacha community

Here [at the dacha] it is a piece of a different life. It is impossible
to compare this life with the life you live the rest of the year.

—Veronika, fifties, Iablochnyi Sad (Apple Orchard) dacha community

The dacha is, in general, a place of refuge from the usual problems.

—Mila, thirties, Nadezhda (Hope) dacha cooperative

In summer, it may appear that all of Russia has gone on vacation. The
bustle and noise of daily life in towns and cities noticeably ease with the
departure of residents to public parks, summer camps, cottage communities, and tourist destinations elsewhere. The pace of life slows down as
people meander aimlessly through the dense thickets of parks and forests,
nap on blankets spread along riverbanks, or read while absently pushing baby carriages containing contentedly sleeping infants through city
parks. Formal business attire gives way to gently faded and patched work
clothes and bathing suits. Businesses reduce services, or sometimes close
their facilities altogether, for several weeks to accommodate the absences
of their employees. Lines shorten in banks, post offices, and grocery stores
in the aftermath of the mass exodus of urbanites who have crammed into
packed buses, trains, and cars to head out of town. The only shops and
restaurants that seem to attract a lively, or even increased, business are cottage and garden supply stores selling lawn equipment, patio furniture, and
seeds and garden supplies, and outdoor cafés offering cold beer, *shashlyk*
(shish kebabs), and snacks. Conversations among relatives, friends, co-

workers, and strangers alike focus on holiday plans, as people exchange tips on the best sites for sunbathing, the trains likely to be less crowded, and new recipes for garden-fresh produce.

Russians' appreciation for summertime pursuits reflects a serious sense of purpose that requires careful attention throughout the year. In the depths of winter Russians are already thinking ahead to summer as they consult almanacs to determine the optimal time to schedule their time off and plant their gardens. Before the snow has melted, seedlings are pushing up in containers on kitchen windowsills, waiting to be replanted in gardens as soon as the ground is soft. Families savor the dwindling supply of pickles, preserves, and dried mushrooms from last year's harvest and wax romantic about the coming year's yield. Travelers consult tour books and make budgets to set aside sufficient funds for a holiday trip. Travel agencies fill public spaces and stuff private mailboxes with glossy advertisements and hire young women to stand outside metro stations and distribute brochures. Stores selling home and outdoor goods expand their selections with the latest in travel clothing, sporting gear, fishing and hunting supplies, lawn furniture, and outdoor grilling equipment. Bookstores set aside ever larger sections to accommodate the rapidly growing selection of books, magazines, newspapers, and other media devoted to every aspect of summer life imaginable: travel guides; publications on hunting, fishing, hiking, and bicycling, as well as more exotic "adventure sports"; guides to cottage design, repair, and decoration; books on gardening and flower arranging; and cookbooks for garden foods.

Among the multitude of possible leisure pursuits, one activity stands out as perhaps the most recognizable aspect of Russian summer culture: visiting the dacha, or summer cottage. Simultaneously beloved and reviled, dachas possess an undeniable and curious power that compels Russians of all classes and generations and from all parts of the country to leave the comfort of their homes, sit (or stand) for hours while packed in overcrowded and overheated buses and trains or trapped in their cars in the gridlock that surrounds large cities and small towns alike, and then devote themselves to even longer hours engaged in the exhausting manual labors of gardening and home repairs, all while swatting incessant mosquitoes and flies, dragging buckets of water from a well, and availing themselves of pit latrines. Dachas are not simply a prime destination for summertime, however; for many they are the only conceivable destination, a sentiment captured in the comments of Mila, a professional in her early thirties: "As soon as dacha season approaches, people start longing for it. The only thing that interests them is the dacha. No longer do other people's problems interest them."

For Russians, dachas belong to a world distanced from ordinary life, a sentiment captured in the phrases "another planet," "refuge," and "a piece of a different life" that appear in the epigraphs to this chapter. This sense of a world apart is reinforced both visually and viscerally. The here-and-now urban reality of anonymous crowds, massive blocks of generic apartment buildings, and ever-present dust and pollution contrast sharply with the quiet coolness of endless green forests, the fairy-tale qualities evoked by gingerbread-style cottage decorations, and the drowsy laziness brought on by the summer heat. The value of the dacha as refuge evinces powerful qualities of a self-indulgent privacy, a sensibility underscored by the rest of Mila's comments: "Even though during the depths of the winter season everyone is living with other people's problems, in the summer they live only with the problems of their own dachas."

The enchanting qualities associated with dachas can be deceptive, however, as accounts of peaceful solitude disguise the more mundane, and even irritating, realities of this world. Mila's idyllic depiction of dacha life is a case in point: the dacha she describes as a "refuge" is in fact a two-room bare-bones cottage and tiny garden plot sandwiched among a cluster of older, more substantial cottages and gardens. To access the garden and the front door, she and her husband must walk through the yards of their neighbors. Irina's comments about the stress-free, otherworldly natural setting in which her dacha is located similarly obscure the reality that her cottage is located only a few hundred meters from a busy railway line and thus constantly in full view of train travelers. Antonina, like several other devout dacha enthusiasts, eventually confessed her secret relief at having sold her dacha, thereby ridding herself of the nuisance of keeping up with her garden and visits from friends. More than one acquaintance has also planned a vacation abroad with the specific purpose of recovering from their time at the dacha. Such attitudes illustrate the fundamentally paradoxical nature of dachas. Even as dachas are valued for the leisure and pleasure associated with them, they also require hard work and dedication in terms of time, energy, and labor. As friends and acquaintances emphasized repeatedly, dacha life is exhausting and frequently downright unpleasant. Yet complaints about the difficulties of dacha life are not enough to dissuade Russians from heading to their dachas or, more intriguingly, from voicing their beliefs that the dacha life is relaxing, pleasurable, and desirable.

An account of contemporary dacha living, this book ponders what makes this lifestyle so meaningful and appealing and why Russians claim to feel such a strong affinity for their dachas, even as they grumble about the aches and pains that result from gardening and the annoyances of hosting a seemingly endless stream of visitors. The dacha world in all its richness and complexity symbolizes and encapsulates a meaningful life—a "good life"—that draws inspiration from and plays out through the natural environment in which it is situated. This ideal "good life" stimulates the senses, animates the imagination, and affirms feelings of belonging to a community of people who share a similar set of experiences and sensibilities. At the same time, this "good life" is not relegated to the peripheries of Russian social life as might be imagined with leisure activities, but instead extends into the most ordinary and fundamental parts of Russians' everyday worlds.

Even though the types of activities that occupy Russians at their dachas—hiking, swimming, napping, picnicking, mushroom and berry picking, and visiting with friends—closely resemble the activities that engage cottagers elsewhere in Europe (Bren 2002; Hervouet 2007; Löfgren 1987),[1] Russians such as those described in this book are quick to insist on the distinctiveness of the Russian dacha phenomenon. These claims of cultural exceptionalism coincide with a protectionist ethos according to which the less savory aspects of dacha life become the shared secret of "insiders" who can collectively poke fun at them while shielding them from the less empathetic gaze of "outsiders." These exceptionalist and protectionist orientations derive from a geographic, or even ecological, nationalism in which Russia's natural environment is the source from which a uniquely Russian nation emerged and to which it is biologically, socially, and spiritually best suited and most attuned. Hence dachas, as institutions that are both culturally and environmentally derived, encapsulate and project the country's social history and heritage in ways that are intimately familiar to people across Russia and across generations.

My project in this book is both to provide a detailed ethnographic account of "dacha life" *(dachnaia zhizn')* and to show how this lifestyle is not peripheral to Russian social life but is in fact a central, even ordinary, part of Russians' everyday lives at the personal, community, and even national levels. As will become apparent in the chapters that follow, dacha life, and the natural settings and qualities with which it is linked, are both microcosms of and conduits for fundamental issues in today's Russia: the politics of national identity and nationalism, the transition to capitalism, projects of social transformation, and the legacies of socialism, among others.

In this book I propose to take the dacha seriously as a cultural institution that engages and refracts broader social concerns. My discussion will

FIGURE 1. A typical dacha community consists of colorful wooden cottages.

move beyond immediate descriptions of contemporary dacha life and show how Russians appreciate dachas for their power to make sense of the larger world around them. This project of taking dachas seriously will also entail relocating them from their apparent exile on the periphery of scholarly treatments of Russia. Despite the importance and centrality of dachas in Russian life over the past several centuries, and despite the obvious preoccupation with dachas demonstrated by Russian elites, artists, and ordinary citizens alike, accounts of dacha life have been largely overlooked as a topic of serious scholarship and reserved primarily for more popular accounts of "Russian culture" such as those that appear in newspaper articles and travel writing. Although dachas are not completely excised from scholarly analyses, they are primarily limited to discussions of the value of dacha gardens in Russia's subsistence economy or used as a colorful backdrop for other topics (Clarke 2002; Ortar 2005; Struyk and Angelici 1996; Zavisca 2003).[2] Only rarely have they been taken seriously as subjects of their own, as in Stephen Lovell's historical study of pre-Soviet and Soviet dachas (2002, 2003), Caroline Humphrey's account of post-Soviet dacha architectural styles and socioeconomic differentiation (1998), and Ronan Hervouet's work on dacha life in Belarus (2003, 2007).[3] As will become apparent, this oversight not only suggests an intellectual devaluation of dachas, but, more significantly, it obscures the productive and essential contributions of dachas and dacha enthusiasts to fundamental and vital processes of nation and state building.

THE GIVENNESS OF DACHAS

Etymologically, the word *dacha* comes from the Russian word *dat'*, "to give." According to historian Stephen Lovell, the word *dacha* can be traced back to the eleventh century in Old Russian, with the medieval origins of the word indicating "the result of a gift bestowed publicly." By the seventeenth century *dacha* had come to signify land distributed by the state (Lovell 2003:8). These historical and linguistic underpinnings of the word *dacha* were details that numerous informants emphasized when asked to describe dachas. In one particularly revealing response Angela, a third-generation dacha enthusiast, referenced the verb *dat'* in her explanation that Russians view the dacha as something that is "given" to them by someone else rather than something that they purchase themselves, a sentiment that she observed was apparent in the fact that Russians often refer to their dachas as *dannii* (sing.), the past participle construction of *dat'*, meaning "was given or having been given."

In more practical terms, the term *dacha* has evolved from referring to a parcel of land to indicating the residence erected on that land, and more precisely to a recreational summer home in the country (Lovell 2003:8).[4] Lovell locates the origins of the modern notion of the dacha as a leisure-oriented residence in the land reforms initiated by Peter the Great at the beginning of the eighteenth century. One component of Peter's project of transforming Russia's wilderness into urban spaces entailed allocating land for housing developments, a practice that established suburban regions where summer cottages were built (Lovell 2003:9). Between the early eighteenth century and the mid-nineteenth century, dachas, which could be either rural or suburban plots of land, continued to gain significance, eventually becoming formally established as part of the summer culture of Russian elites (Galtz 2000; Lovell 2003). In the second half of the nineteenth century, the emergence of a middle class in Russia and the development of leisure as a form of conspicuous consumption shifted cottaging and other recreational activities into the mainstream (Gorsuch and Koenker 2006; McReynolds 2003). The transformation of dachas into a mass phenomenon for virtually all segments of society was cemented in the Soviet period, when dacha plots were allocated to workers, in part as remuneration and in part as an incentive.

Issues of allocation, as well as public debates about the politics of allocation, are persistent themes in dacha practices. The emphasis on the fact that the land has been given rather than procured through an act of taking or buying underscores a notion of property ownership based not on active acquisition, but rather on receipt. When asked to describe how they came to be dacha owners, informants responded with the year of allocation and then an indirect object construction using either *dali,* the past tense of the verb "to give," or *dannii,* the past participle form of the verb, in order to indicate property "that they gave [us]." These linguistic forms reveal two important details about how Russians conceptualize dacha ownership: first, that dacha property is a gift bestowed on them; and second, that there is a sense of rights and entitlement associated with dachas, as signaled by the use of the undefined third person plural to indicate the subject—the "giver"—which is understood to be the state.[5] Perhaps just as revealing, however, is what Angela observed about Russian attitudes toward the long-term ownership of these properties. Angela noted that Russian lacked a corresponding notion of disposing—or "giving away" *(pridat')*—a dacha, primarily because there was no legal provision for disposing of dachas. "No one gives away [a dacha]" *(Nikomu ne pridat'),* Angela commented. With this observation, Angela illuminated both the theme of dacha owners being recipients but not agents of disposition, as well as the pervasive sense that dacha life is so inherent to Russian culture that its elimination is inconceivable.

Nevertheless, even as dacha access corresponded less rigidly to social status, clear differences persisted between the summer homes of the Soviet political elite and the summer work cottages of ordinary citizens. The association of dachas with upper-class lifestyles persisted into the twentieth century, as the word *dacha* officially denoted the spacious and luxurious summer homes of the country's elite, a trend that has continued into the post-Soviet period with the privately owned brick mansions surrounded by high stone walls and security cameras (and even a moat in one remarkable instance that I observed outside Moscow) of Russia's nouveaux riches.[6] Mirroring suburbanization trends of the nineteenth century, large single-family residences are colonizing the Russian countryside as the financial capital of Russia's present-day middle class increases and tightly bounded urban centers give way to suburban sprawl. Gradually, the homogenous McMansion architectural styles that characterized the villas built during the early post-Soviet years are being replaced by contemporary American-style *"taunkhausy"* (townhouses) and Northern European–style *"kottedzhy"* (cottages).

The summer cottages inhabited by ordinary Russians, by contrast, have typically been far more modest and rustic. Moreover, even though *dacha* is the colloquial and most recognizable term for these cottages, most Russians were quick to point out that *dacha* is actually an official administrative designation reserved primarily for the larger country residences of the elite. By contrast, the smaller, more basic cottages owned by the majority of Russians were officially classified as functional structures associated with personal plots in a collective garden community. In interviews, when I first asked respondents about their dachas, most immediately corrected me by describing their cottages as a *sarai* (shed), thus indicating both the dwelling's small size and its function as an all-purpose storage and preparation space, and reflecting the fact that many cottages started out as storage sheds that have since been updated, winterized, and perhaps expanded slightly to include a bed. Yet after making such a distinction, respondents typically continued by describing their cottages as dachas.

Most cottages consist of one or two multipurpose rooms that serve as both living and sleeping space. Some cottages have just enough space on a table top for a hot plate and an electric kettle, while others are accompanied by a separate building just large enough for a tiny kitchen with a hot plate or occasionally a miniature stove, a small table, and a set of stools or spindly chairs. Although most structures have electricity, indoor plumbing is rare. In most cases, cold running water is provided only through an outdoor spigot in the yard. Outhouses vary in sophistication from a pit latrine with a plastic or wooden toilet seat to a hole cut in a board placed over a bucket that must be emptied in the woods. In recent years bio-toilets have become more popular and affordable, although they have not yet become the norm. Viktoriia was one of the first residents in her dacha community to install a bio-toilet in her cottage, a detail that several mutual friends proudly related to me. At the encouragement of her friends during my visit to her dacha, Viktoriia led me up the narrow staircase in her dacha to show off the bio-toilet that she had wedged into a small alcove. She confessed, however, that although the bio-toilet was a more comfortable alternative to her outhouse, she found the latter far more convenient and hence used the bio-toilet only rarely.

These rustic cottages are marked by a mismatched sensibility, as they are typically outfitted with the outdated but still usable remnants of the occupants' urban lives. Lumpy mattresses, old couches, frayed linens, dented pots, and chipped dishes enjoy new life at the cottage. Interior walls are usually covered with outdated calendars, travel posters, pictures of famous authors and historical figures, and wallpaper remnants. During the Soviet

FIGURE 2. A typical dacha living room is a multifunctional space for drying clothes, watching television, and resting.

period, the type of building materials that could be used in these structures was tightly regulated. To prevent citizens from using their cottages year-round, officials passed laws preventing occupants from insulating them or building second stories for storage or living space. Residents stuffed newspapers and rags into the spaces between the walls to fill cracks and provide a bit of protection against the elements. In an era where "everything was forbidden but anything was possible," enterprising individuals and local inspectors engaged in cat-and-mouse games. Just as quickly as cottage residents could install thicker insulation and create secret attic crawl spaces, the local inspectors would arrive to rip out the insulation and ladders up to the upper spaces, only to have the cycle repeat. Despite the simple nature of these plots and their buildings, most Russians refer affectionately to their cottages as *dachas*, thereby linking their cottages to a more expansive ideal of summertime leisure that is not exclusive to Russia's elite.

For most Russians, dachas cannot be understood separately from their gardens, as evidenced by Russians' use of the word *dacha* to refer to both the cottage and its cultivated land. Gardens actually predate cottages, as gardening came into existence in Russia before the seventeenth century,

when Russian Orthodox monasteries used gardens both for medicinal purposes and for making religious principles of sacred and profane physically
manifest (Ely 2002:31; Likhachev 1988). These gardens also satisfied the
more practical need of feeding monastery communities (Likhachev 1988).
Since the seventeenth century, Russian gardening practices have under-
gone many changes that reflect changing cultural sensibilities and material needs, with gardens ranging from aesthetically oriented landscapes
and pleasure spaces for elites to utilitarian kitchen gardens *(ogorodi)* that
served as supplemental, or even primary, sources of food for their owners.
It was during the twentieth century that garden plots became particularly
significant both for their role as critical food sources and for their role in
supporting the physical and social health of the nation. During the recurring food shortages that plagued the Soviet Union, dacha gardens were
seen by both state and citizen as a vital part of the national food supply
system. Dacha gardens were valued not just for their material benefits but
also for their symbolic value as conduits of essential national qualities. The
soil of dacha gardens was believed to produce foods that were superior in
taste, quality, and healthfulness to foods grown outside Russia. Today,
the considerable investment of money, time, and energy necessary for gardening has influenced a shift in the value of gardens from a site for food
production to a location for the performance of class status. Consequently,
the decisions that Russians make about how to design their gardens—
and whether they use their gardens for food at all—offer a compelling
vantage point for understanding the economic and cultural issues facing
Russians. Even as Russians debate among themselves what their dacha
gardens should look like, the consensus remains that gardens are essential
to the dacha experience.[7]

Although precise figures about dacha use in Russia are difficult to access,
there is compelling evidence for popular depictions of dacha use as a widespread, perhaps even universal, feature of Russian life. In a country with a
population of approximately 141 million, the chairman of the State Duma's
Construction and Land Use Committee reported in 2008 that almost thirteen million families had dacha plots (Malpas 2008). Beyond legal ownership, mass dacha use is evident in the availability of dachas for rent and the
practice of many Russians of visiting relatives and friends at their dachas.
In the course of my research, virtually every person with whom I talked
affirmed that they participated in the dacha life, regardless of whether they
owned a dacha. Russians who live abroad and have vacation cottages in
their adopted homes claim that they prefer to return to Russia for the dacha
experience because there the dacha experience is more authentic, enjoyable,

FIGURE 3. Dacha gardens are densely planted with a variety of fruits, vegetables, herbs, and flowers.

and meaningful. Even citizens of other formerly Soviet countries suggest that their own vacation cottage cultures do not resemble and cannot fully capture the experience of the Russian dacha world.

NATIONAL NATURES

Geographically and ideologically, dachas are inseparable from the natural environments in which they are situated, even though those natural environments vary tremendously from pristine forests to weedy meadows overlooking murky ponds to patches of postindustrial wasteland alongside busy highways. Nature, as it is accessed and experienced through the dacha world, is not a singular entity but rather a flexible concept that simultaneously encompasses both ecologically and geographically defined locations and imagined, symbolic states of being. Hence nature is as much an idealized, experiential state of being as it is an actual place defined by ecological features. Friends and acquaintances repeatedly assured me that no matter the travails involved in traveling to the countryside to reach their dachas, and no matter how cold, wet, or otherwise miserable the weather, the natural setting was the most desirable place to be. A poster that appears throughout Moscow's metro system depicts this vividly with a simple scene of brilliantly colored autumn leaves and the caption "In nature there is never bad weather." This seemingly simple sentence suggests a set of deeper values that infuse both popular representations and official discourses about why Russians cherish natural spaces.

Nature is, first and foremost, a space where personal, social, and national health is emphasized and most readily realized. Family relationships and friendships are strengthened by the intimacy of encounters behind cottage walls or in the forests, and bodies are fortified by the fresh air and fresh foods taken directly from the ground. Children learn about natural cycles of life and death by arranging solemn funerals for pets and wild animals. For post-Soviet citizens long accustomed to an intrusive government, the intimacy and privacy attributed to nature fosters a sense of distance and security from the reach of the state. This distance informs a powerful ethos of personal freedom and independence that is manifest in practices of self-reflection, critique, and disregard for the highly structured systems of regulations and oversight that constitute everyday life. As a result, Russian nature becomes a place where many things are officially forbidden yet anything is possible. In full view of strategically placed signs listing federal regulations banning campfires, motorized vehicles, swimming, fishing, and picking protected flowers, citizens can be observed cutting down trees, digging up plants, burning trash, riding their Jet Skis in fragile waterways, and swimming in cholera-filled lakes.

Beyond opening up an alternate realm for daily life, the privileged place of nature derives from an ideology of a national self that is grounded and rooted in the physical landscape, thereby inducing a physiological nationalism in which individuals claim to feel physical and biological connections to the homeland. While such bio-symbolic connections among earth, bodies, and the nation are apparent in the identity practices of other formerly Soviet societies (Schwartz 2006), the immediacy and magnitude of these correlations for Russians is manifested in daily linguistic usage: the root *rod,* meaning "family" or "genus," is common to the Russian words *rodina* (homeland), *priroda* (nature), *narod* (a term for "nation" that conveys the idea of "the folk" or "the people"), *rodit'* (to give birth [to]), and *rodnoi* (relatedness).

By conveying qualities of relatedness, cultivation, and generation, these terms evoke processes of reproduction that are simultaneously social and biological. These qualities are captured beautifully in the comments of one of Nancy Ries's Russian interlocutors: "*Rodina* is habitat, nature, soil— but it's a very *fermenting* thing. Upon or within it history takes place;

legends, values are born. *Narod* grows out of these two things" (Ries 1997: 29).[8] Margaret Paxson draws a similar connection in her discussion of the significance of *rodnoi:* "There is a relationship between the sense of being rodnoi, that of coming from the same rodina, or motherland, or being from the same narod, or people. But the term is far from being simply descriptive of affiliation; it has a profound set of emotions associated with it. . . . It is a term with earth and soil in it, as well as ancestral rootedness" (Paxson 2005:53).[9] Christopher Ely observes similar connections in the work of nineteenth-century intellectual commentators who emphasized the primordial and filial connections of biology and sentiment between the Russian landscape and its inhabitants (Ely 2000). In his analysis of the comments of A. S. Shkliarevskii, a Kievan doctor who invoked maternal tropes in his own interpretations of Russian landscape, Ely writes that "Motherhood carried the suggestion that the entire nation could be understood as an interrelated family group, held together by an emotional connection to the shared mother, the land" (Ely 2000:261).

The intrinsic connections between nature and nation have been reinforced throughout Russia's history as nature has repeatedly been the setting for the enactment and interment of national issues and political struggles. Over the past two hundred years alone, Russia's political history has been daily evinced by the forests and fields that continue to preserve and shelter the secrets of the dead, whether it is in the fields of Borodino where Napoleon met his match in Russia's army, the forests outside Ekaterinburg where the Romanov family was executed and hastily buried, or the forests and fields in western Russia that continue to give up the remains of the dead, both Soviet and German, from the Great Patriotic War (Tumarkin 1994).[10] Nature has also consistently provided places of refuge, asylum, and even political mobilization for a diverse set of Soviet and post-Soviet political actors: dissidents, political exiles, Pioneer youth brigades, post-Soviet youth organizations such as the pro-Kremlin group Nashi and Orthodox Christian nationalist youth religion camps, neofascists, and punks, to name but a very few.[11]

This packaging of land, kinship, and identity, and the production of a nation grounded simultaneously in geography and biology, crosscuts multiple spheres in Russian culture and social practice. Associations of land, identity, heritage, and emotion came up repeatedly in my interviews, particularly during discussions about Russia's peasant heritage. This complex of ideas is captured poignantly in the comments of Larisa, a sixty-year-old teacher, in her response to my question about why Russians are content when they travel to their dachas in the countryside:

Well, the first reason this is the case is because ... we are all peasants ... Our country, it is a peasant one in ideology. The second reason is that we have always had strong patriarchal relationships [otnoshenie] in Russia. The first person [in our family] who lived here and started building things was my grandfather. Once he went on his pension, he loved to build all of the peasant roots, although he himself had spent his life being a member of the *nomenklatura*.[12] And then you have to understand that he gathered everyone around him. He had two sisters, who had been widowed at a young age and left with two small children after the war [World War II]. And my grandmother also had widowed sisters who raised their children here. And Grandfather gave them all advice and provided a place for all of their children. In general, our grandfather was the unifier [ob'edinitel'] of the clan ... Everyone came together—relatives, our friends; this resulted in a continuation of the patriarchal life. Four generations of the family lived together here: my great-grandmother, my grandmother and grandfather, my parents, and my brother and I. We all lived together ... It wasn't just that I liked it, but that our life seemed natural [mne kazhetsia estestvennym nasha zhizn'].

For Larisa, the intimate relationship that she experiences with the countryside cannot be separated from her intimate family relationships and her heritage. Biological, cultural, and familial continuity all coexist symbiotically and unsurprisingly. More significant, the natural settings in which the dacha world exists refract multiple registers and dimensions of space, time, and belonging. It is this "kaleidoscopic" capacity (Richardson 2008) that renders dacha experiences accessible and knowable to Russians from diverse backgrounds and experiences and that imbues them with a uniquely Russian heritage.

HOMO DACHNIK

The exceptionalism ascribed to Russian dacha practices extends to descriptions of the individuals who partake of the dacha world. Dacha enthusiasts are dubbed *dachniki* (sing. *dachnik*), a flexible term that can include both individuals who own their own dachas and those who rent a cottage, a space in a cottage, or even a section of a dacha garden. In the course of my research, informants rarely distinguished between these groups but rather used *dachnik* to describe themselves, their friends and relatives, and anyone else who used a dacha. In this book I will therefore follow the lead of my informants and use the terms *dachnik* and *dachniki* to refer to anyone who participates in dacha life.

Because allocation of dacha plots during the Soviet period was most frequently managed through workplaces or party affiliation, dacha communities were typically extensions of already existing relationships that were transplanted from the city to the countryside. In smaller cities like Tver, where several workplaces might share allocation rights within the same few dacha communities, dacha residents were acquainted with one another through multiple and frequently overlapping networks of work, neighborhood apartment blocks, and their children's school communities. Hence, in most cases dachniki have generally known their neighbors well, with multigenerational relationships extending for more than fifty or sixty years in some cases. As dachas tend to be the center of extended networks of family and friends, dacha life is a multigenerational affair. Retirees typically live at their dachas continuously during the summer months, often accompanied by grandchildren and family pets sent to live in the countryside while parents work in the city. College students and working adults divide their time between their jobs in the city during the week and their cottages on the weekends and during their vacations. Hence dachniki range in age from toddlers to spry great-grandparents in their nineties. The dachniki who are most faithful about spending time at their dachas, however, tend to be adults between their thirties and their seventies, as these are the persons who are most able to commit time, energy, and money to their dachas.

More significant than demographic features such as these are Russians' descriptions of dachniki, which suggest that they constitute a unique population readily identifiable by their physiology, beliefs, and practices. In particular, dachniki are described as wearing ragged clothing and having a disheveled appearance from living in the countryside without modern conveniences, and as having a stooped posture from constant gardening and carrying sacks filled with yard tools and seedlings. While these caricatures of dachniki are certainly visible in any dacha settlement or on any suburban train during the height of dacha season, they are more than simple stereotypes. Rather, these traits are widely recognized and celebrated as part of a distinctively Russian character.

More than a century ago, writer Maxim Gorky pondered the nature of Russian dacha enthusiasts. In his play *Dachniki,* often translated as *The Summer People* or *Summerfolk* in English, Gorky portrays a typical day in the life of a summer dacha community as a means of illuminating the larger social tensions that were emerging in Russia at turn of the twentieth century and the end of the Tsarist period. The primary characters in the play are a group of friends and relatives who have left their homes in the city to spend the summer at their cottages in the countryside. These characters represent Russia's newly emerging class of middle-class professionals—doctors, lawyers, and writers. Neither nobility nor peasant, these characters occupy a transitional position between the world of the city and that of the country, and between Russia's past and its future. Holding the play together is a series of arguments among the various characters as they debate the nature of a meaningful and productive life, their place within this world, and, most importantly, the nature of their existence. Affairs of the heart, intellectual anxieties, and family politics all preoccupy the dachniki and serve as allegories for these larger issues of social transformation. Observing these interactions is a secondary set of characters who comprise the community's year-round residents, the locals who must tolerate the summer visitors who descend in droves to soak up the sun and fresh air, suck up the berries and mushrooms from the forests, and leave the detritus of their everyday lives strewn about their surroundings.

Throughout the play, both the locals and the visitors try to discern the essential qualities of this new breed of person represented by the dachnik. One set of qualities emerges early in the play when two locals who work as watchmen and provide general assistance for the dachniki discuss the various people who have arrived for the summer.

> Kropilkin: "And at that dacha over there—who has rented that one?"
> His fellow watchman Pustobaika responds: "An engineer. Suslov."
> . . .
> Kropilkin: "They are all new, aren't they? None of them were here last summer?"
> Pustobaika lowers his pipe: "They are all alike. All the same."
> Kropilkin sighs: "Of course. . . . They are all ladies and gentlemen . . . oh, yes!"
> Pustobaika: "Dachniki—they are all identical. I have seen them for five years—more than I can count. They all seem to me like bubbles in a puddle on a rainy day . . . they rise up and then they burst . . . rise up and burst. . . . That is the way it is."
> . . .
> Kropilkin: "So? Who are they, really?"
> Pustobaika: "It is very simple: They are all dressed up in their finery and—they talk . . . all sorts of words, whatever they feel like . . . they yell, they bustle around as if they have something to do . . . or as if they are angry. . . . Well,—they deceive each other. One of them imagines 'I am honest, of course.' Another imagines 'I am smart' . . . or the one over there, 'I am a miserable fellow' . . . whatever they feel like, that is what they imagine for themselves." [Gorky 1906:45–47]

Later, in act IV, Gorky allows the dachniki themselves to debate the real nature of their identities. This question crystallizes in an argument among several dachniki. Zamyslov, an assistant to the lawyer dachnik, comments, "We are all complicated people." Varvara, another summer resident, counters with, "We are not the intelligentsia! We are something else. . . . Those of us who are dachniki in our country . . . we are some kind of transients. We bustle around, searching for a place in our lives where we can feel comfortable. . . . We do nothing and talk a disgusting amount" (Gorky 1906:164–65).

A few moments later, another dachnik, Mar'ia L'vovna, joins the conversation with a passionate speech:

> We should all be living in a different way, friends! Children of weavers and cooks, children of healthy laborers—we should be living differently! In our country there have never been educated people connected with the masses, the blood of the generations . . . and we ourselves created our complete loneliness, this anxious fussing, and internal division against each other. . . . This is our own drama! But we ourselves created it, we deserve all the torment that we have given ourselves. Yes, Varia! We do not have the right to fill our lives with moaning. [Gorky 1906:168–69]

As the acerbic comments of Gorky's characters reveal, dachniki are easily identified by their slothfulness, pettiness, and general unpleasantness. Dachniki are also interchangeable, a quality that contributes to the larger cultural sense that dacha enthusiasts belong to a distinctive breed. Gorky's caricatures are not merely satire, however, but rather tap into an even deeper truth about the dacha experience. Gorky's Russian audiences find the depictions humorous because they are familiar. Beneath Gorky's cynical descriptions is a candid appraisal of the reality of life at the dacha, where the intimacies of nature and the cramped quarters quickly lead to disagreements and contempt. Squabbles and anxieties become the private and fiercely guarded secrets of the insiders in this world. At the same time, these more complicated, nuanced depictions of the realities of dacha life threaten the more idyllic representations of dacha life. Hence, in their outward expressions Russians are often quick to emphasize images of harmony and pleasure while disguising the seamier aspects of dacha life. In fact, when visitors come to a dacha for the first time, established dacha rituals effectively divert their attention to the enjoyable elements while obscuring the complications. Only over time, as strangers become intimates, does the reality of the dacha emerge. As will become clear, these secrets are the privately held, insider knowledge of an entire nation, and the collective preservation of these secrets is itself a crucial part of national consolidation and reproduction (Herzfeld 1997).

The dachniki described in this book represent a broad cross-section of Russian society in terms of their social, economic, and demographic diversity. This diversity illuminates the extent to which Russia's post-Soviet economic transformations have affected its citizens unequally. Most of my informants were educated professionals—doctors, lawyers, teachers, professors, historians, geologists, computer programmers, engineers, architects, musicians, and artists—whose occupations afforded them a certain amount of prestige and social status.[13] Their personal financial circumstances, however, were greatly dissimilar as a result of a post-Soviet context in which financial remuneration is no longer connected to workers' social or moral value to society but rather to their financial value to a market economy. These economic differences were compounded by generational differences within and among families. In some cases, retirees who had previously enjoyed significant social prestige and earned high wages but were now receiving pensions that had failed to keep up with inflation were drastically impoverished in comparison with their employed children and grandchildren. In other cases, retirees who continued to receive pensions that included supplemental amounts for special service to the state or for disabilities found themselves earning more than their children and grandchildren, especially offspring who worked in state-run enterprises. The dachniki I interviewed, then, represented a broad cross-section of Russia's changing economic classes.

Informants tended to downplay these distinctions, however, by deemphasizing economic comparisons with neighbors or relatives and instead accentuating commonalities of background, personal beliefs, and social networks. In the case of families, economic differences between relatives were minimized through emphasizing the cooperative nature of family dynamics. Such deflections, however, should not be interpreted as evidence that differences, particularly economic differences, do not matter to dachniki. As will become apparent in subsequent chapters, even though dachniki may attempt to conceal such differences from the gaze of outsiders, dacha communities are far from internally unified, and dacha affairs illuminate fissures and provoke antagonisms.

Although upper-class dachniki have attracted considerable public attention in Russia because of the large villas they have constructed and the ostensibly ostentatious lifestyles attributed to them, these individuals are not the focus of this book. This is in part because I did not have access to wealthy Russians through my social networks, and in part because popular sentiment among dachniki holds that these individuals are not legitimate members of the social class comprised of "ordinary dachniki." Upper-class dachniki did reside in several of the dacha communities I visited and where I interviewed residents, but my friends and acquaintances claimed not to know these neighbors and that they were unable to arrange meetings with them. Upper-class dachniki did not live such isolated existences as to be removed from local gossip channels, however, and informants were usually keen to share stories and personal opinions (largely negative) of these neighbors.[14] Hence while the dachniki discussed in this book claim to be distinguished by a shared middle-class sensibility, it is important to recognize that this invocation of a common identity and social experience is a strategic element of the dacha experience itself, one that both complicates and enables Russians' claims about dacha life as a universal Russian experience.

DACHA METHODOLOGY

How does one do research on dacha life? That is a question that I have been asked repeatedly during the course of this project. Perhaps surprisingly, it is a somewhat difficult question to answer, and not because there are different methodologies one must employ. To be sure, learning how to sample multiple varieties of pickles, jams, and homemade liqueurs is a bit like learning how to taste wine: one must always be able to comment knowledgeably on the taste, consistency, and color of the tidbits being offered, and also to ask questions about where the food was procured, under what conditions, how much labor was involved, and how many jars were needed. Developing a tolerance for buzzing and biting mosquitoes and perfecting one's berry-picking skills are also helpful. But these challenges aside, dacha research is difficult because it can be hard to convince one's colleagues that studying how people go on vacation is in fact a worthy inquiry. And here at least, as I argue later in this book, it is important to note that dacha life, and the natural life more generally, as much as it may seem to resemble leisure and recreation, is anything but that. Dacha life is hard work.

Although I did not originally set out to study dachas, this project has been with me since the very first trip that I made to Russia in 1995. By the second week of that first visit, I had already gone *na dachu* (to the dacha) after my landlady, Anya, invited me to accompany her on a week's visit to her friend Tanya's dacha several hours outside Moscow. Although I was not a summer cottage novice, having visited friends and family at their summer cottages in the United States and Finland, nothing had prepared me for my first dacha experience. The preparations leading up to that trip were all consuming and, frankly, a bit terrifying in their intensity. During the week preceding our departure, Anya was in a constant frenzy as she cooked meals that she left for her adult son, collected large glass jars that would become containers for pickles and jams, and studied the train timetables to determine the optimal route and travel schedule. The night before our departure, Anya inspected my backpack and removed most of my clothes in order to create space for food (including a large boxed cake!), empty jars, and other supplies that we would bring to her friend. On the morning of our departure, we were up early in order to travel across Moscow before the crowds filled the metro and train stations. Nonetheless, we still found ourselves on a completely packed train, and it was only several stops later that we were able to find seats. Once the train was underway, a palpable sense of excitement filled the air, as friends and strangers alike began talking and swapping stories about dacha adventures and berry-picking conquests. As the train jolted and swayed between stations, elderly men juggled fishing poles and buckets, while elderly women kept an equally firm grasp on both their wheeled carts and small grandchildren. Dogs of all sizes nuzzled the legs of their fellow travelers as they searched for small spaces in which to curl up and nap. There was a shared sense of camaraderie and anticipation that was contagious.

Within an hour of our arrival at the dacha, we were deep in the forest, wearing buckets tied around our necks to hold the sweet, plump raspberries that we picked off overloaded bushes. Our days were spent collecting and nibbling raspberries and blueberries, while our evenings were spent following Tanya, our hostess, as she searched for mushrooms. Late at night we ate boiled sausages, drank black tea sweetened with fresh raspberry jam, and processed berries into jams and garden-fresh tomatoes and cucumbers into pickles. By the time I left Russia at the end of that very first and very short two-month trip, I had found myself *na dache* (at the dacha) three times, for almost one-quarter of my time in the field. I was, not surprisingly, hooked.

Since that first magical dacha trip, I have spent considerable time visiting friends and acquaintances and *their* friends, acquaintances, relatives, and co-workers at their dachas. I have spent perhaps even more time ambling through forests and parks with friends while enjoying the fresh air, looking at plants and flowers, and snacking on ripe cherries, apples, and wild strawberries that we picked along the way. Although I was dimly aware during my initial excursions to dachas, forests, and other natural spaces that there was "real" ethnography happening all around me, I was so caught up in the distracting joys of relaxing and enjoying nature with my friends that I did not consider pursuing a dacha project seriously. Because dacha visits offered necessary breathing space from the hard work of my urban fieldwork, I did not consider being at the dacha "real" fieldwork; it was my mental health break from my fieldwork. It was colleagues, friends, and relatives back home who were bitten by the "dacha bug" through the accounts with which I regaled them and who prodded me to realize that dacha life was not as removed from the realities of ordinary daily life as it might seem. Rather, the notions of temporal and spatial distance that my fellow dachniki and I so eagerly embraced in order to separate ourselves from the bustle of the city and the problems of our work lives merely obscured the fact that dachas, gardens, and natural spaces are deeply enmeshed in the realities of everyday life.

Between 1995 and 2005 I conducted fieldwork in Moscow. Although my research during this period focused primarily on other topics, dacha life was never very far away, as it emerged repeatedly in the conversations and experiences of my informants and my repeated visits to informants' dachas. During even the shortest stints of summer fieldwork I typically made several dacha visits. In summer 2005 I returned to Russia for three months of concentrated fieldwork to supplement the copious amounts of dacha-related material that I had gathered over the preceding ten years. At the invitation of a friend, I spent the summer in Tver, where I was warmly welcomed into an extended network of dachniki. Tver is a midsize city of approximately 250,000 residents, located along the Volga River approximately 120 kilometers northwest of Moscow. Tver's geographic location acquired special significance during the Soviet period and greatly influenced the composition of the city. Citizens who fell out of favor with the Soviet regime—especially intellectuals and political figures—were often banished from Moscow and forbidden from living within 120 kilometers of the city. As the first big city beyond Moscow's zone of exclusion, Tver became home to many artists and intellectuals, which in turn fostered the growth of other professional classes. At the same time, Tver's location along several rivers and in the midst of a region rich in natural resources has encouraged a strong industrial sector. As a result, Tver is marked by striking demographic and socioeconomic diversity.

Normally Tver is a bustling city with a lively street life oriented around the historic district, the universities, and the city's picturesque riverbanks. On summer weekends, however, Tver becomes a ghost town. Lines at the post office and the stores disappear, and the city's busy streets empty, making it possible once again to cross the streets without worry. Yet as the city's center empties out, the periphery becomes more clogged, as the cars, buses, and trains heading out of Tver to the nearby cottage communities overflow with passengers making their way to their dachas and the nearby rivers and forests. The larger Tver region is also home to numerous sanitariums, recreational facilities, and summer camps (sing., *lager*), including the compound on Lake Seliger where the pro-Kremlin political party Nashi holds its annual summer retreat for patriotic Russian youth.

During my summer 2005 fieldwork I based myself in the Nadezhda dacha collective, an established community that was a twenty-five-minute train ride from Tver and the summer home of many Tver residents. I made additional visits to several other dacha communities ringing Tver. I interviewed informants at their dachas, on the train, and at their homes. I also met with residents of other dacha communities from the Tver and Moscow regions at their homes or in public. I quickly discovered that doing dacha research was "easy" in that people were eager to talk with me about their dachas. Iuliia, the aunt of a friend, was my hostess that summer. Iuliia kindly took it upon herself to organize interviews for me. She quickly discovered, however, that she had a waiting list of people who wanted to share their thoughts and experiences, and her role as my social secretary expanded far beyond what any of us had expected. Other friends who described my project to their acquaintances reported similar responses. Even though some professed to despise the dacha life, all nevertheless had strong opinions on the subject. In short, I had stumbled upon a topic that my informants found both fascinating and exciting. Typically anthropologists worry about gaining access to informants and not being able to collect enough material by the end of a year-long fieldwork trip. In my case, however, I could not schedule all the interviews that were available to me, and I am still collecting and writing up data. Today, several years after that fieldwork period, my friends report that their acquaintances are still hoping to be interviewed. Clearly, there is something going on with dachas.

Since 1995 I have formally visited at least thirteen different dacha communities around Moscow and Tver, with additional informal visits to and through smaller dacha communities several hours to the northwest and northeast of Moscow, outside St. Petersburg, and in the outskirts of Tver. During visits to informants' dachas and their homes, as well as during random conversations with other people, I have been presented with photographs and accounts of many more dacha communities across Russia. These dacha communities range from small settlements of fewer than one hundred dachas to large settlements of more than several hundred cottages, and they consist of both collectives that were established in the early Soviet period and settlements established in the post-Soviet era. In some cases, dachniki owned their land and cottage outright; in others, dachniki continued to rent their property from the state. Often these two types of ownership coexisted within the same community, and I had to tease out which neighbors owned and which rented.

All in all, I have probably talked with several hundred individuals about dachas, dacha life, mushroom and berry picking, and nature more generally. These conversations came about both during formal interviews, primarily during my 2005 fieldwork, and in the course of informal conversations with acquaintances and strangers. As I quickly discovered, dacha-related topics came up repeatedly and often spontaneously in my conversations with others, as it did during a chance encounter with the woman who worked at the front desk of the dormitory where I lived in Tver as she was cleaning herbs she had picked on her way to work, and when interviews I was conducting on completely unrelated topics somehow circled back to dacha-related issues. The taxi drivers who ferried me to and from the airport upon my arrivals to and departures from Russia were particularly eager interlocutors, as our trips were almost always complicated by the endless crush of dacha-related traffic on Moscow's highways during the summer.

Conversations about dachas were also not restricted to Russians living in Russia. Russian émigrés who have attended lectures I have given on this subject, Russian students in my classes, and Russian friends of acquaintances have all sought me out to share their perspectives. Even my husband has become an inadvertent research assistant to this project: in the course of his work as a chemist he frequently collaborates with colleagues at other universities and companies. On occasions when he has worked with Russian scientists and mentioned my research to them, he has quickly found himself on the receiving end of lengthy discourses on dacha life. In essence, dacha life is a ubiquitous part of everyday life for Russians no matter where in the world they live.

During the course of this research I have accompanied friends and acquaintances on a wide range of activities related to the dacha experience. In many cases a visit to someone's dacha was the primary encounter, but the idea of a "visit" does not fully capture the variety of activities that might take place *na dache,* nor does it capture the sense that dacha visits were highly ritualized. It is important to point out that these rituals were not done specifically for the visiting ethnographer, but they were in fact a standard part of the dacha experience that hosts provided to all guests.

A simple day trip to visit acquaintances at their dachas typically involved a journey by some form of public transportation (bus, tram, train, or some combination thereof) from the city to a stop somewhere in an otherwise unremarkable rural setting, usually identified only by vague directions such as "look for the big boulder" or "ask the driver to let you off at village such-and-such," even when there did not appear to be a village anywhere in sight. Reaching one's destination was invariably a collective enterprise that involved asking fellow passengers, the bus driver, and random passersby where to get out and which direction to start walking. In most cases I was met at the drop-off point by my acquaintances, who then escorted me to their dachas, a trip that always involved a ten- to fifteen-minute walk through meadows and forested areas. Along the way, hosts detailed the history of their communities, pointed out the cottages of their friends, indicated recent changes in the architecture or arrangement of the community, related all of the local gossip, and kept a sharp eye out for mushrooms or berries to be scooped up as we walked. Commentary is itself a critical element of the dacha rituals, thereby enabling a tremendous amount of information to be imparted more or less spontaneously.

A typical dacha visit might include the following sequence of events: Upon arrival at the dacha, hosts invite guests to sit down for tea and sweets, or perhaps a light lunch, depending on the time of day and the length of the journey to the dacha. A "light lunch" entails an assortment of fresh vegetables and herbs (tomatoes, cucumbers, radishes, dill), usually picked from the host's garden, as well as sliced meat, cheese, and bread. Additional activities during the dacha visit include a guided tour around the host's garden, during which the host provides a lengthy commentary on the specific varietals of fruits, vegetables, and flowers that have been planted and the techniques of cultivation. Often hosts lead guests on guided tours of the community and to a local riverbank or meadow. Sometimes a formal mushroom- or berry-picking excursion is included as well. Upon departure, guests often find themselves being urged to accept a bag of fruit or vegetables to take home with them.

My dacha-related research trips also included visits to informants' apartments, which followed a similarly ritualized itinerary of looking at dacha-related pictures and artifacts, inspecting the collection of preserves and pickles that were stored throughout the apartment, and sampling those preserves and pickles and, when available, homemade wine and liqueur. I also participated in mushroom- and berry-picking excursions; long walks around dacha communities and through nearby villages; and endless trips on trains and buses loaded with dachniki and campers. Finally, no research on Russian-style organic life would be complete without a trip to the *banya* (Russian steam bath), which I enjoyed at the dacha belonging to a friend of my hostess Iuliia.

Despite the centrality of dachas to the experience of a nature-related

FIGURE 4. Dacha tours are group ventures, as friends and neighbors appreciate the flowering plants and vegetable gardens.

good life, these cottages were not the only spaces in which this good life could be accessed. Hence my dacha visits took place alongside visits to nature preserves, forests, public parks, historic estates, and monastery gardens throughout and outside Moscow, Tver, St. Petersburg, and other small towns outside these cities. Material was also gathered during visits to markets (where I engaged in informal conversations with sellers and buyers of "natural products"), garden centers, food exhibitions, and even cemeteries. During interviews and informal conversations alike, my informants made reference to this broader range of settings and experiences that constitute the nature-infused good life evoked by dachas. In short, because this good life is just as much a state of mind as it is a lifestyle grounded in a real physical space, it can be accessed in multiple realms, even in the midst of large cities like Tver, St. Petersburg, and Moscow.

JOURNEYING TO AND THROUGH THE DACHA WORLD

There are two primary organizing themes to this book: nature and intimacy. Because of the centrality of nature to dacha life, my discussion will draw on nature themes as both topics of analysis and organizing motifs. In particular, I would like to note my deliberate use of "natural" and "organic" to emphasize a Russian ideal of geographically inspired nativism, and phrases such as "natural living" and "organic living" should be understood to indicate these multiple meanings. Additionally, attention to the aspects of intimacy attributed to the dacha world will illuminate the multiple inflections of insiderness and outsiderness that are both intrinsic to this lifestyle and have sustained it across time and space.

My exploration of Russia's dacha world entails a journey to and through a multiplicity of spaces, times, and experiences. The journey begins in chapter 2 with an exploration of the significance of place to the dacha experience. On the one hand, Russians feel at home in nature, and this comfort and familiarity reveals a particularly Russian inflection of geographic nationalism. At the same time, the dacha experience is rife with physical and social discomforts, a reality captured effectively by Russian social critics. This recognition of the simultaneously pleasant and unpleasant qualities of dacha life invites both a rethinking of place not simply as a setting but as a dynamic, phenomenological experience and a rethinking of dachas not simply as sites of leisure but as forms of meaningful labor.

Chapter 3 continues these themes of meaningful activity, comfort, and discomfort by focusing on why Russians engage in unpleasant, labor-intensive, and increasingly expensive activities such as gardening and provisioning while claiming that they derive deep personal, and oftentimes spiritual or soulful, satisfaction from them. The answer, I suggest, has to do with an organic lifestyle that rests upon different structures and experiences of time and activity; work that is done on one's own time and for one's own benefit, such as gardening and cottage repair, is interpreted as leisure and relaxation. In chapter 4 I describe the activities of gardening and foraging that are part of the dacha lifestyle and explore how the value that Russians place on "natural foods" reveals concerns with personal satisfaction, social well-being, and spirituality. Natural foods become reference points for discussions about the physical, social, and spiritual health of Russian society and its citizens.

Chapter 5 moves beyond gardens to address the sentimental attachments that Russians claim to feel for their dachas and for the countryside more generally. These sentimental feelings typically take the form of nostalgic reminiscences and encapsulate a larger and more contentious set of debates about the nature and direction of the past, present, and future in today's Russia. These themes are continued in chapter 6, which explores how seemingly out-of-the-way places such as forests, villages, and dacha communities might be better understood as at the center of Russian daily life. In particular, I suggest that it is in the natural world that we see the new values of a Russian postsocialist modern democracy—the ideals of freedom, autonomy, liberty, and civil association, in particular—emerging most vividly and with greatest effect. The natural life, especially as it is experienced and contested in the forest and at the dacha, emerges as a form of civil society that shapes daily life in Russia. Finally, in the conclusion, I describe recent developments in the dacha lifestyle and offer thoughts on the impact of these changes not just for Russia's ongoing social transformation, but also for an emerging field of post-postsocialist ethnography.

CHAPTER 2

Intimate Irritations

Living with Chekhov at the Dacha

From the moment I arrived in Sakhalin until today it has been
warm and bright; sometimes there's a light frost in the mornings
and one of the mountains has snow on the top, but the earth is
still green, the leaves have not fallen and nature all around is
smiling, just like May at the dacha.

—Anton Chekhov, in an October 1890 letter to his mother describing
  his observations of Sakhalin Island (Chekhov 2004:38–39)

At the end of summer 2005, I was invited by Veronika to visit her at the
dacha that she shared with her elderly widowed mother, Zinaida, in the
Nadezhda dacha cooperative. During the summer, Veronika and Zinaida
occasionally shared the dacha with Veronika's grandchildren and assorted
nieces and nephews. Accompanying me on this visit were my hostess Iuliia
and her niece Angela. Although Veronika was a bit older than Iuliia, the
two women had grown up together in the dacha community, and their
families knew each other well. Veronika and Zinaida had been looking
forward to our visit, and when we arrived Zinaida bustled to light the fire
in the samovar so that we could have proper tea.

Although the visit was ostensibly for the purpose of a formal interview,
our discussion quickly veered far from the questions I had prepared and
turned into an animated informal conversation among close friends. Over
several hours, our discussion ranged far and wide over such topics as the
weather, the cottage's broken television antenna, the fresh berries gracing
the table, and the latest family news (including an update on the dating
life of the visiting teenaged granddaughter, much to the girl's dismay as
she hurried through the sitting room on her way to visit friends). Worried
that our digressions were taking us too far afield from a serious conversa-

tion about the dacha, Veronika periodically exerted her right as hostess to interrupt our chatting so that I could ask the next question on my list. Typically, however, within a few seconds of my having posed a question, the conversation once again veered in a new direction. The several hours that we spent together were lively, to say the least.

Our conversation was interspersed with reminiscences by Zinaida about her long history at the dacha. She and her husband had been among the very first to receive allocations in the Nadezhda community. They were fortunate to receive a particularly desirable plot of land on the edge of a small hill overlooking the river, and in the late 1940s, after her husband had returned from the war, they built the cottage and outbuildings by hand. During those early years, Zinaida recalled, they traveled to Nadezhda with friends and family, often enjoying picnics along the riverbank. To show us what the area had looked like some sixty years earlier, Zinaida pulled out a stack of old black-and-white photographs.

The dacha life captured in Zinaida's photographs was multigenerational, the images depicting a young Zinaida and her husband in their twenties with their young children, surrounded by friends, grandparents, and elderly great-grandparents. Some photographs, such as images of the older generations posed formally dressed in suits and their veterans' pins and badges, documented special events celebrated in the nascent dacha community. Most photographs, however, captured the everyday dacha life, such as the images of the same grandparents and great-grandparents sitting on a bench in the meadow and attired more casually in summery dresses and lightweight summer work pajamas. Other images caught several generations together, including laughing grandchildren who were lying on the grass on the riverbank or sitting around a large outdoor table and eating bowls of soup. There were photographs of fishing gear and a freshly caught fish lying on the riverbank, of a very small child holding several huge mushrooms over his head, and even of the family cow grazing in the tall grass by the river's edge.

The longer our conversation continued, the more deeply Zinaida delved into the past, reminiscing fondly about the pleasures of the fields, the river, and the family get-togethers. I commented that during the course of my research, I had observed that nostalgia seemed to be an essential quality in dacha stories. Veronika immediately responded that yes, this was true, and that I must be referring to the feelings that are evoked by the end of the dacha season: "In the beginning of the season, there is enthusiasm. But [later there is] sorrow . . . Of course there will be sorrow." Iuliia added, "When summer comes to an end, then there is real sorrow." The topic of sorrow then took a somewhat unusual direction, as Veronika commented that she was especially troubled by the end of this particular season because of the amount of time she had spent shopping for nice, special-occasion clothing during the summer. She felt that these efforts had been wasteful, because when she arrived at her dacha, all she needed were her old work clothes: "You don't need anything more than that. That is the way it has been, ever since the old days. God knows that it has always been that way." Iuliia quickly added, "And it was even that way back during Chekhov's day" (i.e., the late nineteenth century).

Certain constants characterized my dacha fieldwork: riding the train with ankle-licking dogs; endless family photographs of dacha picnics; lazy rambles through forests and meadows; overflowing baskets of fresh berries, mushrooms, tomatoes, and cucumbers; intense, hours-long philosophical discussions; and Anton Chekhov, one of Russia's greatest and most beloved writers. I quickly discovered during interviews and informal conversations that no matter the topic under debate, it usually was not long before Chekhov made an appearance. In fact, during the course of this research project, countless colleagues, friends, and strangers alike advised me to begin this book with Chekhov. It was Chekhov, I was assured repeatedly and enthusiastically, who truly understood and best captured the nature of dacha life in all of its intensely visceral, passionate, and oftentimes conflicted glory and who could best help non-Russians truly understand what it was like to spend time at a cottage in the countryside.

For my acquaintances, Chekhov was a key informant—a person who, in anthropological terms, possesses extensive knowledge on a particular subject, can communicate that knowledge effectively, and enjoys widespread respect and acclaim for that knowledge. Writing at the end of the nineteenth century, Chekhov drew attention to the social issues of the times by focusing on the everyday affairs of ordinary people. Dachas were a recurring theme in his work, and in particular they were used as a setting for his critical commentaries on the pressing social issues of the day: the rise of populism, the consequences of the emancipation of the serfs, the beginnings of industrialization and urbanization, and the class tensions heightened by these changes. Both Chekhov's plays and his short stories are characterized by a strong ethnographic sensibility that critically illuminates the social and moral conflicts that confronted Russians who were living in a period of acute social and political transformation. More important, Chekhov's work is infused with a profound ability to express the lived experiences of everyday life and to elicit in readers a sense that Chekhov's characters' experiences are their own. Chekhov's writings make the world come alive in ways that are palpable and undeniably real.

Although Chekhov was perhaps the most frequent guest to our conversations, he was occasionally joined by other artists, such as fellow writers Maxim Gorky and Leo Tolstoy and painters such as Ivan Shiskin, each of whom focused on themes of nature and country living in their works. In an interview with another longtime Nadezhda resident, my elderly interlocutor Vladimir reflected expansively on the significance of Russian forests as the generous provider of food, shelter, and life's pleasures more generally by referencing poetry: "Where do all of these things come from? From the forest. It is all from the forest! Firewood comes from the forest, of course [Drovishka iz lesa, vestimo]." Vladimir's concluding phrase—"Drovishka iz lesa, vestimo"—invokes a line from a poem by N. A. Nekrasov. The phrase appears in a conversation between a city gentleman and a peasant youth about the origins of firewood: "Where did the firewood come from? From the forest, of course." Beyond making frequent references to literature and to specific artists in order to explain dacha life, friends and colleagues also arranged visits to the nearby dachas of artists such as Isaac Levitan, who had lived in the Tver region, and to Abramtsevo to visit the dachas that had been used by artists such as Sergei Aksakov, Valentin Serov, Mikhail Nesterov, and Viktor Vasnetsov, all of whom employed nature themes in their work.[1]

For Russians such as my informants, art is a cherished medium for accessing and appreciating the dacha world. Over the past several centuries, dachas and the natural settings in which they are located have inspired many Russian artists both in the themes they have chosen and in their productivity. Beginning in the early nineteenth century, the evolution of dacha lifestyles encouraged an entire genre of dacha literature that has continued to the present, with pieces ranging from Aleksandr Pushkin's "Egyptian Nights" and Nikolai Gogol's "Old World Landowners" from the early nineteenth century to Viktor Slavkin's play Cerceau more than 150 years later. Masha, Iuliia's close friend and neighbor in Nadezhda, is a graphic artist for one of Russia's most prominent fabric companies. Her specialty is nature designs, and she frequently bases her designs on the mushrooms and berries she gathers in the forest near her dacha. Masha also paints for personal enjoyment and presents sketches and watercolors as gifts to her friends in the dacha community. Iuliia owns several of Masha's works, including a striking watercolor featuring mushrooms that hangs on the wall over the kitchen table. One summer morning, one of Iuliia's new lilies bloomed so spectacularly that she invited her neighbors in the dacha community to come for a visit and look at the flower. News of the flower spread quickly through the community, and Masha soon arrived with her painting supplies and an easel so that she could paint its picture. Masha's friends commented, only partly in jest, that they would not be surprised to see the flower turned into a fabric pattern. The aesthetic dimensions of the dacha world are also evident in more ordinary activities such as the skits and stories that children create and perform for one another and their families as part of their summertime play, and in the late-night suppers with friends that turn into spontaneous musical interludes that extend into the wee hours of the morning.

The idyllic qualities of beauty and pleasure evoked by artistic renditions of dachas and nature are tempered by rueful acknowledgment of the drawbacks and difficulties of these very spaces. At the same time that nature is a generative setting for intellectual, social, and emotional pleasures, it can also be an irritant. For Russians such as my informants, fully appreciating nature by accommodating its complexities requires a visceral, sensual engagement that extends beyond visual or aural perceptions alone. There is a quality of inhabiting nature, and of "having been there," that is necessary for fully appreciating nature in a way that goes beyond a detached observation to convey a feeling of experiencing that reality from the inside. It is the recognition of these elements of dacha life that informants most wanted to convey when they invoked Chekhov, Gorky, and other artists in our discussions.

THE FAMILIARITY OF CONTEMPT

I am going first class [on the boat], because my traveling companions are in second class and I am keen to get away from them. We were all on the road together (three in a tarantass), slept together, and have all got fed up with each other, especially I with them.

—Anton Chekhov, in a June 1890 letter describing his travels in
  the Far East of the Russian Empire (Chekhov 2004:21–22)

Chekhov's deep affection for dachas, coupled with his ability to evoke in profoundly simple prose the essence of living in the countryside, is evident throughout his short stories, plays, and even his personal letters. The care with which Chekhov attends to descriptions of nature—its rivers, soil, trees, plants, animals, and people—is beautiful both for the obvious joy that he felt in these spaces and for the tremendous insight that he offers his readers into the magic and significance of these spaces. In a letter to his family in June 1890, Chekhov describes the Amur River region in breathless, ecstatic prose:

I've already travelled over six hundred miles down the Amur, and have seen a million magnificent landscapes; my head is spinning with excitement and delight. I saw one cliff that would cause Kundasova to expire in ecstasy, were she to take it into her head to oxidize herself at the foot of it, and if Sofia Petrovna Kuvsh[innikova] and I were to arrange a picnic at the top of it, we would say to one another: "You can die now, Denis, you will never write anything better." The landscape is amazing. And it's so hot! It's warm even at night. The mornings are misty, but still warm.

I stare at the banks through binoculars and see masses of ducks, geese, divers, herons and all manner of long-billed creatures. It would be a glorious place to rent a dacha! [Chekhov 2004:26–27]

In pieces such as these, Chekhov's appreciation of and delight in the beauties and comforts of nature are clearly evident. Yet even as these qualities appear repeatedly in his writings on dacha living—such as in the opening lines of his short story "Dachniki," in which he writes, "The still air was thickly suffused with the fragrance of lilac and bird cherry" (Chekhov 1885 [1996])—depictions of physical natural beauty are tempered by the realities of the social relations that take place in their midst. Idyllic nature is layered with complications and tensions, so that beauty and comfort are complicated affairs. In Chekhov's writing, dacha living, much as it was later presented in Gorky's play *Dachniki,* is never fully restful, never fully desirable, and never fully solitary.

What makes Chekhov's dacha writings so compelling is his shrewd awareness that dachas belong to the realm of ordinary life, and as such are not immune to the trials and conflicts that crop up elsewhere in the course of everyday activities, an insight that also characterizes Gorky's play *Dachniki.*[2] Both writers' perceptive character studies unveil dachniki as real people with real flaws who are muddling through the messiness of real life, dealing with jealousy, impatience, overwork, boredom, and the annoyances provoked by the forced intimacy of cramped quarters filled with relatives, friends, and strangers. Their accounts remind readers that ostensibly leisure-oriented activities such as gardening, hiking, cottaging, and even socializing are not for the faint of heart but are, in fact, difficult, exhausting, and even distressing exertions. It is this intimate familiarity in both Chekhov's and Gorky's affectionately teasing representations of dacha life that resonates so strongly with Russians.

Gorky's play offers a glimpse into a typical day in a dacha community at the turn of the twentieth century, as his middle- and upper-class dachniki wander aimlessly into and out of the woods. Musical interludes, poetry recitations, and theatrical performances erupt spontaneously, while emotions flare up and then simmer down as the characters alternately argue with and snub one another over such issues as love, lust, work, social strati-fication, and the meaning of life. This is not a romantic view of nature but a close-up reality check that reminds viewers that even in the woods, even at the cottage, life is messy and tense; the dacha is never an escape.[3]

The emotional tensions evoked by these disagreements force Gorky's dachniki to recognize that the intimacy of cozy dacha life is scarcely as pleasurable as one might imagine. In Act II, one dacha visitor, Vlas, con-fesses the extent to which he dislikes the other summer residents in whose company he finds himself:

> I am sick of this, Mar'ia L'vovna, I feel ridiculous. . . . I do not like these peo-ple. . . . I do not respect them. . . . They are so pitiful and small, like mosqui-toes. . . . I cannot talk seriously with them. . . . They evoke in me a nasty desire to take on an affect, but to take an affect that is more honest than theirs. . . . My head is clogged with all kinds of rubbish. . . . I want to moan, to curse, to complain. . . . It seems that I will start to drink vodka, go on a drinking binge! I cannot live among them or live like them. . . . I will become deformed . . . and I will poison myself with banality *[Ia otravlius' poshlost'iu]*. Here they are . . . do you hear? They are coming! Sometimes I look at them with terror. . . . Let us go! I want to talk with you so much. [Gorky 1906:87]

In a scene later in the play, the doctor Dudakov announces his readiness to leave the dacha by saying, "At some point we were going to find one another loathsome! And now it has happened—we find one another loath-some! Vlas, he got it absolutely right, Olga! He got it! And now it is time to go home" (Gorky 1906:181). Several moments later, another character, Varvara, announces her departure with a bout of histrionics: "Yes, I am leaving! I am going far away from here where everything is decaying and falling apart. Far away from you loafers! I want to live! I will live and do something . . . unlike you. . . . Unlike you! Oh, damn you all!" (Gorky 1906:192). Gorky ends the play by allowing Shalimov, the resident writer, the penultimate word: "Calm down, my friend! This is all just rhetoric and hysteria . . . believe me. Do not fuss about it!" (Gorky 1906:194).

In his short story "At a Summer Villa," Chekhov similarly explores the complications of enforced social intimacy at the dacha through the lens of sexual tension. The story begins with the arrival of an anonymous letter for Pavel Ivanitch Vyhodtsev, "a practical married man who was spending his holidays at a summer villa" (Chekhov 2007:157). The anonymous letter purports to be from an amorous secret admirer who invites Pavel Ivanitch to meet for an evening rendezvous in the old arbor. Pavel Ivanitch spends the day pondering the invitation and wondering whether the letter is a joke or perhaps a legitimate invitation from a love-struck girl or eccentric widow. He remembers seeing a beautiful young lady in the dacha community and wonders—even hopes—that she might be his secret admirer, even as he contemplates whether meeting her would violate his marriage vows. As evening arrives, Pavel Ivanitch decides to venture out to meet his admirer. He takes great care dressing himself, and when his wife asks about his activities he tells her that he has a headache and has decided to cure it with a walk.

Pavel Ivanitch makes his way to the secluded arbor and, in trembling anticipation, steps inside, only to discover that there is already another person waiting. Much to his surprise and annoyance, the other person is the brother of Pavel Ivanitch's wife. The younger man, Mitya, is a student who is staying with them at the dacha. For several tense moments Mitya and Pavel Ivanitch argue with one another, each trying to convince the other to leave. Pavel Ivanitch claims that he needs the secluded space because he is unwell and needs to take a nap, while Mitya claims that he needs the privacy to think about his dissertation. In the midst of their disagreement, a woman's face briefly appears in the opening to the arbor and just as quickly disappears. Angry that Mitya's presence spoiled his tête-à-tête with the young woman, Pavel Ivanitch storms out and returns to the cottage.

At dinner, Pavel Ivanitch and Mitya eat in sullen and hateful silence. In response to his wife's smile, Pavel Ivanitch turns to her and crossly asks why she is smiling. Looking at Pavel's petulant expression, his wife bursts into laughter and asks him if he had received a letter that morning. When Pavel Ivanitch denies it, his wife playfully teases him and demands that he confess before revealing that she had sent the letter. She then reveals that she had sent Mitya an identical letter before divulging the reason for the subterfuge:

> "But what could I do? Tell me that. . . . We had to scrub the rooms out this evening, and how could we get you out of the house? There was no other way of getting you out. . . . But don't be angry, stupid. . . . I didn't want you to be dull in the arbour, so I sent the same letter to Mitya too! Mitya, have you been to the arbour?"
>
> Mitya grinned and left off glaring with hatred at his rival. [Chekhov 2007: 161]

With wry humor, Chekhov demonstrates a keen awareness of what really takes place at the dacha. In this case sexual tensions reveal how the solitude and restfulness promised by a country cottage far away from the hubbub of the city vanish abruptly as that small cottage fills with family, friends, and other visitors. For wives and mothers, the fantasies of freedom and abandon promised by vacation are quickly sabotaged by the constant presence of husbands, children, and houseguests underfoot and the hard work of managing a household. And despite the allure of an escape from "real life," dachas are in fact where the true character of everyday life and ordinary people can be seen most clearly. The dacha is where passions can become reignited, tensions can flare, and family members and friends can tease each other. As Chekhov so poignantly demonstrates, dachas are spaces where pleasure and discomfort, relaxation and work, solitude and socializing go hand in hand, and life, although filled with joys and comforts, can also prove wearying and exhausting.

What makes dachas so unique, appealing, and immediately familiar to Russians is this recognition that despite the very real challenges and annoyances that characterize dacha life, there is a prevailing current of good humor. Dacha living is an experiment in absurdity, and it is precisely this absurdity that dachniki recognize and appreciate, both in their own experiences and in the accounts of writers such as Chekhov and Gorky. This combination of hilarity and exasperation is what my friends and acquaintances wanted to impress upon me when they repeatedly invoked Chekhov in their own narratives about dacha life and when they insisted that this book could not be written without including Chekhov's dacha stories.

Of all of Chekhov's dacha writings, the piece that perhaps best captures these sentiments and issues is his short story "Dachniki" (1885 [1996]).[4] This is the piece that my friends and acquaintances specifically insisted I include in this book.[5] "Dachniki" is a tale of dacha pleasure and disillusionment, told from the perspective of two young newlyweds who have retreated to the dacha to begin their married life. The story begins with the young lovers having walked from their cottage to the railroad platform for an afternoon stroll. As they walk along the platform, embracing, their affection for each other and for their natural surroundings is apparent. The moon, who is jealous because of her own solitary, maidenly state, watches them grumpily.

In anticipation of another pleasurable evening together, Sasha asks his new bride what they will have for dinner. Varia replies, "*Okroshka* [a summertime soup] and chicken. . . . There is just enough chicken for two. And also the sardines and salmon that came from town." The sound of an approaching train excites Sasha and Varia, and they decide to wait for it to come into the station before heading back to their cottage and their supper. Sasha happily tells his wife, "Living with you is so wonderful, Varia, almost impossible to believe how wonderful." As the young couple stand on the platform, they hear something unexpected from one of the train's windows: "Oh, oh! Varia and her husband have come to meet us! There they are! Oh Varenka! . . . Varechka! Oh!" Two young girls jump out of the train and eagerly embrace Varia. They are followed by a stout older woman, a tall, gaunt gentleman, two school-age children, the governess, the governess's grandmother, and all of their assorted luggage.

"Oh, here we are, here we are, my friends," says the gentleman, shaking Sasha's hand. "The tea must already be heated up! I am sure you scolded your uncle for never coming out here. Kolia, Kostia, Nina, Fifa . . . children! Kiss your cousin, Sasha! We all came to see you, perhaps for three or four days. I hope we will not be a bother?" Upon seeing their relatives, the young couple is horror-stricken. Sasha immediately visualizes what will happen next: he and Varia will need to give up their three rooms, all of the pillows, and all of the blankets to their visitors. Even worse, "the salmon, the sardines, and the soup would be slurped up in an instant, the cousins would tear out all of the flowers, the ink would be overturned, there would be a constant din, the aunt would spend the entire day complaining about her illnesses (both the tapeworm and the pain in the pit of her stomach) and about the fact that she was born Baroness Von Fintikh . . . "

At this Sasha looks at his new bride with hatred and whispers to her, "They came to see you . . . damn them!" Varia responds to her husband with equal hatred and rage: "No, they came to see you. . . . They are not my relatives—they are your relatives!" Varia then turns to greet the visitors with a smile, saying, "Welcome, my dears." With that, Sasha turns to his relatives, hiding his angry expression, and greets them equally warmly, "Welcome, dear family."

At that, the moon comes out from behind the cloud and "it seems that the moon smiles; it seems that she is happy that she does not have any relatives."

ANIMATING PLACE

With sympathetic but tart humor directed at the tensions provoked by the intimacies of dacha life, Chekhov and Gorky highlight the familiar paradoxes of this world, where solitude is illusory, self-centered pleasures are fleeting, and a getaway that is supposed to be restful is not. To focus only on dacha life as fertile soil for critical commentaries of Russian social life, however, is to overlook the significance of the locatedness of the dacha realm. Place is critical to the dacha lifestyle, not simply as a physical, geographic location but as an experiential dimension of its inhabitants' lives. The dacha world exists as a "place-world" (Basso 1996:6) of mutual constitution and inhabitation: both dacha places and their residents reside in and belong to one another and are mutually shaped by this reciprocal inhabiting (Casey 1996:24). Keith Basso describes this "process of inter-animation" as a mutual relationship in which "as places animate the ideas and feelings of persons who attend to them, these same ideas and feelings animate the places on which attention has been bestowed" (Basso: 1996:108, 107). Bodies are essential to the materialization and enervation of spaces as simultaneously lived and living places, a point that Edward Casey makes in the observation that "just as there are no places without the bodies that sustain and vivify them, so there are no lived bodies without the places they inhabit and traverse. . . . Bodies and places are connatural terms" (Casey 1996:24).

In other words, the daily life that occurs at the dacha is inspired and shaped by its setting, so that Russians perceive the nature and quality of life at their cottages as remarkably different from the encounters and experiences that take place elsewhere, in the more "ordinary" spaces of daily life. Like their fictional counterparts, my dachniki informants contended that the dacha realm encouraged a fuller expression of behaviors than was possible in other realms. Life is better at the dacha because it is lived more completely, in multiple registers, unlike life in the city, which dachniki blame for reducing them to unthinking, unfeeling automatons. From claims that they experience lowered blood pressure and more restful sleep at the dacha to the assertion that they enjoy deeper personal contemplation and heightened, more vivacious sociality (whether positive or negative), dachniki suggested that a multidimensional, authentically human existence was more accessible at the dacha than in the city. This notion that dachas make possible a fuller range of humanness appears in a scene in Act I of Gorky's play *Dachniki,* in which the characters debate what makes their lives meaningful. One character, Kirill Akimovich Dudakov, a doctor, engages this theme by explaining why he has not met his obligation to visit a nearby facility for adolescent criminals: "We all have so many things to do . . . why? For example . . . I tire myself out. I loafed about in the woods today—it relaxes me . . . somewhat . . . but I am always on edge" (Gorky 1906:37–38). In this short passage, Dudakov expresses multiple and conflicting orientations: exhaustion, boredom, agitation, relaxation, and perhaps even remorse about not keeping his obligations, tempered with the pleasures of self-interest. It is at the dacha that all these moods are possible, that they can coexist, and, perhaps most important, that they add up to a deeper, richer, more complex person.

Recognition of the dynamic, phenomenological qualities of place illuminates the significance of the activities that dachniki pursue at their dachas.

Although dacha-related activities are most commonly identified as forms of "leisure" or "recreation," the qualities of passivity, triviality, or diversion typically attributed to these categories do not adequately capture the reality of dacha life. Conventional definitions have contributed to the marginalization and trivialization of these categories, such that leisure has been set in opposition to labor, and most notably to the value-producing qualities attributed to labor (Koshar 2002; Parker 1983; Stebbins 2004). From this perspective, labor is privileged as a type of activity that is inherently active, productive, and regulated, whereas leisure is presented as a form of nonwork and an escape from activity and structure (Koshar 2002). Travel is especially suited to this orientation because it adds a spatial dimension to the retreat from work.

These dichotomies, however, not only disguise the reality of leisure, but they also misrepresent the nature of labor itself. For historian of leisure Rudy Koshar, such binarisms are inappropriate because they ignore the extent to which "labor and leisure are intertwined, the one reciprocating the other's contradictions and tensions" (2002:15). Koshar suggests instead a perspective that recognizes the mutual constitution and overlap of these two domains, particularly in how they each engage time as something to be managed and consumed. Both leisure and work entail the active, deliberate, and purposeful use and control of time (2002:4). Robert Stebbins takes this perspective further with his observation that the leisure/labor binarism fails to accommodate the nature of one's personal relationship to the expenditure of time; specifically, it is the degree of intensity and commitment with which practitioners take up certain activities that characterizes leisure and labor (Stebbins 2004). For Stebbins, aspects such as degree of commitment and enthusiasm demonstrate the insufficiency of approaches that privilege the more utilitarian, pragmatic, and even financial benefits that are presumed to adhere to labor (2004:xii). By diverting attention away from the material in favor of personal or social traits, Stebbins demonstrates how hobbyists and other leisure enthusiasts can, in fact, approach their activities with the same sense of seriousness, purpose, and responsibility normally associated with work.

With this crucial observation that both leisure and work can inspire devotion among their practitioners, Stebbins suggests considering leisure as a serious activity marked by "earnestness, sincerity, importance, and carefulness" (2004:50). Yet Stebbins is careful to recognize that the hard work of "serious leisure" is not necessarily pleasurable; rather, it is fulfilling (2004:1), a subtle distinction that resonates with the paradoxical condition of Russian dacha life as simultaneously bothersome and desirable. Stanley

Parker similarly makes the point that analyses of the relationships between leisure and labor must not fall into the trap of presuming that "problems" are exclusive to labor and not characteristic of leisure as well (1983:xii).

In the case of Russia, the dynamic qualities of "serious leisure" acquire spatial dimensions by being grounded in physical locations, with a special emphasis on natural settings. Russian leisure activities historically have entailed active engagement with the places in which they are situated. Already by the seventeenth century, pleasure gardens offered Russia's nobility the opportunity to appreciate nature as both an aesthetic object and a setting to be engaged physically (Ely 2002; Floryan 1996; Likhachev 1998). By the second half of the eighteenth century, Russia's elites were importing foreign garden styles, most notably the more "natural" style of unruly English gardens, the carefully symmetrical formalism of French gardens, and the deliberately antiquarian orientation of Italian gardens. They were also traveling abroad on tours of gardens and garden towns, each of which provided a different means of engaging with place (Roosevelt 1990). Other outdoor activities such as hunting, picnicking, and boating were frequent themes in both literary and artistic treatments of summer life, and biographical accounts of Russia's writers and painters were similarly marked by frequent mention of travels and parties in the countryside. By the end of the nineteenth century, leisure activities were no longer the exclusive domain of elites as members of the emerging middle class took up landscape touring, mountaineering, hiking, camping, bicycling, spa visits, and tourism (Ely 2003; Layton 2006; McReynolds 2003, 2006).

These trends continued into the Soviet period, when socialist officials promoted leisure activities as essential, even compulsory, to the development of well-rounded, productive, and fulfilled citizens. Tourism and other leisure activities were intended to be "purposeful," which entailed both work and personal development and served the interests and needs of both self and state (Gorsuch and Koenker 2006; Maurer 2006). To accomplish these objectives, socialist planners formalized the structures of leisure through oversight and regulation of citizens' activities. Through such measures as prescribing proper hygiene practices, home decorating styles and techniques, cooking and eating habits, and bodily comportment, socialist planners promoted an ideology of everyday life that "would combine work, self-improvement, and pleasure in one" (Koenker 2006:119; see also Buchli 2000). The disciplining capacity of daily activities was extended to the realm of leisure, where activities such as tourism were intended to teach socialist citizens how to engage with the world and other cultures around them (Gorsuch 2006; Koenker 2006; Purs 2006; Vari 2006). Diane Koenker also notes that the highly routinized, organized, and focused orienta-tions of "proletarian tourism" were envisioned as means to "discipline the unruly, chaotic, and risk-taking proclivities of Soviet youth" (2006:125). By the 1970s, the emphasis on productive activity had weakened associations of restfulness with tourism (Gorsuch and Koenker 2006:3).

Spatial location emerged as a key element in the pursuit of these activi-ties. On the one hand, the movement in and through places that was enabled by tourist travel was a form of nation-building, an activity through which citizens became intimately acquainted with their own country in its geographic form, and a form of national expansion, whereby tourists were agents through which national values were transmitted elsewhere (Gorsuch 2006; Koenker 2006; Vari 2006).[6] On the other hand, socialist planners realized that disciplining tactics for cultivating productive action could be effectively implemented in physical settings such as schools, public squares, cultural centers, parks, and sports halls (Buchli 2000; Crowley and Reid 2002; Reid 2002). In a study of the Moscow Pioneer Palace, a center dedi-cated to the educational, cultural, political, and recreational development of children, Susan Reid writes that "this exemplary 'socialist space' was to promote their [i.e., children's] self-realization as fully rounded individuals, at the same time as developing their communist consciousness and collec-tive spirit" (Reid 2002:142).

The enactment of daily activities, including leisure, was thus wholly intertwined with the politics of the state. Louise McReynolds suggests that one outcome of this intertwining of leisure and politics was the reconfigu-ration of recreation, so that "*recreation* means just that, the possibility to re-create the self" (2003:300). Such bodily regimes were presented as a means to improve the healthfulness of socialist citizens while simultane-ously harnessing these healthier and more efficient bodies for the greater productivity of the socialist state. By aligning the rhythms and routines of citizens' bodies with those of the state, socialist planners emphasized the productive, purposeful nature of citizens' actions. Yet at the same time, such efforts further complicated distinctions between work and leisure because they "faced the perpetual dilemma of balancing pleasure and pur-pose" (Gorsuch and Koenker 2006:2, 6).

Today recreational activities continue to be a vital component in Rus-sians' post-Soviet lives, either as a form of escape from the challenges of daily life or as an opportunity to claim their position in this new world, even as the diversity of such activities has expanded exponentially as a result of the dramatic political and economic changes in Russia. The increased financial resources of the country's middle- and upper-class citizens, coupled with political changes resulting in the lifting of restrictions on foreign travel, have made travel abroad and hobbies requiring expensive equipment (such as golf, scuba diving, and hang gliding) or specialized knowledge (such as wine tasting, wilderness hiking, and antiques collecting) more commonplace. Yet despite post-Soviet trends toward leisure pursuits as enactments of personal consumption preferences, the emphasis on structured, deliberate activity continues, as evidenced by the proliferation of guidebooks, instructional manuals, and courses teaching the proper enjoyment of these activities. Even informal pickup games of table tennis, badminton, or soccer require careful enumeration and discussion of the proper rules and format, as I have repeatedly discovered.

Natural settings are among the most desirable realms for cultivating and regulating productive bodily activity. The healthful qualities of fresh air, clean water, homegrown foods, and simpler living associated with nature were key to the popularization of spas, sanitariums, and health resorts (McReynolds 2006:32).[7] At the same time, hiking, camping, mountaineering, bicycling, skiing, canoeing, and other recreational activities represented opportunities for merging citizens' personal pleasure with state goals (Bren 2002; Maurer 2006).[8] In the case of socialist children, Pioneer camps were an effective medium for using organized, purposeful leisure to cultivate healthy, disciplined youth. Susan Reid describes Pioneer houses and camps as channels for "[bringing] up future citizens of communism, fit in mind and body," because it was "through exposure to nature and vigorous regimes [that] young people's bodies and wills were tempered" (Reid 2002:143).

Over the past century, dacha-related activities have occupied an intriguing position vis-à-vis these structured, purposeful pursuits. In the logic of socialist body regimes, gardening and cottaging represented additional techniques through which the state could cultivate individual citizens' bodily performances and harness them for the benefit of the nation. As recreational spaces, cottages and gardens provided citizens with opportunities to eat, sleep, and relax in physically and socially healthy ways, thereby increasing their effectiveness as workers.[9] Socialist states also benefited materially by taxing citizens on the produce they grew and the livestock they raised on their garden plots. During periods of shortages, socialist officials expected citizens to use their gardens to supplement the meager supplies available in state stores and markets.

Notwithstanding the value of cottages and gardens to state interests, individual citizens appreciated them for very different reasons. Specifically, Russian citizens found dacha pursuits personally fulfilling and meaningful because these were activities that one did for oneself, *not* for the state. Even though cottaging and gardening activities were often far more labor-intensive and exhausting than official work activities and mandatory community-enhancement activities such as the paradoxical "involuntary voluntarism" of Soviet public-service activities known as Subbotniki, dacha-centered activities such as planting, weeding, harvesting, and foraging were perceived as being purely voluntarily and done for one's own benefit. Even though dachniki criticized the taxes that were levied against what they grew in their gardens and the enhancements they made to their cottages, they perceived their personal activities as a means to reclaim the labor of their own bodies and pursue interests that were free, or at least distanced, from the official regulating efforts of the state.

Within this context, leisure activities are most relaxing and restorative when they entail not a retreat from activity but rather its embrace. Vladimir described it in this way: "People really [like] it here for the active rest [aktivnyi otdukh], when you are not working [kogda ne rabotaet]. But today when people go on holiday [v otpuske], when they are resting [otdokhnut], they will be working." Here Vladimir suggests a significant distinction between work, rest, and active rest. For rest to be meaningful, it cannot consist of mere emptiness or absence of activity, but instead it must entail activity done for another entity—an employer, a nation, or oneself. But it is only when this activity is done for oneself that it is pleasurable and restful. Hence, "active rest" is no less laborious than regular work, but it belongs in the realm of pleasure because it is self-oriented work.

This embrace of deliberately active, labor-filled rest is understood as a personal choice, no matter how coercive it might, in fact, be. An example of the importance of personal choice can be seen in popular attitudes toward gardening versus participation in another key national institution: the Russian Orthodox Church. During the course of my fieldwork, Russian believers who did not regularly attend Orthodox services most frequently cited the onerous bodily regimens of Orthodox rituals—long periods of time spent standing or kneeling on hard concrete floors, often in poorly heated churches—as the reason they did not formally practice their faith. What was particularly curious and revealing was that many of these same individuals voluntarily spent even longer periods of time kneeling, squatting, or hunched over in their gardens or around berry bushes without similar complaint. This was particularly noteworthy among elderly informants. The behavior of the elderly father of my friend Alla was typical of this perspective. In his late eighties and frail, Alla's father rarely left the family's apartment, except to walk the six kilometers back and forth from the family's dacha.

Russian acquaintances joked that the bodies of elderly dachniki were permanently marked by the telltale crouch into which their limbs had ossified after years of gardening. In a conversation with Angela and her colleague Margarita about the physical consequences of toiling in a garden, Angela commented that hard work in the garden is evident in the bodies of elderly people because they are always hunched over and they have problems with their blood pressure; even so, elderly people continue to do this work despite the toll it takes on their bodies. One issue of a dacha magazine included a section on improving one's health at the dacha that focused specifically on bodily postures. The article addressed basic dacha tasks—tending beets in a garden, picking apples from a tree, planting flowers, cutting branches off a tree, and digging a hole—using cartoon figures to illustrate the correct and incorrect ways to do each activity. All of the characters in the illustrations were clearly middle-aged or elderly, and they included a babushka (elderly woman) wearing a head scarf (Kalachev 2004:47–49).

This insistence on active, rather than passive, leisure that one chooses for oneself was captured beautifully by the sign for a fishing supply store in Tver. Named Dom Rybaka (House of the Fisherman), this shop sold a reasonably wide assortment of equipment for fishermen of all ages and experience levels—rods, reels, lines, hooks, bait, and nets—as well as other summer sporting gear such as soccer balls, swimming gear (goggles, fins, snorkels), camping equipment (camping chairs and sleeping bags), and hunting-themed decor items. Most striking was the store's slogan, printed clearly beneath the store's name: "Wares for an Active Vacation" (Tovary dlia aktivnogo otdykha).[10]

In a context in which the appropriation of labor by the state transformed work into something official and public, dacha activities represented an opportunity for ordinary citizens to redirect and reappropriate their own labor to suit their own interests and needs. This orientation resembles the self-directed appreciation of work captured in Stebbins's notions of "serious leisure" and "occupational devotion" (2004), although, as we will see, dachniki such as my informants associate this reclamation of one's activities, time, and body from the state as a form of "soulfulness." Activities done for oneself are described as "for the soul" in recognition of the simultaneously physical and psychical satisfaction that comes from working for oneself and under conditions of one's own choosing.

It is this explicitly active, self-oriented engagement that makes the relationship between dachniki and dachas meaningful, a detail captured in Casey's observation that "the living-moving body is essential to the process of emplacement: *lived bodies belong to places* and help to constitute them. . . . By the same token . . . *places belong to lived bodies* and depend on them" (1996:24; emphasis in original). Hence dachniki and their dachas are symbiotically linked in a mutual relationship of enervation that is continually constituted and reinforced through dachniki's active labor in this space. The dacha world is inhabited fully as an experiential realm in which topographies are sensed and felt through the most intimate spaces of the body.

THE INTIMACY OF DISTANCE

A simultaneously physical, psychical, and topographical realm, the dacha world exists as a dimension that is fully present to its inhabitants, a point underscored in dachniki's observations that they felt more alive, more attuned to the world around them, and more human at their dachas. How, then, can this notion of presentism and immediacy be reconciled with the perception that dachas, and leisure life more generally, belong to a dimension that is set apart from everyday life? In actuality, these two perspectives are not mutually exclusive but constitute another paradoxical feature of dachas. Specifically, it is these distancing tactics that foster the construction of the dacha world as an enchanted place—"another planet."[11] The values and qualities that are believed to characterize the dacha world derive directly from rhetorical tactics that locate it elsewhere, in a state of exceptionalism separate from the banalities of everyday life.

In other words, distancing maneuvers operate as protective devices to shelter the paradoxical realities of dacha life from the gaze of outsiders who are presumed to neither understand nor appreciate them. True access to the absurdities of the authentic dacha world—to its "ontological wildness" (Casey 1996:35)—is reserved for those insiders who know these dirty secrets and can value them appropriately. By keeping secret the paradoxes of dacha life, Russians collude in a project of national self-identification and belonging that is projected both outward and inward. Michael Herzfeld's concept of "cultural intimacy" is instructive for understanding how people find in dacha secrets alternative visions of what it means to belong to the nation. Building on Anderson's concept of "imagined community," Herzfeld observes that ideologies of nationalism are always founded on "resemblance, whether biogenetic or cultural," with the result that all citizens are ascribed to a formalized singularity, so that differences, or "variant cultural readings" in Herzfeld's terms, are dangerous to this mythology of similarity (Herzfeld 1997:27). Difference does not disappear, however, thereby forcing societies to find ways to cope with it, most often through concealment. Concealment thus requires members of that society to engage in a collective act of secrecy in order to prevent national embarrassment. Herzfeld suggests that these acts of protective secrecy inspire among insiders a form of intimacy that is simultaneously rueful and affectionate (1997:28). As a result, nations selectively cultivate and present two images of themselves: a positive expression of national identity for outsiders, and a more complicated set of traits that are immediately familiar to insiders. Underlying "cultural intimacy" is a normalizing project that recasts those qualities that would otherwise be embarrassing when projected to outsiders into traits that insiders view affectionately and even proudly. More significantly, these traits become "ordinary" and even expected within this arena visible only to insiders.

The relational logics of representation evoked by cultural intimacy illuminate the significance of the distancing tactics at play in Russians' attitudes toward their dachas. Russians emphasize the separateness of the dacha sphere in order to segregate the paradoxes and turmoil that take place there from the realm of the ordinary, the normal, and the publicly visible. This allows Russians to acknowledge to themselves the ordinariness of the discomforts of this sphere while insisting to outsiders that these same problems are somehow exceptional. More importantly, the insider status afforded by sharing in the collective secrets of dachas is reassuring because it indicates one's membership in a select social group. Hence, at the same time that these trials and tribulations are the criteria by which authentic dacha experiences are evaluated, it is the "fellowship of the flawed" (Herzfeld 1997:28) forged among those who collectively protect these secrets that distinguishes Russia's dacha lifestyle from cottage cultures elsewhere.

Russians who invoked writers such as Chekhov as a shorthand for their dacha experiences and advised me that any discussion of dacha life would be incomplete without including Chekhov's story "Dachniki" were imparting both a message about the overall quality of the organic lifestyle and a subtle warning. Dachniki's relationships with the dacha lifestyle are complicated and often bittersweet. Pleasure and pain, joy and misery, are inextricably linked: it is not possible to participate in dacha life without encountering the full spectrum of experiences. As the comments of dachniki suggested, disentangling them would be counterproductive, as this would violate the authenticity, meaningfulness, and ordinariness of the experience. Yet at the same time, these travails reveal the vulnerability of the dacha world and its place in Russian heritage. The self-deprecating and often sardonic humor that tinges accounts of the dacha world can be read as both a coping mechanism and a protective impulse of insiders. It is their recognition of these internal conflicts through humorous, but no less pointed, accounts that makes the dacha stories of Chekhov and Gorky resonate so strongly with dachniki. Chekhov and Gorky are not just narrating fictional dachniki, but rather they are telling the story of every dachnik. While dachniki may laugh together or commiserate about their challenges at the dacha, it is another thing entirely for that laughter to come from outsiders who do not share the same visceral and emotional connection to that experience.

CHAPTER 3

The Pleasure of Pain

Gardening for the Soul

During the summer months in the country you cannot help relaxing; you dress casually in loose-fitting clothes, so that you can sit on the ground, make your way through the scrub and nettles on the riverbank, get wet in the rain and then dry out again in the wind and sun. The same thing with shaving. You tire of shaving every day as you do in Moscow, and you give it a miss for four days. A reddish stubble appears on your cheeks along with a great many whiskers which have lost their colour. You do not look quite like a convict on the run, but you are no angel either.

—Vladimir Soloukhin, "Tittle-Tattle: Small Unintentional
   Mystifications" (Soloukhin 1988:108)

When [Russians] go to their dachas in the countryside, they are content. But when they have to get there by *elektrichka* [commuter train], they are miserable.

—Svetlana, aged fifty-five, to the great amusement of her
   dacha compatriots

In the 1990s, dacha stories were rife with narratives of need, misery, and suffering juxtaposed against the satisfactions associated with dacha life. During the periodic economic uncertainties that had emerged in the initial post-Soviet period, dachas became particularly important as a part of Russia's subsistence economy. Newspaper accounts documenting the consequences of inflation, fluctuating exchange rates, and unpaid salaries and pensions focused heavily on how Russians were again resorting to their gardens to sustain themselves through these difficult times. The accounts of financial decline that were presented by the media, especially by Western sources, focused on desperate acts of thievery and retaliation occurring in dacha communities across Russia.

Among my acquaintances in Moscow, Tver, and elsewhere in Russia, there were frequent conversations about how their survival through Russia's long winters depended on their ability to stock a sufficient supply of preserves made from foods taken from their gardens and the forests.[1] In the mid-1990s, my landlady Anya planned to fill an entire wall of her bedroom with canned tomatoes, cucumbers, and berry preserves. Anya's goal was not an unusual one but shared by many acquaintances, even after Russia's economy had begun to recover. Underlying all of these narratives was a sense of misery and suffering, especially the miserableness of the formal economy with its pitiful pensions, the rising price of food, and the threatened increase in public transportation costs.

The theme of misery has continued to color dacha narratives into the 2000s, although the precise nature of this "misery" has shifted. Instead of lamenting the price and scarcity of food, Russians complain about the cost of maintaining their dachas, planting their gardens, and buying jars and other supplies for preserves, as well as the time required and the annoyance involved in traveling to and from their dachas. As the number of cars on Russian roads has grown exponentially, so has the time spent in traffic jams on highways originally built to accommodate a fraction of the traffic. People who previously hopped in their cars on Friday afternoons for a quick drive to their dachas now wait until early Saturday morning to depart and then return earlier on Sunday afternoons, thus decreasing the amount of time that they spend in the countryside. For Russians without their own car, the thought of spending several hours on a hot, crowded suburban train, with its hard bench seats and tiny windows that at best allow only a tantalizing hint of a breeze to pass through, is equally horrifying. Elderly informants in particular complain about the physical hardships of traveling long distances by public transportation and on foot. One friend, a woman in her mid-eighties and in poor health, finds that she must spend two to three days in bed recuperating for every trip she takes to her son's dacha. Despite her complaints and the obvious toll that these journeys take on her physical health, she valiantly struggles on and refuses to miss out on these visits to the countryside.

Over the past ten years numerous friends complained that the hassles of their dachas had become so onerous as to outweigh their benefits, and they had sworn off using their dachas on a regular basis. Several announced their intentions to sell their dachas in order to rid themselves of the burden. Such threats were rarely carried out, however, as most friends have held on to their dachas and continue to invest time, money, and energy into the very activities that they claim have tormented them for years. Beneath the compulsory rhetoric of agony and dread that infuses dacha accounts exists a persistent optimism that dacha trips are, in the end, worth the aggravation and expense.

Russians' ambivalence about dachas raises intriguing questions about what makes them ascribe such different qualities to their summer retreats and how they reconcile these differences. The reason Russians most frequently cite for pursuing this lifestyle is their conviction that life in nature is more peaceful and relaxing than ordinary life, especially when that ordinary life is characterized by formal work schedules and apartment living. Repeatedly, respondents informed me that the reason they liked going to their dachas was because one can "live well" *(zhit' khorosho)* there. A conversation among several Nadezhda residents captured this sentiment nicely:

> *Viktoriia:* Russians have a certain yearning—to go to one place, the dacha.
>
> *Masha:* At the dacha, you sleep well. Here you can sleep so well [*vysypats'ia mozhno khorosho,* i.e., get your fill of sleeping so that you are refreshed]. In the city you do not sleep.
>
> *Roman:* In the city, mosquitoes will eat you up.
>
> *Iuliia:* And at the dacha they do not eat you up?
>
> *Masha:* But there [i.e., in the city] there are cars under the windows and someone is always working on them—rrrr, rrrr—rrr, rrr [*makes noises like a car engine constantly turning over*], and there are always drunks walking past.
>
> *Roman:* They are screeching, right?
>
> *Masha:* Yes, screeching. But they aren't just screeching, they're cursing.
>
> *Iuliia:* And here it is the cats screeching.

Konstantin, another neighbor in the Nadezhda community, described his reasons for participating in dacha life in this way:

> We have been living here for a long time. When it starts to get warm, we immediately come out here for the entire time. We live here, well that is, we breathe the air. You yourself know the condition [of the air] in the city? There is dust, it is humid, noisy. And when you go from the dacha to the city—you cannot sleep at night for an entire week. It is impossible to sleep because of the noise, the cars . . . impossible. But here—here you sleep like the dead [*tut spish' kak ubytii*]. It is marvelous . . . The forest is your own.

The specific reasons that Russians give to explain why they engage in dacha life reflect the common view that natural settings encourage individuality and invite each person to personalize his or her relationship with this world, a perspective neatly summarized by one dachnik as "To each his own *[dlia kazhdogo]*": the forest for one person, the river for another, berries for yet another, and finally the company for others. In response to this description, Masha wryly replied, "To each his own cross [to bear] *[kazhdomu svoi krest]*." Several individuals even remarked how much their cats loved going to the dacha, thereby including the needs and desires of the nonhuman members of the family. Roman emphasized this personal specificity in this way: "It is very individualized *[Eto ochen' individual'no]*." It is this variety, informants insisted, that is part of the appeal and value of dacha life: everyone is free to pursue his or her own interests and pleasures, and no one can impose their preferences on others. Svetlana stated, "It is a piece of a different life. Besides, it is as if everyone who comes here is engrossed in their own worlds [and] can choose what they desire most of all . . . [People have] the opportunity to choose what is their favorite."

The value of individualized experiences for overcoming the apparent miseries of dacha life was made apparent in Valentina's response. Like her neighbors in Nadezhda, Valentina has invested considerable time and money into her garden. Well into her seventies, she has also devoted significant physical energy to the backbreaking work of planting, weeding, and maintaining her stunning garden. During my first visit to her dacha, Valentina led me on a guided tour of her beautiful flowerbeds, matter-of-factly describing the amount of work that her garden had required. When I complimented her on the loveliness of the garden and commented that it must have been an exhausting project, she replied simply that for her, the most important thing about her garden was that it was "for the soul *[dlia dushi]*."[2]

Valentina's invocation of soulfulness illuminates an important detail about the ways in which seemingly paradoxical qualities of misery, hardship, contentedness, and even pleasure can coexist. The commingling of pleasure and pain is a recurring theme in Russian culture. The experience of being miserable, or at least engaging in publicly recognized performances and recitations of personal misery, carries symbolic power in Russian social practice and can, in some cases, reward the subject of this misery with a sense of satisfaction and even personal pleasure (Ries 1997).[3] The tales of woe and hardship told by dacha enthusiasts closely resemble the accounts of "heroic shopping" that Nancy Ries has recorded among

Russian consumers in the perestroika period (Ries 1997). Like Ries's consumers who complained about the length of time they stood in line, the difficulty of finding particular items, and the hardship of repeated trips across town just to complete their shopping, dachniki lament the long and unruly lines at the train station ticket counters, the overcrowded train cars, the heavy bags they lug through the woods, the number of mosquito bites they have incurred, and so on. And just like Ries's consumers, for whom tales of "heroic shopping" become ammunition in social competitions, dachniki try to outdo each other with their stories. Misery is not just something to be endured but something to be borne proudly.

What these complaints suggest, first of all, is that suffering is not necessarily wholly undesirable. Suffering can, in fact, bring benefits and even pleasure. Second, practices of suffering, including carefully crafted performances of that suffering through complaints and the presentation of insect bites and other wounds, reveal that the nature of soulfulness, of doing something "for one's soul," is not simply an existential or spiritual experience but rather a corporeal one. Both dachniki's complaints about the misery of gardening and cottaging and their passionate enthusiasm about the joys of these same spaces emphasize the very practical, bodily qualities of these activities: loss of time and physical exertion on the one hand, and improved physical and mental health on the other. This point was revealed in a discussion about whether dachas were a place of rest and relaxation *(mesto otdykha),* when Masha exclaimed wistfully, "Oh what kind of relaxation there is at the dacha!" Valentina tartly replied, "There really is no relaxation at the dacha." Agreeably, Masha consented, "No relaxation at the dacha! . . . No kind of relaxation at all!" Valentina then quickly complicated the nature of relaxation, confusing pleasure and suffering: "It makes no difference, you are relaxing with your soul and body *[Vse ravno otdykhaesh' dushoi i telom].*" Soulfulness, then, as it is enacted and experienced in the organic life, is a multisensory, full-bodied, and fully embodied experience that simultaneously encompasses both pleasure and misery.

This visceral soulfulness derives from a particularly Russian conception of geographic nationalism, a connection made explicit by one of Nancy Ries's Muscovite informants in this statement about *dusha* (soul): "*Dusha* is the ability to feel very deeply. So you feel deeply, first of all nature, the beauty of nature, the oneness, your own oneness with nature, and this whole feeling of being at one with the landscape means that you are part of the landscape, and that the landscape expresses the same kinds of feelings that you experience yourself" (quoted in Ries 1997:30).

The concept of *dusha* is almost impossible to translate either linguistically or culturally (Pesmen 2000), as it encapsulates a range of experiences that are simultaneously existential and physical: suffering together through long, dark winter nights, reading and passionately discussing Russian novelists and philosophy, roasting oneself in the *banya* (steam bath) with friends, and feeling connected to one's nation and co-nationalists. As Dale Pesmen has documented, *dusha* is more than a religious concept but is rather an expansive quality or entity that encompasses both "a myth, a notion, an image, a consoling fiction, and a nationalist trope" as well as the "*ways* in which people did things and *what* they did" (Pesmen 2000:12; emphasis in original). *Dusha* is both universally shared and personally experienced. Attention to the corporeal qualities of *dusha* underscores the significance of a full-bodied, sensory, and deliberately active engagement with the world to Russian philosophies about meaningful living. In this sense, the visceral quality of soulfulness as described by dachniki suggests a more direct, more immediate relationship with the natural world of the dacha.

THE SIMPLE LIFE

Leisure activities such as cottaging and gardening, and rural living more generally, often inspire ideals of simplicity: simpler times and simpler places. The value of simplicity registers in the minimalism of physical space, especially when it comes to dacha structures and their furnishings. Although dacha cottages are frequently the repositories of cast-off and worn items from people's apartments, there is an understated elegance to these items' reuse in dachas. Decorations are functional, and often multifunctional. Outdated calendars with photographs of world cities, reproductions of famous paintings, and depictions of scenes from well-known fairy tales (*skazki*) can serve double duty as art and as patches covering holes in peeling wallpaper. Baskets filled with berries, mushrooms, or the garden's bounty are transformed into centerpieces on a kitchen or sitting room table.

As the comments of my informants revealed, the physical size of one's dacha was less important than its capacity for leisure and socializing. Anton described his dacha as a *malenkaia domushka* (little house), using the diminutive form of *domik,* which is in turn a diminutive form of *dom* (house), as a further indicator of both the structure's size and the affection he felt for it. He continued by asking, "Who needs something big? You put in a bed, a table, bread, and salt—you don't need anything more than that. You eat and sleep. That's all."[4] What was especially fascinating was the way in which even as informants privileged smallness over bigness, the simplicity of dachas also evoked qualities of expansiveness. During the Soviet era of pervasive housing shortages, the theme of the magically expanding apartment appeared both in Russian imagination, such as the enchanted apartments that expand into ballrooms in Mikhail Bulgakov's *Master and Margarita,* and in daily practice. As Svetlana Boym and Katerina Gerasimova have documented in their accounts of Soviet communal housing practices, citizens found creative ways to use partitions and furniture to transform cramped apartments into multipurpose living spaces (Boym 1994; Gerasimova 2002).

The pleasures of the simple life extend beyond the immediate confines of the dacha cottage and its garden and into the surrounding meadows and forests, as residents in dacha communities find numerous ways to pass the lazy days of summer. In the forested area just outside the Nadezhda community, for instance, local residents had cleared out a space for a volleyball court where, as Inga remembered, she and her friends played so often that they were practically professionals. Today the volleyball court still sees regular use by neighborhood children, as does the half-sized soccer pitch, complete with nets on either end, which has been scratched out of an open, marshy area. Svetlana fondly recalled the table tennis skirmishes that she enjoyed in her youth: "Oh, we really entertained ourselves. We had a table where we played table tennis. That was when we lived in the big [communal] cottage. I played table tennis with Sergei Ivanovich [a friend of the same age who had been born in Tver and became a well-known Russian poet] and I beat him! Oh, here I am reminiscing about my youth, and I'm already fifty years old."

Even artistic productions and exhibits found their way to dacha communities. During the socialist period, traveling theaters moved through dacha communities, setting up their stages and performing for a few days before moving on. Some communities erected tents in a small clearing in the forest where they showed films to local dachniki, a practice that Margarita and her friends recalled fondly when reminiscing about when their children were younger. As Inga described it, "The children were running all over the place. They were not interested in coming in and sitting on the benches, but they did want to look inside the projector. It was all free! And everyone would search it out straight away. We were all watching films under the tent." Although local municipal agencies no longer entertain residents with films and concerts, neighbors gather informally in one another's cottages to watch television or films on video cassette or DVD. Riverbanks are an appealing gathering place for car owners to park their vehicles and turn up their stereos for music to accompany their sunbathing, swimming, and campfires.

Such leisure activities were not restricted to regular dacha residents or dacha communities, however, as I learned one afternoon when my friend Ksenia invited me for a walk around Tver. As we set off on our stroll she told me that she needed to run an errand. We stopped at the sporting goods section of the local department store, where she purchased a pair of table tennis paddles and balls as a birthday present for her son. As we were walking over the bridge that crossed the Volga, Ksenia turned to me and suggested that we test the paddles before she gave them to her son. We stopped at the park that extended along the riverbank but discovered that all of the table tennis tables were already occupied, as were the basketball hoops and volleyballs nets. We continued walking through the neighborhood, looking for a free table, until we eventually made our way to the yard in front of Ksenia's apartment building. There, in the middle of a patch of dirt, covered with broken bottles and other trash, was an available table. After clearing the trash and leaves off the table, Ksenia removed a net and clamps from her handbag and attached them to the table. With our table properly outfitted, we began to play, eventually attracting a small crowd. On a separate occasion, Ksenia and I carried badminton racquets and a shuttlecock to the tiny courtyard behind a local school, where we spent the afternoon playing under the watchful eyes of a family of goats who lived in the neighboring yard. In the courtyard we were competing for space with a teenage couple practicing their tennis serves against a wall, several bike-riding children, and a young mother aimlessly pushing a pram around the edges of the courtyard while chasing her toddler, who was repeatedly trying to catch our shuttlecock.

I soon learned that Ksenia, like many others, routinely carried sporting equipment in her bag during the summer in case the opportunity to play a match or two presented itself. The ability of Ksenia's handbag to expand magically to hold table tennis balls and paddles, badminton racquets, and even bundles of freshly picked herbs and mushrooms was not unusual. Other friends and acquaintances regularly carried swimming attire, towels, shuttlecocks, racquets, books, and other leisure implements in their purses, backpacks, briefcases, and plastic bags. In public, it is not uncommon to catch a glimpse of similar collections in strangers' bags and briefcases.

These preparations reveal a curious truth, which is that spontaneity requires careful planning. In turn, this planning reveals a tension between structure and nonstructure, particularly as these tensions play out in struggles between state and citizen to manage and control the routines of daily life. As will become apparent in the following section, to the extent that Russians perceive nature as a protected space beyond the reach of the state, the schedules, rules, and norms that organize this realm are reinterpreted and experienced as unstructured.

TIMEKEEPING

The struggle to manage the structures and activities of one's own life appears perhaps most compellingly in the experience of temporality. Time is also perhaps the dimension that most immediately and unmistakably conjures up dacha life as something qualitatively distinct from those forms of life constituted by officially organized and sanctioned forms of leisure, work, and school that people lead when they are outside nature. As Russians are quick to point out, time exists differently in natural spaces than it does in other settings, especially fast-paced urban spaces. Russians like my landlady Anya, whose constant refrain was *"bystro bystro!"* (quickly, quickly!), complain about the constant hustle and bustle of their lives in the city. Friends and acquaintances lament the fact that there is never enough time to meet friends, go to the cinema, or read a good book. In recent years, mobile telephones have become ubiquitous, not only because of the shortage of telephones in public housing, which continues to be a problem in some regions, but because people find themselves so busy that they cannot schedule activities in advance. Mobile telephones thus represent a lifeline for friends to catch each other for a few moments to chat or even arrange a spontaneous visit to a café.

This sense that society is increasingly speeding up has been intensified by Russia's embrace of North American–style business practices, with their regimented working hours and time clocks supervised by managers, as well as the migration of upper- and middle-class professionals to new housing complexes in the suburbs. Although these residences boast modern conveniences such as state-of-the-art appliances and proximity to high-end food and other markets, their distance from the city center has meant that more workers must now spend additional time commuting to work, either by car through the ubiquitous traffic jams that ring both urban and rural communities, or by multiple forms of public transportation. As a result, Russians complain that not only do they lack adequate time for themselves, but they also have less control over their ability to plan their time.

Complaints about the rapid and dizzying pace of urban life are not, of course, exclusive to Russia, but rather have been associated with a postmodern, global, hyperconsumerist world more generally (see, e.g., Barber

1995; Harvey 1989; Inda and Rosaldo 2002; Petrini 2001a). In many cases, this speeding up of daily life was initially heralded as a desirable form of progress. Like their capitalist counterparts elsewhere in the pre–World War II era, the Soviet Union became a leader in promoting efficiency techniques to harness and maximize the labor of its citizens. What was unique about the Soviet case was that despite official efforts to implement time-saving measures such as assembly lines, workplace shops and canteens, and the outsourcing to specialists of personal tasks such as laundry, cooking, and childcare, the realities of everyday Soviet life meant that time was frequently wasted and in short supply. Queues, a necessity in shortage societies such as the Soviet Union, were emblematic of inefficiently used time. Soviet citizens could never predict where they would be at any particular time because of the unpredictability of shopping and the long lines of passengers trying to shove their way through subway tunnels and into overcrowded subway cars. As Russian friends have repeatedly joked, "Russian time" is always at least fifteen minutes late.

Soviet citizens responded to the arrhythmia of daily life by developing strategies to put time to multiple purposes. To accommodate frequent shortages of food and consumer goods, citizens incorporated personal activities into their work schedules. Periodic breaks and midday meals became opportunities to go out shopping, while office spaces and supplies could be conscripted for unofficial second jobs. Citizens who worked in lucrative food, consumer goods, or construction industries could divert supplies for their own personal benefit. Consequently, these dual uses of time, and the resulting sense of dual ownership of time by state and citizen, meant that time was a pawn in the daily struggles between state and citizen, as both parties battled to determine and control its parameters, its rhythms, and the uses to which it was put.[5]

Natural settings offer a striking contrast, both in terms of how time is regulated and controlled and in terms of how temporality is experienced. Russians insist that there is simply something very different about the way time proceeds and is experienced in the countryside, as both the pace of life and the flow of time there follow very different rhythms than they do in the city. Not only does time have a palpably different feel in nature, but it also seems to follow very different trajectories. The seasonal rhythms of the organic life proceed quite differently from those enacted by capitalist work time in sterile offices governed by official clocks. Dietary habits change, particularly in the summer. In this season, the bland cafeteria food or instant soups that office eaters depend upon for their lunches shift to accommodate the progression of seasonal fruits and vegetables, freshly picked from gardens and forests. Bodily movements also change noticeably in natural spaces, as people who otherwise hurry along city sidewalks and rush to catch public transportation slow their pace to wander languidly along grassy paths. In the summer, the long days of endless sunshine affect not only *what* is possible but *when*, as activities continue on long into the evening. Although many dachniki rely on scheduled trains to reach their cottages, others use minibuses and other informal modes of transportation that do not adhere to regular schedules but are dispatched when there are enough passengers heading in the same direction. Curiously, even though this might mean that travelers find themselves waiting for extended periods of time, often accompanied by unhappy children, and even unhappier cats in their travel carriers, rarely have I overhead complaints. Instead, there is an air of anticipation and relaxation, as people nap, chat, or read to fill the time.

Seasonal cycles also affect the making of long-term plans. Although Russians insist that their city lives are so complicated that they prevent advance planning, those same individuals make their dacha plans months in advance, often in consultation with farmer's almanacs, to accommodate seasonal changes and growing seasons. Even local municipalities recognize that dacha season is different and adjust community affairs accordingly. Public transportation is one such area that is reorganized for dacha season, with the expansion of roadways to ease congestion caused by dacha traffic and the addition of minibus lines *(marshruti)* that transport passengers directly from the city to their dacha communities. The transportation needs of dachniki are reflected in fluctuations in railroad and bus schedules, with more trains running during the summer months. Public utilities undergo similar adjustments as local municipalities change the rates that they charge residents for public utilities. Ivan, the president of the Nadezhda cooperative, provided to all of the residents in the cooperative certificates (sing. *spravka)* that they could present to the Tver utilities department in order to receive a discounted rate for their apartments during the summer. The discounts were justified on the grounds that during the summer, dachniki were not using their apartments and thus should not pay for utilities during that time. When Angela related this news to me, she explained that "dacha time is an officially recognized excuse" for modifying utility schedules.

In the late 1990s, I experienced a moment of enlightenment about the importance of dacha time as a different mode of temporality. During an interview with Oleg, a thirty-year-old father of two small children and a midlevel manager at a company in Moscow, I asked him to explain why he and his wife found their dacha useful. At that time, Russia's economy had not yet fully recovered from Russia's 1998 economic crisis, and Oleg and his wife had both told me on separate occasions that they relied on their dacha garden as a significant supplemental food source for their own family.[6] They also routinely sent care packages of garden foods to his wife's parents, who lived in another former Soviet republic. Hence I expected Oleg to refer to provisioning in his answer. As Oleg responded to my question, however, he departed from the subject of supplemental food supplies and mentioned that he enjoyed going to his dacha to sleep. Elaborating further, he explained that he sometimes spent several hours in transit simply to get a good night's sleep—no matter how brief—at his dacha. To explain why he preferred spending several hours driving back and forth to his cottage to spending those hours at home in his own bed, Oleg framed his response around time. He told me simply that at the dacha, "time moves differently [vremia idet po-drugomu]."

After this conversation I began to pay attention to how my Russian informants related to time in the countryside. One family immediately took off their watches as soon as they arrived at their dacha and kept their clock tucked into a discreet corner of the kitchen that was not easily visible. Yet somehow, without looking at their watches, my friends seemed to know when to start walking for the train, arriving on the platform just minutes before the arrival of the Moscow-bound suburban train. During the week that I spent with Anya and Tanya at the latter's dacha, I observed as they spent hours trudging through the forests to pick baskets of raspberries in the heat of the day, then stayed up until the wee hours while they talked and made raspberry jam and canned pickles, only to be up again before the sun rose, bright-eyed and bushy-tailed and apparently suffering no ill effects from their labors.[7]

Members of the Kuznetsov family told me that the casualness of dacha life meant that neighbors could drop in uninvited at one another's cottages late in the evening without worry about waking or offending their unexpecting hosts. In fact, these acquaintances insisted that at the dacha unexpected visitors were always expected, no matter the time, a belief that was borne out repeatedly at other dachas, where friends and strangers alike dropped in for a chat, a cup of tea, or directions to the nearest train station. Equally revealing was an occasion when the Kuznetsov family invited me to visit them at their dacha. My hosts informed me that the visit would be for the weekend and that we would leave Moscow on Friday afternoon after work. Given the importance that my hosts placed on scheduling the dacha trip around their work schedules, I understood this to mean that we would return to Moscow on Sunday evening so they could return to work on Monday morning. Instead, as Sunday evening rolled around with no preparations for departure in evidence, I awkwardly asked my hostess when we were leaving. She looked at me with great surprise and replied that we were not leaving for another couple of days. As I quickly discovered, her summertime definition of "weekend" was only loosely based on the calendar or work commitments.

Inga likened life at the dacha to a timeless existence, a social world that existed in a different temporal reality. In her description of the dacha community where she, her parents, and many other Tver residents had long spent their summers, Inga reflected, "Everyone went there and spent the entire summer there." Continuing, she qualified her statement by adding a curious detail: some would only go to the dacha for the weekend. For them, this "little piece of time, where you dashed there, ran around, then dashed back home like a refugee," was akin to spending the entire summer at the dacha.

As I have come to appreciate, and as anyone who has spent time at a Russian dacha or in the Russian countryside knows, there is something palpably different about dacha time and dacha life. In the countryside, as people sit around the table and drink endless cups of tea sweetened by fresh raspberry jam, talk politics, reminisce about the past, and putter in their gardens, time ceases to exist as an explicit structuring framework for daily life. This is even truer in the northern parts of the country during summer, when it seems as if night will never come or it arrives for only a brief moment before quickly disappearing. Time is perceived as unbounded and capable of moving forward, backward, and even outward, qualities that are particularly apparent in the persistent nostalgia that colors dacha life. Activities must also be spontaneous, or at least convey the impression of being unstructured and unprompted, a belief affirmed by the plans made by Ksenia, who had scrimped for months in order to save enough money to send her teenaged son to camp *(lager)* for several weeks. Although Ksenia regretted that she could not afford to send him to camp for a longer period, she argued that the relatively brief time her son spent in nature would be just as beneficial as a longer stay. When the end of her son's session approached, Ksenia decided to make the two-day train trip herself and collect him, unannounced, from camp a few days early. When I asked how her son would know to meet her earlier than originally planned, she shrugged off my question and replied simply that her son would know.[8]

One woman in her thirties stated that she did not enjoy going to Pioneer camp when she was a child, precisely because of the structured activities. She recalled that the camp schedule was highly organized around multiple activities that were supposed to be forms of leisure. She found, however, that the overstructured time left her little time to rest and enjoy herself. She reflected that in Soviet-era youth camps, time for resting or time for oneself was considered dangerous because it allowed the opportunity for independent thinking. For her, Pioneer camp represented a struggle over the control of time and leisure waged between the individual and the state, and she preferred to spend time at her family's dacha where she felt freer to determine her own schedule and choose her own activities.

Calling attention to the structures of time is the height of rudeness, as I discovered with the misunderstanding that had stranded me (delightedly, I admit) at the Kuznetsovs' dacha for an extended period, and with my question about how Ksenia and her son would be able to meet at camp. Yet even though the structures and markers of time should be neither apparent nor acknowledged, time does not cease to exist. Rather, its textures and rhythms become manifest and experienced in other ways, such as by acquaintances who claimed never to consult a watch yet arrived at the train station on time, or another acquaintance whose internal clock alerted her, without fail, to her favorite soap opera on television. For that single hour every afternoon, she adhered to the routines of media time; as soon as the program had ended, however, the television was returned to its place in the corner and the regime of the clock faded away.

The lack of a need to wear a watch came up in a conversation with Irina, who explained that when one was at the dacha, a more primitive, intuitive sense of time took over, as human cycles became aligned with natural cycles:

> Yes, yes. Time goes completely differently, that is exactly true. In the first place, [time] goes according to the sun. You understand, the entire time [you are at the dacha] you do not look at your watch, but you look at the sun and see where the sun is going. Therefore you go around the dacha without your watch. In the off chance that there is a bit of water [i.e., rain], then it messes things up. But in other words . . . there is a piece of primitive life *[tam kusochek pervobytnoi zhizni]*, because really to some degree you are merging with nature. Right? That is, you live like [nature] tells you. Not like we think about it for ourselves. And time goes along differently. Sometimes a bit longer, and sometimes completely quickly; for example, weekends go by like minutes. You think, good grief, once again I have blown an entire week. And the thing is, it is not obvious, it is good, quick. Time runs in a different way; that is absolutely correct.

Veronika similarly invoked natural rhythms in her reflections on the movement of time:

Differently, of course [time moves] differently, of course, that is precisely it, of course. In the first place, here you get up with the morning—here I get up at 6:30, once in a while at 6.

Judging by the reactions of her friends and neighbors who were sitting nearby—including Iuliia, who whispered the word "*Koshmar!* [Dreadful!]"—this was not seen as a universally desired practice. Veronika continued:

And when I am here, I immediately get started working on things, even if the sun has not yet risen. And here I come to my senses [i.e., become self-aware], when there is time—two hours, and I do not need to feed anyone . . . Somehow everything just goes very quickly. In the second place, you simply cannot do anything here with clean hands [i.e., idle hands]. I cannot go around for five minutes with idle hands . . . Something needs to be fixed or needs to be pulled out, then you need to go wash your hands and so it is as you walk around . . . all day. Those idle hands—look, they are dirty once again. Again you go and wash them—and again they are dirty . . . Of course, this is all wonderful. *[She sighs.]* It is good here.

Most commonly, time slows down and lengthens beyond conventional structures. Valentina stated that dacha time brings "a longer day. A longer day, yes, a longer day." This slowed-down tempo and the extended nature of time enable dachniki to engage the world around them more fully and with more awareness. Konstantin, Iuliia's next-door neighbor at her dacha, stated, "The rhythm [of time] slows down." His sister Natalia, who was visiting for the weekend and listening in on our conversation, interrupted and elaborated on Konstantin's point by referring to her working life away from the dacha: "It slows down, of course. Where is there to rush off to? Nowhere . . . That's good . . . I arrive at work—it starts at eight A.M., and I have only remembered my name at seven A.M. And I would not remember it if my children did not call after me!"

Anton is a doctor in his late thirties. He and his wife have only recently bought a tiny cottage and an equally tiny plot of land at the edge of the Nadezhda community and are working diligently to make this dacha their own. Anton's perspective on dacha time echoed Natalia's thoughts when he responded to my question about whether time moves differently at the dacha:

Yes, yes, absolutely. What it means, first of all, is that [in everyday life] the day flies past in an instant—flies past in an instant *[mgnovenno proletaet]*. And then, when you are living at the dacha, you are included in the cycle of the year. Here, it turns out, all these seasons are dacha seasons—they accumulate one on the other. They would seem to be a separate life. Life in the city—it seems like a separate life. There, there are only fragments of summer—they are pasted together. Life there in the city, it seems like a film—like a montage . . . And you know what is interesting? If you spend part of the day in the city, and then you come here to the dacha, then the day gets longer . . .

Responses in a group interview that I conducted with several of Iuliia's friends in Nadezhda reveal the extent to which people recognize the different tempos and patterns of dacha time and find them exciting, even provocative. When I first asked these friends whether time moves differently at the dacha, they all responded excitedly, talking simultaneously before eventually allowing one another to speak: "*Da, konechno* [Yes, of course]." "*Da* [Yes]." "*Bezuslovno* [Without question]." "*Konechno* [Of course]." "*Sovershenno tak* [Absolutely so]."

Masha: Only [the question really] is why [does time move differently]?

Roman: And how does it fly differently *[letit po-drugomu]?*

Svetlana: [responding to Roman's question] What do you mean, how? Because . . . well, you do not work.

Masha: In the city everything is all so artificially organized, right? You need to get up at 8 in the morning, go there [i.e., to work] at 9, finish up at 5 . . .

Svetlana: Of course!

Masha: And then you go to the store.

Svetlana: Complete . . .

Valentina: [finishing Svetlana's sentence] . . . freedom.

Svetlana: There [i.e., at the dacha] there is not a daily schedule.

Iuliia: You go out with the *elektrichka* and forget everything that happened in the city. There and then *[Tut zhe].*

Masha: I am my own mistress [i.e., master].

Iuliia: Yes . . . And time stretches on in a different way *[techet po-drugomu].*

Svetlana: You pass through into a different time and into different dimensions *[izmerenie]* of times and spaces. And stop there with different people. Do you understand? Here at the dacha no one ever pushes and tells me: "Babulia [diminutive for *babushka*], what are you doing here? Go home and do not bother me!" *[laughs]* And when I am in Moscow, I am constantly hearing "Babulia, come here. Babulia, come over here. Babulia . . . "

Masha: [finishing Svetlana's thoughts] There [i.e., in the city] you are constantly hurrying around, you need to force [your way] through *[prorvat'].*

Svetlana: Here it is completely something else—you yourself are different. It is not just time, but you are different.

Masha: You suddenly notice the heavens, you remember that the air is tasty.

Valentina: And there are stars above you . . .

Svetlana: And therefore the days are very short.

Masha: And if there is still a bonfire going by the river, then it is everything! . . . In any case, it is such happiness!

Roman: Ah, do you remember how it used to be with us? They used to come to see us and immediately they would sleep for two days.

Masha: Yes, that is true.

Roman: Here the air is something different.

Iuliia: It is an exercise [in dealing] with oxygen, yes, of course!

[Everyone talks simultaneously.]

Masha: And when they all arrive here—they sleep! They sleep for probably an entire week. Yes: they eat, sleep, eat, sleep.

Finally, the words of Vladimir, a dachnik in his late seventies, perhaps best of all sum up the themes that emerged repeatedly in dachniki's opinions about the flow of time at the dacha:

> Yes, of course, time goes differently here. In the first place, well, I do not know, I am not a doctor [i.e., scholar], I cannot really explain, but here you do not need as much time in the sun and to rest. Sometimes we come here to sleep; [we sleep] peacefully; we wake up in such a good mood and recover [i.e., get ourselves back on track] . . . *[He's quiet while he ponders further.]* All around us there are so many old trees, this peaceful place; and here I have planted many of those trees myself, especially the pine trees . . . I really like that kind of tree, because they always have leaves, see them? They hang so peacefully there, and if you look closely, [you can see] the leaves trembling. Here I sit in my little window and watch them. And in autumn they turn red and purple . . .

Vladimir continued by describing the trees that he and his son have planted over the years, how these trees have made the area around his dacha such a peaceful place, and the family memories that he associates with these trees. For Vladimir, time at the dacha exists not within discrete institutional categories such as minutes, hours, days, or even weeks. Rather, this mode of time stretches out expansively over seasons and years; a sense of timelessness is manifest at a personal, visceral level. Just as revealing is the sense of personal ownership that emerges in Vladimir's reflections. Temporal rhythms exist precisely because he expended his own time and labor to create the markers—trees—by which these rhythms proceed.

The simple act of planting trees illuminates the importance of autonomy and personal control over one's activities as essential elements in these forms of timekeeping, both in distinction from and as responses to the co-optations of time that take place in the non-dacha lives of Russian citizens. Pleasure, then, is very much tied to the ability to control one's time and one's activities outside the conventional, official structures of daily life. In many respects, it is in dacha time that Russians actively reconfigure the structures of everyday life, thereby calling into question distinctions between suffering and pleasure, work and relaxation.

STRESSING THE STRESS-FREE LIFE

During one summer visit to Moscow, I was invited on a walking excursion around Moscow's Bytsovskii Prirodnii Les (Bytsovskii Nature Forest) by Maxim, a specialist on Russian ecology and a biology professor at one of Moscow's universities. Knowing of my interest in dachas and natural spaces, Maxim thought I might enjoy seeing one of the city's largest and, in his view, most beautiful nature parks. As we entered the densely forested park, Maxim called my attention to the large signs posted along the pathway. The signs welcomed visitors and outlined the various rules governing proper behavior in the forest. By way of commentary, Maxim explained that the reason Russians like forests so much and visit nature preserves such as this one was because they relieved "stress" (Russian: *stress*). When people entered the forest, Maxim continued, they felt their stress disappearing.

As we strolled deeper into the forest, Maxim frequently interrupted his narration of the various plants and trees around us to remark on the other people we encountered and how it was evident from their behaviors and expressions how much they loved this space. It was not simply the space, however, that Maxim found so significant, but rather the combination of fresh air, bird songs, trees, plants, and the river that wound through the forest. He confessed that he found it difficult to reconcile the sheer beauty and scope of nature in this park with the fact that it was located within such a highly urbanized setting as Moscow. He finished by relating that in recent years a local organization had proposed to establish a zoo on the park grounds but that local residents had successfully protested the plans on the grounds that a zoo would ruin the atmosphere of the forest and attract too many visitors. With this reference to the zoo controversy, Maxim acknowledged a central issue in popular conceptions about structure and order within natural settings. What made the zoo problematic was that it would introduce an institutional structure at odds with that of the natural order of the park. Even within the park, formal and informal rules governed proper behavior, as did the ecological structures of trees, shrubs, and waterways, which facilitated the transmission of certain sounds, sights, and smells while masking others. A zoo situated in the midst of the forest would disrupt the flow of these sensory cues as well as introduce manmade structures that would reorient the bodily experience of moving through this seemingly natural landscape.

The complicated and frequently contradictory nature of structures in natural settings became apparent during a trip to visit Iuliia's ophthalmologist friend Anastasiia at her dacha. Anastasiia promoted a casual attitude at her dacha: as soon as she arrived she immediately stripped down to her undergarments and ran around the lawn barefoot, despite the stinging nettles that had taken over most of the green space in the yard, and she urged my female companions and me to shed our outer layers of clothing and be free (*svobodno*). Despite this air of uninhibited freedom, Anastasiia also had a clearly defined sense of order and propriety. Even as she encouraged us to pick and eat as many berries as we liked from her overflowing currant bushes, she gave us explicit instructions on which side of the bushes we were to pick the berries from, which berries were best, and the proper way to hold our buckets in order to catch the berries. When she sent us into the nearby forest to collect birch branches for use later in the banya, she gave us explicit instructions on the types and sizes of branches to collect. My two companions and I set off for the woods just outside Anastasiia's fence, where my companions stripped branches off the young birch saplings. My companions joked that because they were not banya experts like Anastasiia, they would likely pick the wrong branches and be scolded upon their return. Not surprisingly, as soon as we arrived back at the dacha, Anastasiia took one look at the branches we were holding and rebuked us for not following her directions.

Anastasiia's insistence on structure continued during the rest of our short visit, with various admonishments about gardening and setting the table for lunch, and then escalated when we moved on to the banya. The banya was located in a separate little building in the yard, close to the back fence. Shortly after our arrival, Anastasiia had opened the banya and lit the fire underneath the stove. The building contained two small rooms: a small anteroom containing a bench lining one wall, a tiny table in the back corner, and a row of hooks hanging on the wall; and a second small room that was the steam room. This room contained two benches arranged against the back wall as a set of ledges, a bench along the front wall, and a large metal stove that took up most of the rest of the tiny space.

To prepare the banya, Anastasiia instructed us to fill multiple buckets with water drawn from the well. She poured the water into a tank attached to the stove so that it would warm as the fire burned. When the water was heated, Anastasiia then ordered us in her no-nonsense voice to remove our

FIGURE 5. *Banyas* such as this one typically contain an outer room with a table and chairs for drinking tea and eating snacks and an inner room where the stove is located and the steam bath takes place.

clothing in the main house, drape towels and sheets around ourselves, and then walk back to the banya. Inside the steam room, there were two towels spread out on the top bench. Taking each of us in turn, Anastasiia told us to lie on our backs on the bench with our hands crossed over our bodies. She allowed that if we preferred, we could bend our knees, although it was apparent that she did not necessarily recommend this tactic. But the most important thing, she insisted, was that we were to lie perfectly still.

When my two companions and I were finally arranged to her satisfaction in our respective places on the benches, Anastasiia poured hot water from the stove onto the hot coals, sending up a thick cloud of steam. It was difficult to breathe, especially as the hot steam picked up the smell of birch and carried it through the air. My nostrils burned so painfully that it was easier to breathe through my mouth, although then my lungs began burning, making it difficult to breathe deeply enough to get sufficient oxygen. The bottoms of my feet were burning from the intense heat. Judging from the mutters and squeaks of my companions, they were experiencing similar discomfort. Whenever one of us moved, Anastasiia scolded the offender and sternly instructed her to be quiet and still. After one of the other women had taken all she could for the moment, she got up and scurried out, Anastasiia's scolding ringing through the air. Shortly afterward, when I could no longer breathe, I hurriedly got up and tried to exit the banya. In my haste and confusion, I stumbled on the rickety stool at the bottom of the benches. Although I fell backward into the bench, rather than into the hot stove, I nonetheless received a stern scolding from Anastasiia about how I had not climbed down the benches "accurately" (akkuratno).

As I stood in the anteroom, gasping for breath, I was quickly joined by the other two women who were visiting with me. Eventually Anastasiia came out and ushered us over to the table, where she poured scalding tea to be mixed with fresh raspberry jam. Over tea with jam we chatted about mutual friends of Anastasiia and the two other women, my research project, Anastasiia's lifelong love of the banya, and any other topic that came to mind. Anastasiia asked each of us probing questions about our medical issues—issues that rarely come up in North American conversations between acquaintances, but that apparently were acceptable in the banya, where all modesty disappears.

After we had enjoyed our tea, Anastasiia informed us that each of us needed to undergo at least three sessions in the banya, and that our banya experience would be incomplete and unsuccessful if we did not complete all the sessions. With that pronouncement, she herded us back into the banya for our second round. During our second and third encounters, we took turns lying on the top bench and getting whipped with the birch branches, which had been soaking in boiling water on the stove. The heat only intensified during these subsequent rounds. And despite the discomfort that I and the two other women were experiencing, Anastasiia insisted that we stick it out, claiming that with time it would get easier as our "organisms" grew accustomed to the heat (and we got over our panic). After the final round of steaming and being whipped, Anastasiia brought in plastic pails, soaps, and loofah sponges. She filled the pails with boiling water, giving one to each of us so that we could bathe. Bathing, I quickly discovered, was a similarly regimented activity, as I was given detailed instructions from each of the women about how to use the loofah properly. When it came time for us to scrub one another's backs, I was again corrected for not scrubbing properly.

Although many of the criticisms and instructions directed at me were undoubtedly because of the fact that I was unfamiliar with banya rituals, I was not the only person singled out for such instructions. If anything, the advice I received was far less critical than that directed at my companions, who were chastised for not following procedures properly and informed they were thus not likely to receive the full benefits of the banya. As we laughed together at being on the receiving end of such pointed advice, my companions good-naturedly reflected that Anastasiia's version of the dacha life seemed to be quite organized and complicated.

The frictions that emerged at Anastasiia's dacha highlight a deeper set of concerns about the extent to which the experience should be structured or unstructured, and whether it was possible for such a highly rigid and routinized experience to be healthful and dissipate stress. Embedded within these frictions was a more general tension over the nature of leisure in an organic lifestyle. Even as nature was promoted as a space of restfulness, rejuvenation, and recreation, these ideals quickly bumped up against the reality that the organic life is highly ordered and even restrictive in its own way. This sense of order also reveals the pervasive sense that leisure is not a retreat or respite from activity but is instead necessarily an active practice that requires continuous and meticulous attention to how one conducts oneself physically and mentally.

This insistence on structure and regulation while perpetuating an illusion of nonstructure and even autonomy illuminates some of the problems of trying to disentangle distinctions between suffering and pleasure, between work and relaxation, and even between leisure and relaxation. The Russian words used to distinguish between the activities of the organic life are difficult to translate into English because their English equivalents do no not adequately capture the same qualities. The Russian word most commonly used to describe what people do at their dachas and in the forests is *otdokhnut'*, the verb for "to rest or relax." This form of rest or relaxation is a complicated one, as came through clearly in a conversation about rest at the dacha with Veronika, her mother Zinaida, and Iuliia:

> *Veronika:* What do you mean "rest"? For two months we are tending to things, tending, and tending. There is no time to rest *[Otdykhat' nekogda]*. We arrive, and everything is already overgrown, Melissa. The grass here is up to your waist. Everything is up to your waist. Even though my friend mowed three times, so that it was apparent that you could see the house, but then . . . You know, I am up to here with grass. It is so much work!

> *Melissa:* What distinguishes work *[trud, rabota]* from leisure *[dosug]* at the dacha?

> *Veronika:* Nothing distinguishes work from leisure. Here there is both work and leisure—they are, in essence, one and the same. I cannot imagine what leisure might be: is it to lie here by the river? Frankly speaking, I could not imagine doing that. When guests come to visit me, we go somewhere with them, so that in general, that is always what is going on here. Leisure—that

is crosswords, books, and whatnot—how could you do all of that here at the dacha? Now, thank god, the television is broken—that is a really good thing . . . I do not know, it is probably a good thing for Mama [i.e., Zinaida] to take a rest *[otdokhnet]* from her incessant soap operas.

Iuliia: I would die, straight away [i.e., from having soap operas on constantly]. It is good to welcome guests to the dacha. Here it is really like a big holiday. And for what? It is all for our guests.

Veronika: It is especially a holiday for us. A never-ending [holiday].

In a sense, Veronika's and Iuliia's observations echoed those made by Gorky and Chekhov a century earlier. Perhaps it is also significant that it was Veronika, her mother Zinaida, and Iuliia whose comments about Chekhov inspired the preceding chapter. In any case, what these statements illuminate is the extent to which the organic life is simultaneously enjoyable and a nuisance, for oneself and for others, structured and unstructured, desired and despised.

In this last section, I want to turn to one final event that at first glance might appear out of place, but in fact, I would suggest, highlights the overlapping and multiply transecting elements and dimensions of temporality, place, work, leisure, pleasure, and suffering that are immanent in the organic life.

SLOW LIVING

After a long, hot day of doing nothing special at the Nikolskii family's dacha, Angela, her husband Misha, Angela's father Sergei, and I found ourselves lounging in their dacha's small front room, which served as a combination mudroom, storeroom, drying room, library, and living room, aimlessly searching through channels on the small television in the hope of finding something of interest to watch. We chanced upon a comedy festival that featured amateur acting troupes of young people from all around Russia. The vast majority of the eight- to twelve-person groups consisted entirely of young men; only one or two featured young women. Gender stereotypes and sexual innuendo were the primary topics of the sketches, and all of the sketches were variations of each other. None of us was particularly enthused about the program until a very different troupe appeared. This one presented a sketch about McDonald's as an elite restaurant—*Elitnyi Makdonalds*. Knowing of my interest in the topic, my hosts were quick to draw my attention to this sketch.

The sketch began with a table covered with a tablecloth and a man's voice booming *"svobodnaia kassa"* (available cash register), an immedi-

FIGURE 6. Although meals at the dacha may be simple affairs made from freshly picked garden produce, they are always occasions for celebrating the company of family and friends.

ately recognizable phrase first introduced into Russia by McDonald's.[9] The maître d' guided a male customer to a table and handed him a menu. A moment later the waiter approached the table and waited for the customer to place his order. The customer requested a "hamburger and large cola." The waiter then made a grand show of writing several pages of notes in his notepad. When the customer belatedly added "with ice," the waiter gave him an exaggeratedly exasperated look and ripped from his notebook all the pages on which he had written. A second waiter then carried out a silver tray, on which was balanced a two-liter bottle of soda and a wine glass. A third waiter approached with a silver tray topped by a silver cover. He lifted the cover and presented the customer with a hamburger, still in its wrapper. The customer was then handed a knife and fork. Another waiter lit a candle on the table, and a violinist approached and played for him. At this moment, Angela, with whom I had earlier in the day had a long discussion about Slow Food philosophies, turned and commented that this was "Slow Food." Suddenly, a waiter shouted *svobodnaia kassa!* The other waiters quickly snatched the food, wine glass, and utensils from the table and dumped them in a McDonald's-style trash can before rushing the customer away from the table and off the stage. As the actions signified, the brief interlude of "Slow Food" was quickly replaced by "fast food" again.

Both this comedy sketch and the circumstances in which I viewed it were striking for what they revealed about the complicated nature of competing temporal modalities. On the same day that my hosts and I had debated the nature of meaningful living, as represented specifically in the Slow Food ideology, these themes were presented to a national audience as a commentary on the nature of Russian life today. As the actors in the amateur comedy troupe suggested through their performance, Slow Living could only be a momentary and illusory experience that would be quickly replaced by "life as usual"—that is, by Fast Living.

These tensions between different modes and tempos of being emerged vividly in a conversation that took place during a group interview I conducted with Iuliia's friends. In response to a question about what people do at their dachas, my companions engaged in a long discussion and enumeration of the essential elements of dacha life: gardens, nature, forests, fresh air, and relaxation *(otdykh)*. For the most part, all of the individuals were in agreement with each other, and the lively discussion evoked frequent asides to explain inside jokes and stories. The conversation was delightfully rowdy, free-spirited, and unified, in the way that happens when close friends get together and have the opportunity to remind each other of shared memories. Yet the conversation shifted notably when Roman, a relative newcomer who had married into the community some twenty-five years earlier rather than growing up in the community, ventured the observation that dacha life had changed over the years. In response to the romanticized visions of dacha life put forth by the others, Roman reflected, "Think about it, it is simply that earlier people themselves were different." Apparently in agreement with Roman's comment, Iuliia clarified, "Well, it was during the Soviet period." Roman elaborated, "People were different, but now money has caused all of those relationships to be lost." As if in confirmation, Iuliia suggested, "It was a completely different country then." Roman responded, "Yes, a different country, and a completely different era."

Disagreeing with both Roman and Iuliia, Masha argued, "No, it really is the case that our dachas were created in that period and they have continued up until now . . . Nothing has changed." Svetlana, however, saw things differently: "No, it really was a different country." By way of agreement, Iuliia added, "In a different life." Undeterred from her perspective, Masha continued to insist that there had not been any changes: "But a dacha is always a dacha—nothing has changed with dachas at all!" Valentina, the eldest member of the group, responded: "In another century!" But Masha continued to insist, "The way it was is the way it will always be! . . . The way we lived is the way we live now."

Until this moment, the various points raised by the neighbors sitting around the tiny kitchen table had all been met with a sense of consensus. Each person's comments had found enthusiastic agreement and elaboration by others. Yet Roman's and Masha's comments provoked animated discussion and disagreement. This issue of whether dacha life has changed over the past decades, especially between the Soviet past and the post-Soviet present (and future), appeared to be a preoccupation not only for residents of Nadezhda but for many other Russians as well. Although ostensibly about the difference between the past and the present, this debate was about something much larger—the concern with whether the nature, experience, and fabric of organic living, a practical and experiential philosophy of meaningful living epitomized by dacha life, was changing.

These concerns were analogous to those suggested more metaphorically in the McDonald's comedy sketch. In both cases, the matter at hand was the extent to which different modes and temporalities of being could coexist, or whether the slower, more meaningful pace of an organically inspired life was under threat and in danger of disappearing. In many respects, this conflict between Slow Food and fast food captures the extent to which dacha life is a Janus-faced venture that not only involves but rather seems to require couplings of structure and nonstructure, misery and pleasure. The joys and the pains associated with gardening, banyas, and dachas are two sides of the same coin, so that for many the toil, hardships, anxieties, and sadness that are associated with this lifestyle are themselves forms of pleasure. Ultimately, what is most important about this lifestyle is the overall experience that it produces. For dachniki and other outdoor enthusiasts, a soulfully experienced and performed natural life is a deeply satisfying one—physically, emotionally, and spiritually—even as it is physically and financially draining.

CHAPTER 4

Natural Foods

Feeding the Body and Nourishing the Soul

Our short summer has many magnificent gifts; one of these is
the blueberry. If you want good health for yourself, you should
eat plenty of blueberries and not forget about their relatives. . . .
All of the substances of this berry are so harmonically mixed
that they are a real holiday for the [human] organism when
they are eaten.

—(Markova 2005:6)

In early August 2005, the passage above introduced an article about the
social history of the blueberry in Russian life in *Tver Life,* a daily newspaper for the city of Tver. Combining romantic descriptions with practical
information, the article focused primarily on the healthful attributes of
blueberries: they improve vision, especially for drivers and people who sit
at computers, lower blood sugar for diabetics, ease the pains of rheuma-
tism, possess antiseptic qualities, and facilitate recovery from eczema and
burns. The author concluded by writing that "in these days, the blueberry
is at its ripest, although it is already starting to peak. But at the same
time, raspberries are starting to ripen in the forests. Their harvest now is
very good and brings pleasure not only to people, but also to the forest"
(Markova 2005:6).

In midsummer in the Tver region, as in many parts of Russia, blueberries are the currency of daily life. Although berries are not generally sold
in local stores, they are nonetheless widely available and strikingly visible
throughout the city. Aside from a few mosquito bites and the minimal cost
of a train ticket, berry picking is a relatively inexpensive activity, especially for retirees with few demands on their time. Consequently, it is not
uncommon for local residents to hop on the train for a quick trip to the

FIGURE 7. Veteran berry pickers compare containers filled with fresh blueberries.

nearby forest and fill their baskets with several kilograms of berries, both for personal use and for financial gain. So reliable are the berries—and the pickers—that in Tver it is possible to set one's watch and calendar by them: at three o'clock on summer afternoons, the city's previously empty street corners are suddenly packed with enterprising pensioners who have spent the morning picking blueberries and have just arrived on the afternoon train from outlying areas to sell them by the cup.[1] Blueberries are in such abundance that visits to friends' houses invariably result in the visitor being coerced into eating multiple blueberry pastries and taking home a sack (or more) of fresh berries. As the article in *Tver Life* suggests, and as my own experiences in Russia confirm, these rituals happen again and again throughout the summer as each type of berry—raspberries, lingonberries, cranberries, and blackberries—comes into season.

In light of these summer activities, it certainly seems as if Russia has a national obsession with berries. Casual conversations with acquaintances and strangers alike frequently segue into competitive accountings of how many berries have been gathered, their healthful properties, and whose ailments have been cured. Zinaida, the eighty-year-old dachnik whose family history at the dacha was documented in the black-and-white photographs described previously, had this to say about a friend of hers who gathers berries for both personal health reasons and for commercial profit: "[My friend] is a completely sick person when it comes to cranberries. She says that it is intoxicating! She takes her vacation especially for cranberries and [spends] a month in the bogs . . . so that she can collect cranberries."

What are originally intended to be quick walks through the woods stretch into languid strolls as people stop to nibble along the way, a practice that several acquaintances described as the Russian version of eating "on the go" *(po dorozhke)*. Berry bushes turn into social settings as friends and neighbors who rarely see each other in the city during the rest of the year run into each other unexpectedly in the forest and then catch up while picking. Outsiders who have never experienced the thrill of berry picking Russian-style are quickly initiated with the presentation of a pair of rubber boots, a wicker basket, and a laugh at the swarms of hungry mosquitoes that quickly descend on pickers.

The intensity with which Russians pursue berry picking is perhaps matched only by their ardor for mushroom picking. As soon as the snows have melted in late spring and early summer, Russian mushroom hunters take to the forests in search of their favorite fungi, a pursuit that continues until late fall, when the snows start falling again. Russians from all walks of life, income levels, and ages arm themselves with buckets, baskets, and assorted knives before converging on roadways, public transportation, and forest paths, sometimes traveling several hours one way, just to reach the forest and begin the hunt for mushrooms. Even in city parks and nature preserves walkers keep a vigilant eye trained on the leaves and mosses covering the ground. Mushrooms are seemingly everywhere, and it is not uncommon to glimpse a bag of mushrooms nestled inside someone's open tote bag or sitting on a kitchen counter.

Although freshly picked and prepared mushrooms are preferred, dried and pickled mushrooms can also be added to simple meals of potatoes and sausage to bring the taste of summer into the dark of winter. The most ardent mushroom fans mark the passage of time not by calendars and clocks but by drawing on centuries of natural knowledge about the seasonal progression of mushroom varieties. True mushroom experts can predict, often to the day, when different varieties will first appear and in which location. Through informal census keeping of mushroom yields, dachniki track weather patterns and climate change over months and years.

Mushroom knowledge can be an important indicator of social status, as dachniki assured me. Individuals with seemingly supernatural mushroom-spotting skills were celebrated in the stories told by friends and family.

FIGURE 8. Angela is a veteran mushroom hunter.

I often learned about people through the apocryphal mushroom stories that were told about them before we met in person. Tales of amazing bounty or the discovery of a rarely seen but highly prized variety circulate through ever-widening conversational circles in dacha communities and entice neighbors to drop by for a quick peek and to hear the story directly from the source. While most Russians can identify the most common types of mushrooms, only the most proficient aficionados can confidently distinguish among a vast array of seemingly identical-looking mushrooms. Angela and her husband Misha joked that ultimately there are only two types of mushrooms: those you eat, and those you eat just once—a nod to the fact that some mushrooms are in fact poisonous. That comment became a running joke during our frequent forays into the forest in search of mushrooms. As I could only identify one type of mushroom with any certainty, I would call over Angela for her assessment of mushrooms that I had found. "Eat just once" became our code for mushrooms that we should leave alone.[2]

Russians' affection for and preoccupation with mushrooms and berries are not isolated phenomena but belong to a culturally pervasive set of concerns with natural foods *(natural'nye produkty)*. This expansive category includes not only "wild" foodstuffs such as berries, mushrooms, herbs, wild grasses, and fish, but also cultivated foodstuffs such as fruits, vegetables, meat, and dairy products. Although natural foods in Russia are typically most closely associated with peasant farmers and the small kitchen gardens (ogorodi) found at dachas, they are not exclusive to these settings. City parks, grassy medians alongside roadways, tiny balcony gardens, and even large industrial farms can all be sources of natural foods.

Russians' natural food practices present an intriguing alternative to other popular models of natural foods and organics. Like their counterparts in North American and European organics movements (Kaltoft 1999; Thompson and Kidwell 1998), Russian consumers are also concerned with such diverse issues as the nutritional qualities of foods; the use of fertilizers, antibiotics, additives, and preservatives; and the responsible use of agricultural land. The ideologies of food movements such as Slow Food and Food Democracy, which promote local and small-scale food production (see, e.g., Halweil n.d.; Leitch 2003; Parkins 2004; Petrini 2001a), resonate with Russian practices of personal gardening, foraging, and informal exchanges of foods among relatives and close friends.[3] Consequently, it is tempting to equate Russian gardening and natural food practices with these movements.

As we shall see, however, Russian natural foods ideologies differ from these movements in several crucial respects. On the one hand, Russian natural foods philosophies do not represent a widespread, countercultural politico-environmental trend; in other words, Russian natural food practices do not belong to a formal "green" movement.[4] In fact, as will become apparent, popular philosophies of "democracy" are attributed to problems with litter, vandalism, and pollution in natural spaces. On the other hand, Russian natural foods practices also do not typically engage issues of ethical labor practices or support for small farmers beyond occasional acknowledgment of a vanishing agrarian lifestyle as state farms are privatized (Paxson 2005). In fact, discrimination, and racism in particular, is a growing problem in consumers' attitudes toward produce sellers in markets as local authorities and community policing groups target Central Asian and African vendors for abuse and customers claim that they prefer to buy only from "whites" (see also Caldwell 2003). Moreover, the Slow Food emphasis on encouraging a return to more "traditional" economic roles and systems—and to peasant lifestyles in particular—is directly at odds with Russian attitudes about labor. Although peasant life continues to occupy an important place in Russian heritage, and although many dachniki continue to engage in "peasant" activities like "digging, weeding, milking, etc." (Humphrey 2002:137; see also Perrotta 2002:132), few Russians voluntarily identify themselves as modern peasants or adopt a peasant lifestyle. Part of the reason for this is that the "rustic" life associated with peasants signals a backward, even primitive, lifestyle, an especially problematic proposition for postsocialist citizens who see participation in a consumer-oriented capitalist market as the means to achieve a "normal" standard of living (Jung 2009; Patico 2008). Perhaps more important is the long-standing association of peasant life with economic servitude. As Caroline Humphrey notes, "Actual 'peasants' in the early twentieth century may have been far from equal, but today great offence is taken at the idea of working for a private individual and at economic inequality more generally" (Humphrey 2002:153).

Finally, unlike according to Slow Food ideals, in Russian natural foods philosophies the directionality of the stewardship relationship between person and land is reversed, so that Russians look to the land as the caretaker of society rather than emphasizing the moral responsibility of individual citizens to safeguard nature. More generally, Russian natural foods philosophies illuminate some of the shortcomings of food-lifestyle movements such as Slow Food. In many ways, Slow Food promotes a regressive vision of economic development that is at odds with the realities of Russia's market. Specifically, this movement privileges a return to precapitalist practices of small-scale agriculture and personal gardening as antidotes to the shortcomings of global capitalism. Not only will small-scale agriculture and personal gardening restore personal relationships to commercial enterprises, but they will also empower both producers and consumers.

In Russia, however, gardening and foraging practices have been interpreted by both foreign and domestic observers as a shortcoming of the socialist system. Thus, the advantages and successes of market capitalism that are promoted in Russia today are very much connected to symbols of food security and food safety such as well-stocked grocery stores and the proliferation of packaged foods.[5] An added complication that Louisa Perrotta has reported in Russia is the hesitation of former collective farm workers to privatize their individual plots. Perrotta reports that these farmers prefer to align their plots with larger industrial farms because private farming is too risky. Moreover, the distributions of this land are not equitable because they do not compensate for inequalities of location or land resources. Consequently, many farmers see this lack of parity as "undemocratic" (Perrotta 2002).[6]

Hence, while alternative food movements such as Slow Food are instructive starting points for examining Russian natural foods philosophies, the points of divergence between these two approaches are perhaps more revealing. The ideas about labor, tradition, healthfulness, and even fulfillment that emerge in Russian natural foods philosophies are informed by a primordial geographic nationalism in which landscapes and the resources produced by these landscapes convey qualities of sociability and spirituality. In this sense, qualities of healthfulness are both physical and spiritual, a dualism that reinforces the mutual investments of Russians and Russian nature.

ROMANTICIZING LANDSCAPE IN NATURAL FOODS USE

Analyses of gardening and other forms of natural foods provisioning have frequently described these activities as part of Russia's subsistence economy—in other words, gardening is an activity pursued in times of economic hardship (Ries 1997; see especially Zavisca 2003, 788 n. 5). As a result, food provisioning has typically been interpreted as an activity most prevalent among economically disadvantaged populations. There is an element of truth to this. Historically, foods taken from forests, lakes, and personal gardens have been largely outside the control of the state or the commercial sphere and have sustained Russians when the state could not, particularly during the chronic shortages that marked the Soviet period (Ries 1997; cf. Verdery 1996).[7] My interviewees repeatedly commented on the money they had saved over the years by cultivating gardens or gathering berries and mushrooms from the forest. Older Muscovites, particularly those who endured the privations of World War II, remembered how their families survived by making teas and soups from nettles *(krapiva)* and other grasses.[8] One woman related that a common nickname for mushrooms was "peasant meat," an acknowledgment of the importance of mushrooms for poor rural people who lacked access to meat. During the chronic food shortages of the Soviet period, garden plots became significant as supplemental food sources (Clarke 2002:125; Ries 1997). Both rural and urban citizens supported themselves with the food that they grew in summer gardens and other small plots of land, as well as on the balconies and windowsills of their apartments. One report suggests that in the late 1970s, the private agricultural sector contributed as much as "25 percent of Soviet agriculture's total gross production" (Wädekin 1980:1).

This broad category of "private agriculture," however, is ambiguous, as there is frequently little distinction made either in the literature or in practice between the dacha gardens of urban Russians and the personal plots of rural Russians who were engaged in agriculture as a profession.

Although workers on state farms were more likely to keep a cow or some hens or goats for personal use, urbanites with dacha gardens also reported that they kept rabbits for meat and fur and transported these rabbits back and forth from the city to the countryside. The placement of dacha communities near or even in the midst of farming villages also ensured the mixing or overlap of these agricultural spaces. Finally, any citizen who farmed a plot for personal use was liable to be taxed on their livestock and foodstuffs. Whereas the Soviet state claimed that these taxes were meant to ensure the equitable "redistribution" of goods to the entire population, these actions were interpreted by informants as just one more of the state's strategies for ensuring that citizens did not become wholly reliant on their private plots—and hence independent of the state.

Collectively, these details support a widespread view among both Russians and outsiders that the Soviet state depended heavily on private gardens and other forms of personal agriculture to compensate for its shortcomings. Informants frequently confirmed that their personal plots had sustained them when the state could not. In this context, Russians describe their gardens as *dopolnitel'nii,* or supplemental. In a discussion about the importance of dachas, Angela and Margarita agreed that members of the older generation *(staroe pokolenie)* relate to dachas in a *dopolnitel'noe* (supplemental) way. Arkadii, Iuliia's sixty-year-old neighbor in the dacha community, offered a similar perspective:

> [Dachas] are changing. Previously, dachas were . . . how do you say it? . . . supplemental *[dopolnitel'nie].* [They provided] income *[dokhod]* for the family and for the budget. It was, well in practical terms, it was not a dacha but rather a kitchen garden *[ogorod].* The kitchen garden, [that was] where you grew vegetables, fruits, in order to improve your situation a bit *[chtoby nemnoshko, nu, uluchshit' svoe sostoianie].* It was distressing *[bedstvennoe] [laughing].* We have that kind of understanding—a "budgetary" understanding. Wages are low. I have forty years of work service, forty years . . . it is hard to believe . . . and for that I receive two hundred dollars a month. It is truly a disgrace, a disgrace *[pozor].* It is an unpleasantness, you have to understand: my unpleasantness.

Arkadii's wife interjected: "It [Arkadii's pension] is enough for beer, that is all."

The importance of gardening as a source of supplemental food continued into the post-Soviet period, as the uneven development of Russia's economy in the 1990s led to several periods when Russian consumers turned to their gardens to compensate for shortages of goods and high inflation—most notably during the early 1990s and the 1998 economic crisis. During the mid- to late 1990s, Russians such as my landlady Anya and her friend Tanya spent their summers canning vegetables and making fruit jams that would sustain them during the winter, when their pensions were inadequate to pay the high prices for food in the markets.[9] Thus, to a great extent, Russians' reliance on garden foods is often depicted as a marker of severe economic instability and governmental inefficiency. By contrast, the spread of well-stocked grocery stores and produce markets that have come with Russia's capitalist transition have been praised by many consumers, economists, and politicians alike as evidence that the backward socialist economy that once forced its citizens into subsistence strategies such as gardening is quickly disappearing.

Nevertheless, in contrast to interpretations that characterize natural foods provisioning as indicative of economic insecurity, currently in Russia issues of utility are of relatively minor significance for many consumers. In fact, as many informants pointed out, today the expenses involved in preparing and maintaining a garden, as well as purchasing seeds, fertilizer, and tools, far outweigh the cost of buying fresh produce in local markets and grocery stores. In his analysis of the material importance of dacha gardens in Russia, sociologist Simon Clarke suggests that the very idea of "self-sufficiency" that has been associated with the Russian summer garden is a Western myth because, as he notes, "not one household met all of its basic food needs from its dacha: far from being the land of self-sufficiency, self-sufficiency is another western concept that appears not to have penetrated far into Russia!" (Clarke 2002:125).

Consequently, it is necessary to look beyond factors such as cost and efficiency in order to understand the value that Russians place on natural food products. Instead, what is more revealing is how Russians express their appreciation for nature's bounty in terms that suggest an intimate relationship with the physical environment that is colored by ideas of national heritage, sociality, and even spirituality. As Margaret Paxson writes in her study of an agrarian community in northern rural Russia, "the relationship between humans and the land has been, over the centuries, fraught with a range of emotions in Russia—all of them mixed and many of them heady" (Paxson 2005:30). Lovell notes that Soviet leaders' vision of the ideal Soviet person *(Homo sovieticus)* encompassed both the rural and the urban with a person who was "equally at home on potato patches as on the factory floor" (Lovell 2002:107).

Actual and imagined connections to this rural heritage appear strikingly in a pervasive nostalgia for foods that come from rural spaces. Acquaintances claim that village foods, especially fresh dairy products, have a different and preferable taste and consistency than those produced in factories. One woman in her fifties commented, "You will not go to the city for carrots. That is simply for the sake of convenience." Even though traveling to one's dacha or to a village can be time-consuming and costly, many consumers feel that the benefits outweigh the inconvenience. Among my informants it was common practice to travel to nearby villages by bus or train (sometimes with several transfers) to purchase fresh "village" *(derevenskii)* dairy products and vegetables rather than buying those same products in the local markets or grocery stores. In 1995, when cars were still relatively uncommon, one retired couple who owned one claimed that when they were staying at their dacha they used their car several times a week to drive to a nearby village to buy sour cream and *tvorog* (farmer's cheese). Iuliia also walked through the forest or occasionally took the train to another village to buy fresh sour cream, *tvorog*, and milk.

For consumers without the logistical means or inclination to access village products themselves, advertisers have found ways to bring peasant life directly to them by associating their products with images of village life, such as farms, wooden houses, and peasant grandmothers. The brand Domik v derevne (Little House in the Village) is one such example of products that have capitalized on this imagery. Package labels, advertising flyers, and billboards all feature variations on a core set of themes: a traditional cottage, a small pond, trees, and a kindly grandmother, all designed to resemble a child's crayon drawing. In summer 2005 another company advertised its dairy products with a television commercial that began by depicting a young woman, dressed in clothes reminiscent of Soviet-era romantic depictions of happy, girlish peasants, stirring berries into fresh milk. The image then transitioned to a contemporary woman who was tending her cow on the balcony of her apartment. The commercial ended when the view expanded to show that every apartment in the building had a cow pastured on its balcony.

Acts of bringing the village to the city are more widespread than the imaginary lifestyles presented by advertisers. Many Russians grow herbs on their apartment balconies or even relocate berry bushes or other plants from the forest to their apartments. During the summer it is not uncommon to observe passengers on trains, buses, and other forms of public transportation who are carrying berry bushes and young saplings that they have clearly just dug up from the forest. So pervasive is this practice of "relocating" plants that in Moscow, huge landscaped areas are often picked bare by enterprising gardeners. During one two-week period in May 2004, I witnessed firsthand the extent and speed with which such practices occurred. As part of a spring beautification project, Moscow city workers planted huge quantities of blooming tulips throughout the city. In a pattern that occurred repeatedly across the city, workers would finish planting a section in the late evening, and by the next morning that same area would be completely bare. In an effort to reduce these thefts, city authorities had to issue warnings and increase penalties for people who were caught picking flowers. Perhaps not surprisingly, such measures have done little to deter determined transplanters.

In 1990 an American acquaintance who worked in Moscow as a physician catering to North American and European expatriates and wealthy Russians related to me a more extreme example of the lengths to which people might go to transport the village to the city. He recounted an incident involving an anxious New Russian mother who had come to see him about obtaining a medical release for flying. The release was not for a member of her family, however, but for a goat. The woman explained that her child had food allergies, and another doctor had advised her to give the child goat's milk instead of cow's milk. The family was preparing to travel to Spain on vacation, and the mother wanted to take the family's goat with her on the airplane to ensure that her child had healthy milk to drink.

For Russians like these individuals, although the idea of "nature" is most intimately connected with rural spaces, these rural spaces are not necessarily grounded in actual locations. Rather, "nature" is an expansive notion that can be brought into urban spaces, such as with a transplanted goat or cow, as well as with collections of potted plants and herbs on apartment balconies and windowsills, small plots of cultivated and uncultivated land along city roadways, in city parks, and even forgotten corners of parking lots, alleys, and untended yards behind public and private buildings. Thus, as I elaborate further in the following discussion, the roots of "natural foods" in Russian landscape are both physical and symbolic.

ECOLOGICALLY CLEAN: HEALTH, TASTE, AND SAFETY

Both the fervor that marks Russians' attention to natural foods and the extent to which this passion is widely shared among the general population today are legacies of Soviet-era concerns with food safety issues. The modernizing state-building projects pursued by Soviet officials included efforts to improve the efficiency and safety of the domestic food supply through philosophies and methods of scientific rationality. Soviet scientists, chefs, and food services employees participated in the invention and forcible implementation of a "scientific" food regime that encompassed technologies of food production, distribution, and preparation, nutritional standards, culinary principles, and even the social spaces in which food consumption occurred (Borrero 1997). As Rothstein and Rothstein describe in their study of the emergence of the Soviet food services industry in the 1920s, food "radicals" and other proponents of healthful food treated cuisine as a scientific discipline that was based on data from chemistry, physiology, physics, and other physical sciences (Rothstein and Rothstein 1997:184). Particularly notable were the "food futurists," a group that included "food-surrogate enthusiasts and proponents of experimental and synthetic foods" (Rothstein and Rothstein 1997:186). Food thus represented an effective medium for the establishment and dissemination of particularly Soviet notions of scientific progress and modernity.

Despite Soviet officials' efforts to promote scientific food systems as the ideal means to guarantee food quality and healthfulness, many consumers viewed industrially produced foods and public food facilities with suspicion. Soviet customers voiced their dissatisfaction with the appearance of industrially produced foods and complained about finding insects and pieces of debris in their foods.[10] Rothstein and Rothstein write that "the overwhelming majority of cafeterias were places where food supplies were limited and the food was of low quality and inexpertly prepared, where chaos, flies, dirt, and terrible service reigned" (Rothstein and Rothstein 1997:183).[11] Both the state's emphasis on food safety and its inability to maintain these standards fostered a widespread cultural awareness about food quality that has continued into the post-Soviet period (see also Dunn 2008; Jung 2009).

In particular, industrial foods continue to garner consumers' scorn and suspicion, and many consumers interpret the infusion of foreign-produced foods and foreign food technologies into Russia in the 1990s as evidence of the further decline of Russian-made goods (see also Gabriel 2005; Patico 2001).[12] Aleksandra, a thirty-five-year-old mother who prefers to prepare meals completely from scratch, frequently drew my attention to the poor quality of factory foods. On one occasion when we were having tea in my kitchen, Aleksandra brought out a bag of sweets that she had just purchased at a nearby shop. After cutting into the first one, she sighed and held out the candy so that I could see the dried and discolored chocolate in the filling. She put the sweets aside and opened up a fancily wrapped candy bar, only to discover that it, too, was spoiled. Other acquaintances reported that they rarely eat processed foods because the quality and safety of the foods could not be guaranteed. Foods grown on private plots or in natural spaces such as forests and meadows, however, are considered the antithesis of foods that come from state industries and thus represent an appealing alternative.

For Russian consumers, the most important criterion for natural foods is that they are "ecologically clean" *(ekologicheski chistoe),* a designation that is the closest equivalent to "organic" in Russian food practices (see also Mitrokhin 2004:173, Medvednik 2004).[13] Until recently the "organics" designation was relatively unknown in Russia. By 2004, a very small number of food shops in Russia advertised that they carried "organic" food, including foods that carried European organics certifications. In summer 2005, a food shop carrying "organic" foods, mostly packaged products, opened in downtown Moscow just a few blocks from the Kremlin. By summer 2007, it had closed.

In their purest form, "ecologically clean" foods are presumed to be healthy, full of essential minerals and nutrients, and untainted by additives and preservatives. To a great extent, Russian concerns with additives and preservatives are clearly directed at limiting the use of artificial chemicals and industrial pesticides, an ideology that resonates with Western scientific notions of environmentalism and organics. Vladimir, a retired physician in his seventies, stated, "In the garden, everything is under your own hand. Therefore we know that here everything is without pesticides and without any trash. They are ecologically clean products." A married couple in their fifties echoed this theme of purity and safety in their conversation with me. Fedor began by saying, "The side effects of natural foods are less." His wife, Anna, added, "If watermelons and tomatoes [are picked and sold] early [i.e., before they are ripe], then they have too many nitrates, and many people have allergies to them . . . It is very dangerous."

This emphasis on ecological cleanliness and safety was reflected vividly in a 2002 television commercial for a brand of juice named Liubimii Sad (Beloved [or Favorite] Garden). In the commercial a kindly grandfather figure advised a young boy, presumably his grandson, not to drink a second brand of juice because it contained "apple trash" *(iablochnii gadost').* Instead, the grandfather recommended juice from Liubimii Sad, which was ecologically clean and made only of *"natural'nye produkty."* The advertisement concludes with one final pitch that clearly evokes the Russianness of ecological cleanliness when the grandfather says, "take our *[nash]* [juice], Beloved Garden."[14]

The food safety issues underlying Russians' natural foods ideologies in the post-Soviet period transcend issues of hygiene and quality control. Rather, natural foods philosophies reflect pervasive cultural concerns with national values. One such concern is that of economic morality, an issue that became especially apparent during the turbulent 1990s, when Russia's transition to a capitalist market economy was marked by multiple periods of economic instability. Corruption among Russia's financial elite and growing economic disparities within the population further contributed to widespread public fatigue and discontent with capitalism. Of particular concern to many Russians during this period was that neoliberal capitalism, with its emphasis on anonymous market forces and single commodity exchanges, rather than the continuous cycles of gift exchange that characterized state socialist economies (Ledeneva 1998), would damage people's relationships with one other.

These concerns about the dangers of capitalism appeared vividly in natural foods discourses and practices. In particular, informants pointed to "ecologically clean" foods as the embodiment of the spirit of sociality that was associated with Russian economic activities and social life during the socialist period.[15] According to this perspective, "ecologically clean" foods are those that are grown by a relative or friend, gathered and processed as a group activity, and then circulated through personal networks, preferably as gifts. Not only does the personalized nature of these foods make them trustworthy, but it also endows them with attributes of taste, quality, and cleanliness that are believed to be lacking in foods produced by anonymous, impersonal capitalist means. Russian consumers fear that the impersonal and unfamiliar nature of capitalist transactions eliminates this sense of trust and symbolically pollutes the objects circulated through these exchanges, including dacha-grown foods that are sold rather than given away.[16] Cynthia Gabriel reports that one of her Russian informants expressed his suspicion of commercially produced and distributed foods, including farm-grown foods that were sold on the commercial market, by calling them "capitalist food" (Gabriel 2005:186).[17]

Despite the devaluation that occurs when natural foods are commodified, the economic crises of the 1990s are still fresh in the minds of many citizens. People who are afraid of putting their money in the bank invest their resources in their gardens and in fresh foods that they turn into jams, pickles, and homemade alcohol.[18] Russians can turn to these products when their monetary reserves are low, either by using them as "free" foods or by selling them to others. Consequently, even for Russians who are otherwise suspicious of capitalist markets, their hesitations are outweighed by the certainty of the moral and economic value of nature. Natural foods discourses and practices, then, become the manner in which Russians engage and reflect on proper economic activities in the postsocialist world (see also Zavisca 2003).

A second, more fundamental concern that is related to additives and preservatives in "ecologically clean" ideologies has to do with the cultural understanding of Russianness as a quality rooted in the physical landscape. In this geographic nationalism, Russian perspectives on what is "ecologically clean" frame larger discussions about the unique qualities of Russian soil that appeal to and are recognized by the particular physiologies and sensory perceptions of Russians. Although reminiscent of the notion of terroir, which is central to the heritage food focus in Slow Food ideologies (Petrini 2001a, 2001b), Russian geographic nationalism does not emphasize specific geographies to the same degree. While regional differences do matter to some extent, as is evident in branding practices in which names of locations stand in for product names and prices are set according to the regions in which foods were grown or produced (see also Patico 2001), what is more important is the sense of a pan-Russian national landscape that has distinctive bio-national qualities.[19] Informants maintain that Russian soil itself is cleaner and healthier than non-Russian soil and that food taken directly from the ground does not need to be washed or even inspected, a notion of healthfulness that is perhaps best captured by the word *poleznii,* which Russians use to describe the simultaneously healthful and useful qualities of natural foods.[20] Several retired women with whom I once picked raspberries asserted that washing the berries—even those draped in cobwebs or sporting worms—would ruin them. Another woman with a teenaged daughter remarked that natural foods taken directly from the ground and not washed improved the overall health of children. Valentina, a retiree in her late fifties, stated, "In general, all Russians love [their vegetable gardens] because it is possible to take something directly from the dirt bed to the table. It is really tasty . . . It is ecologically clean."

What is especially revealing of this symbolic ideology about the healthful properties of ecologically clean foods, however, is the insistence that Russian soil is clean and pure even when there are clear indications that the soil is contaminated. On two separate occasions I accompanied friends on mushroom-picking excursions, only to discover that the areas where we were walking had been battlefields during the Great Patriotic War (i.e, World War II). When I asked if we should be concerned about unexploded shells, my hosts insisted that these areas were safe. Other respondents confided that even though they gathered berries or mushrooms along highways or in other areas that might be polluted, they were not worried about harmful effects. In fact, as Dale Pesmen reports from her research in Omsk, Russian soil and food products taken from Russian soil are believed to possess purifying capabilities. Pesmen writes that "as purchased food might have been grown in toxic soil or be otherwise tainted, homegrown food was often announced to be 'ecologically clean' because it had been grown upstream of the refinery or out in the country. . . . Vodka and certain mushrooms and berries were offered with the remark that they take radiation out of the system" (Pesmen 2000:27).[21]

Finally, Russians describe local soil as being packed with unique nutrients that give Russian food a taste that is not only distinctive but also preferred by Russians. A university student argued that Russian taste buds preferred foods grown in Russian soil. An older woman framed the connection between ecologically clean foods and national tastes by describing why Russians preferred domestically grown produce: "One time they started advertising soy products here and saying that they were healthy. But it turned out that people were not used to them . . . not even vegetarians."

This conviction that taste preferences are directly correlated with a distinctive national character came through in the following conversation among several dacha neighbors:

> *Vera:* Our *[nashi]* foods taste better, and foreign foods are less tasty.
>
> *Valia:* And here everything is natural *[natural'noe]*.
>
> *Vera:* Everything is natural, yes. And everything is tasty, natural.
>
> *Irina:* We are used to that kind of food.

Examples such as these reveal that Russian perspectives on "ecologically clean" foods index a larger and overlapping set of concerns with healthfulness: healthfulness of the environment, the person, and the nation. But even more than healthfulness, "ecologically clean" designations speak to pervasive concerns about security and trust. In today's Russia, citizens are concerned with such issues as the quality of medical care, personal safety, and economic stability. One woman in her early thirties voiced a perspective that I heard from other informants when she complained that widespread corruption in post-Soviet business practices has resulted in a lack of controls in industrial food production, so that both food quality and food safety have declined markedly. Conventional medicine is also suspect, and many Russians do their best to avoid hospitals and doctors. Friends reported that only people who want to die allow themselves to enter the hospital. These fears have prompted widespread self-medicating with natural foods, homeopathic remedies, and other natural therapies such as acupressure and leeching. Informants who were physicians claimed to prefer natural therapies such as herbal teas and fresh fruits to pharmaceuticals for treating physical ailments. Iuliia's friend Anastasiia, the ophthalmologist, advised her patients and friends to eat blueberries and other natural foods to improve their vision. Iuliia was just one of Anastasiia's friends who claimed that regularly eating these foods helped their eyesight.

Concerns about deception and trust are at the heart of deliberations over what is considered "ecologically clean" when products are sold in commercial markets. Russian consumers who suspect that industrially produced and commercially marketed foods and beverages are tainted put their trust in nature instead. As one man in his late fifties commented, "Here there is no kind of guarantee. Here no one is certain if foods have additives, if they are healthy or poisonous. And then it becomes clear, it turns out that at all the firms there is no one responsible." A married couple put it more simply in their comments that natural products were superior to anything industrially produced because it is impossible to deceive nature: "You cannot fool [or cheat] nature [prirodu ne obmanesh']."

Even as natural foods provide symbolically charged commentaries on and antidotes to the capitalist market, they also clearly represent the successes of this very system, thereby effectively framing consumers' ambivalence about the dangers and benefits associated with capitalism. Over the past decade commercially produced natural foods have emerged as a lucrative market niche for enterprising producers selling foods to consumers interested in healthfulness and quality. Stores, restaurants, and cafés specializing in both factory-made and freshly prepared health foods are increasingly common in cities such as Moscow, St. Petersburg, and Tver. Natural foods are explicitly used as a theme on product labels and promotional materials, such as an advertising poster for Blagodar green tea that was hanging on a bus stop bulletin board in Tver. The caption on the poster described Blagodar tea as an "ecologically clean and safe product" and claimed that "anyone who is concerned with their health will choose 'Blagodar' tea." The designation "ecologically clean" routinely appears on product labels for foodstuffs as diverse as vodka, milk, candy, and kvass.[22]

Much like their counterparts during the Soviet period (Cox 2003), today's marketers appropriate natural foods motifs in order to capitalize on consumers' beliefs in the safety and trustworthiness of nature. Such appropriations are not exclusive to commercial enterprises; they also appear in the marketing ploys of informal vendors. While standing on the sidewalk and waiting for the bus that would take us to Anastasiia's dacha, my companions and I watched as a man and woman, both in their late fifties, transformed an overturned cardboard box into a makeshift table on which the woman carefully arranged fresh herbs and tomatoes that she removed from a cloth bag. My companions joined other passersby in admiring the woman's produce, especially her tomatoes, and speculated among themselves about her prices. Eventually one of my companions walked over to the small kiosk next to the bus stop that sold an assortment of produce, bread, and other supplies. She looked up the price of tomatoes that was posted at the kiosk and then walked back and asked the woman with the sidewalk stand what price she was asking. When she returned and reported that the woman's price was almost twice that at the kiosk, my companions discussed the price difference and eventually concluded that the independent seller's tomatoes must be "ecologically clean," a hunch that was subsequently confirmed when we overheard the woman using that phrase to advertise her produce to another potential customer. Continuing their conversation, my companions agreed that "ecologically clean" tomatoes were worth the much higher price.

Yet even the designation "ecologically clean" cannot always overcome consumers' suspicions of foods that have moved through the commercial realm. Russia's growing market in bottled water is a case in point. In the mid-1990s the Russian Orthodox Church launched a series of domestic business ventures that included a line of bottled mineral water. The water was bottled under the name Sviatoi Istochnik (Sainted Springs), and the packaging claimed that the water originated from a holy spring and was blessed by the patriarchate of the Russian Orthodox Church.[23] Subsequently, a wide variety of foreign and domestic bottled waters of varying flavors and levels of carbonation flooded the Russian market. Initially, brand names of these bottled waters highlighted the spiritual qualities of the waters, such as with the Sainted Springs brand, or they incorporated historically and geographically important place names, such as the Georgian mineral water Borzhomi, which is bottled at a famous health resort in Georgia favored by Soviet and post-Soviet elites. More recent products tend to make explicit reference to things from nature such as natural springs, pine cones, and pine trees. Representative examples include the brands Shishkin Les (Coniferous Forest) and Valdai Nature Reserve. The label on bottles of the latter features a seagull flying in front of a pine forest and body of water, as well as a small map and other details about the national nature reserve and the spring that is the source of the water.[24]

Despite these direct allusions to nature—and even to presumably trustworthy institutions such as the Russian Orthodox Church—bottled waters trouble many Russian consumers precisely because of their commercial nature. On one particularly oppressive, hot, muggy day in Moscow, my elderly friend Katerina turned down my offer of bottled water even though there were no other beverages available. Katerina explained that she did not trust bottled water because of an incident several months earlier when she had bought some water at a theater and felt ill afterward. Despite the heat that day, she preferred to travel more than an hour to drink tap water that she trusted at home.[25] The subject of questionable bottled water came up again several weeks later when I was back in Tver and another friend came to visit for tea. Because the tap water in the section of the city where I lived had a strange taste and contained a heavy reddish sediment, many residents either bought expensive water filters or obtained water from other sources, such as the hand-cranked water pump located on the sidewalk outside my building, which was used by many of my neighbors. I preferred to buy five-liter jugs of water at the local grocery store, however, and on this occasion I had stacked several empty jugs in the corner of my kitchen. My friend Nina noticed the empty jugs and commented that Russians are amused by foreigners who buy bottled water in Russia. She explained that commercials claiming that bottled water was cleaner and better than regular water were simply a deception *(obman)* and a marketing tactic. She went on to say that there was nothing inherently better about bottled water and that carbonated water contained additives. She continued by reflecting that during the Soviet period, carbonated waters were not available, and consumers did not buy bottled mineral water. Nina maintained that the best water came from natural springs, which were clean *(chistye)* because they came directly from the earth and therefore were not subject to any type of commercial or industrial intervention.

Natural springs are commonly found in rural areas in Russia and are especially prevalent around dacha communities.[26] My field notes reveal that at practically every dacha community I have visited my hosts have taken me to a nearby natural spring as part of an excursion around the community. These trips to the local springs were not simply for the visiting ethnographer's benefit, however. Both residents of dacha communities and day-trippers plan visits to these small springs to wash their faces and fill jugs with fresh drinking water. In one dacha community, water from the nearby spring is directed into residents' personal water pipes. Many residents in this community transfer this water into bottles that they carry back to the city with them. Natural springs are also common at monasteries and other religious sites, and the water from these springs is believed to possess healing qualities. Visitors line up at the springs with cups for drinking the water or with thermoses and jugs that they fill with water to take home for themselves or for sick relatives or friends.

Clean water became an especially critical issue for residents along the Volga River between Tver and Moscow during summer 2005. A series of mishaps—a train derailment, boat accidents, and burst pipes, among other incidents—leaked oil and other pollutants into the Volga River, which flows directly through Tver and past many of the summer communities between Tver and Moscow. Despite the assurances of local and national public officials that the public water supply was safe, the smell and shiny residue of oil in the water were obvious in the center of Tver and in smaller rivers further downstream. Not surprisingly, this "ecological catastrophe" was a frequent topic of conversation, and many people stopped swimming and fishing in local streams and rivers. Angela and Misha told me that it was unsafe to buy fresh fish at the local markets because of the likelihood that it had been taken from polluted areas of the Volga. Nevertheless, at dacha communities that I visited along the river, residents continued to drink the tap water because they trusted it to be naturally clean.

GIFTS OF THE SPIRIT

When discussing why nature and natural foods are more trustworthy than commercial foods, Russian informants consistently point to the inherent sociality of natural foods. The most desirable natural foods are those that are gathered and processed in the course of normal socializing with relatives, friends, and neighbors and then circulated within social networks. Visits to dachas and apartments invariably involve exchanges of fresh fruits and vegetables from people's gardens, as well as samples from the garden and kitchen. Friends and visitors without their own gardens might be invited to take a bucket of berries or bag of fresh cucumbers home with them. On one occasion, when my friend Nina unexpectedly stopped by and I spontaneously invited her to stay for tea, she presented me with a handful of carrots and a cucumber that she had just picked from her garden. When the sister of another friend arrived for a weekend visit from her home five hours away, she brought with her a huge bag of potatoes from her garden. My friend then spent the next several weeks parceling out potatoes to friends and co-workers.

On the one hand, the circulation of fruits and vegetables is part of a longer tradition of investment and redistribution that was especially important during previous periods of economic instability and food shortages (see Caldwell 2004b; Fitzpatrick 1999; Young 1989). Many citizens survived periods of economic crisis by sharing both fresh and preserved foods (jams, pickled tomatoes and cucumbers, and dried mushrooms, for example) with their friends and family. On the other hand, the exchange of natural foods illuminates a larger set of discourses about the importance of social relations in daily life more generally. Foods that are grown, prepared, and circulated through personal networks are powerful symbols of intimacy and trust. In symbolic terms, natural foods are practical gifts that express and reinforce personal relationships and a sense of community (see also Gabriel 2005). One family celebrates the first appearance of each fruit and vegetable in the garden by cutting them into equal shares so that every member of the family can have a taste. During a summer of abundant blueberries, Iuliia devoted untold hours to baking delicious blueberry pies, cheerfully sacrificing her free time to bake pies for the pleasure of Angela, me, and other friends. Whenever I have left Russia, friends have given me jars of jam or pickles to take with me as a souvenir or memento of my trip and of them. These food gifts clearly have an emotional component for the givers, as is evident in the comments of two women in their forties who had been friends and neighbors in the same dacha community for most of their lives. Talking about why they pick mushrooms in the nearby forest, Vera commented, "I gather mushrooms because my nephew loves them." Irina then added, "I eat mushrooms, but I can give away an entire basket. It is enough for me that I receive tremendous pleasure when I gather them."

At the same time that gifts of natural foods mark and cement relationships between close friends and relatives, they also illuminate a more profound set of relationships between nature and people. In this relationship, nature becomes personified as the caretaker, nurturer, and provider of the people who inhabit it. A conversation among several of Iuliia's closest friends in the Nadezhda community captures these sentiments beautifully. The conversation took place while we were seated around the tiny table in Iuliia's dacha kitchen, enjoying her freshly baked blueberry pastries, freshly picked tomatoes and cucumbers, tea, and other snacks.

> *Melissa:* An acquaintance told me that in Russia there is an expression, "The forest feeds us."
>
> *Svetlana:* Here, take some pirogi! *[indicating Iuliia's freshly baked wild blueberry pastries, lying nearby on a plate]*
>
> *Iuliia: [referring to herself]* The champion blueberry collector.
>
> *Svetlana:* The Aleksandrovs [i.e., another family] take up all the mushrooms from the forest, so that you cannot go to the forest after they do.
>
> *Iuliia: [slyly]* After either the Aleksandrovs *or* the Nikolskiis [i.e., her own family].
>
> *Valentina:* Well, it is not so much about eating them. It is not that we especially need them for food, but rather there is such a great pleasure from finding them.

Svetlana: No, but the forest does feed, of course it does.

Valentina: Sveta [a diminutive of Svetlana], what do you mean by that?

Svetlana: Well, it is that you do it with emotions, and I go off to pick [mushrooms] because my son Misha loves them, and I want to [please] him.

Iuliia: For us, that expression is already an old one, one that is disappearing.

Svetlana: Who [gathers], that is not important, no, that is not important. But the forest gives away, the forest feeds.

Themes of gifting emerged more explicitly in the comments of Vladimir, another neighbor, when he explained Russians' appreciation for nature and natural foods: "It is a love not just for nature itself, but a love for the gifts of nature . . . Yes, a gift, a gift of nature. Mushrooms, berries, communing with animals . . . I will not tell you that the forest is like the spring of life for all people. But in the winter, when you have mushrooms with potatoes that have been cooked just so . . . " Trailing off into a fond reminiscence of the special taste of wild mushrooms, Vladimir and another neighbor began reminiscing more generally about the pleasures of natural foods.[27]

It is as gifts, both given and received, that natural foods are in their purest, most dependable, and most desirable state. And as gifts, natural foods not only serve as practical symbols for culturally transmitted values, but they also forge and preserve intimate ties of trust and affection both between individuals and between individuals and the natural environment. If the gifts of natural foods offered by friends and relatives are directed at material and social well-being, then the gifts provided by nature restore a more spiritual sense of harmony and balance in people's lives. More precisely, there is a clear spiritual quality inherent in Russians' appreciation for nature and natural foods. In a conversation with Elena about picking berries in the forest, Elena stated, "Listen! This is where God lives! Not in a church, but here, here is where he lives . . . Oh, look at me, I've got tears in my eyes." Another woman invoked a sense of spirituality in defining dachas as something "given from God" *(dannaia ot Boga).* This spiritual quality appears in multiple registers, both personal and commercial, including in the meditative, soulful qualities attributed to gardening. This interrelation between soulfulness and nature was on display in the playful promotion used by one Russian beer producer in 2005. Advertisements featured bottle caps from Staryi Melnik (Old Windmill) beer artfully arranged with green leaves in a wooden basket like the ones used for carrying berries and mushrooms, with ripe strawberries lying around the basket. The accompanying slogan read, "A summer without Staryi Melnik is just a soulless accumula-

FIGURE 9. Iuliia's blueberry pies are legendary in Nadezhda.

tion of vitamins [Leto bez 'starogo mel'nika'—bezdushnoe nakoplenie vitaminov]."

Russians' affection for mushrooms is also, in many ways, infused with a deep sense of mysticism and natural spirituality. Although the ability to hunt mushrooms is not limited to those of a specific gender or age, and it can be learned with practice, informants expressed the belief that some individuals have a natural gift of sight or smell that enables them to find mushrooms. Both Iuliia and Angela are masterful hunters with unerring instincts for knowing that there are mushrooms hidden deep under piles of pine needles or in mossy hillocks. It was this trait that Svetlana and Iuliia alluded to in their warning against looking for mushrooms after the Nikolskii family had already passed through an area. Angela claims that she can sense mushrooms, often by their smell, and that this is a gift that she inherited from her grandmother. When Angela was a child, she asked her grandmother to teach her to find mushrooms. In response, her grandmother took her to the forest but refused to point out mushrooms, instead allowing the young Angela to develop her own nose and sensibility.

Although these examples of spiritual foods are not related to any specific religious institution, both organized religious groups and practitioners of more individualistic spiritual practices promote soulfulness through nature and natural foods (see also Mitrokhin 2004:172–73). The Danilovsky Monastery, home to the Moscow patriarchate of the Russian Orthodox Church, operates a small grocery store that sells honey, bread, spices, mead, and other herbal drinks and remedies that have been produced by religious affiliates and blessed by church officials. Some individual churches also sell food and beverages that have been blessed by the priests in their small souvenir kiosks. The sidewalks leading up to monasteries and churches, particularly rural historic monasteries and churches that are likely to attract tourists, are also prime spots for local dachniki to sell fresh berries, mushrooms, pickles, tomatoes, and freshly made pastries.

Until recently, perhaps the largest and most obviously denominationally sponsored natural foods health shop was the one operated by the Hare Krishna community in Moscow.[28] The temple grounds included a small shop and café where visitors who were interested in a holistic and purifying vegetarian lifestyle could purchase both prepared foods and raw ingredients. On Sunday evenings members of the community welcomed the public to a free dinner, where visitors could receive information about the Hare Krishna community along with their free food. On the evening that I attended as the guest of an elderly informant, a woman who identified herself not as a Hare Krishna but rather as a "philosopher" who appreciated the message of spiritual purification associated with the Hare Krishna vegetarian lifestyle, the connections among nature, food, and spirituality were very obvious. My companion, Larisa Antonovna, arrived at the dinner directly from a day in the forest, where she had been gathering herbs, grasses, and twigs that she planned to dry and use later for brewing tea. While we were standing in line, Larisa Antonovna began chatting about the healing properties of food with the young man standing ahead of us. After my friend showed both of us the bags containing what she had gathered from the forest, the man first complimented her and then asked if she would be interested in trading a few handfuls of herbs and twigs for a small container of herbal tea that he had already received from another distribution point in the serving line. Larisa Antonovna agreed, and both seemed pleased with the trade.

Natural foods are also credited with fostering internal balance and harmony. Moscow's Dom Meda (House of Honey), one of the city's oldest and most established health food stores, showcases an extensive assortment of honeys, as well as a diverse supply of other health foods and an impressive collection of aromatherapy candles, incense, oils, crystals, and other paraphernalia familiar from New Age and Eastern religious traditions. Similar combinations of "spiritual foods" and other accessories are also featured prominently in shops such as Jagganath and Tretii Put' (Third Way), which feature cafés alongside their offerings of mystical and meditation-oriented wares. One chain of drugstores sells herbal teas that correspond to the signs of the zodiac as well as the Chinese lunar calendar. Descriptions on the boxes claim that each tea is specially blended for the particular needs of individuals who were born under those signs.[29]

In the past several years popular interest in mystical and meditation practices has been reflected in growing enthusiasm for principles of harmony and feng shui, which have been promoted as models for the interior design not only of people's apartments, but also their gardens and cottages.[30] A summer 2005 issue of the newspaper *Toloka v Rossii* promised to provide "healthy advice for dachniki and owners" with a special series of articles entitled "Feng Shui: The Path to Harmony and Happiness." One article focused specifically on ways to organize and use a vegetable garden to achieve "harmony with nature *[v garmonii s prirodoi]*." In response to readers' interest in creating a "medicinal plot *[griadki]*," the author made recommendations for creating an "apothecary garden" of herbs such as basil, bergamot, chamomile, jasmine, and lavender. A separate article in the same issue, titled "A Pharmacy with Your Plot," gave suggestions for preparing fruits and vegetables with medicinal qualities before promising readers that the next issue would be devoted to fruits, vegetables, and other plants with medicinal qualities.[31] At the same time these articles appeared, principles of feng shui and other "New Age" movements were becoming evident in informants' gardens, such as that of one woman who had carefully arranged her flowerbeds around a series of sundials and fountains.[32] More common were the small reflecting pools that many dacha owners were installing in their gardens.

NATURAL FOODS AS COMFORT FOODS

For many Russians, the importance of natural foods for crafting a sense of identity, community, and spirituality has been amplified in the post-Soviet period. Over the past fifteen years Russian society has been radically transformed with the introduction of new forms of economic activity and cultural trends from abroad. In particular, as market capitalist models of impersonal business relationships replace socialist-era practices that relied on long-term informal networks, many consumers lament the loss of personal relationships, trust, and quality. In the case of foods, because commercial foods are produced through anonymous institutional processes, they are presumed to be dislocated from the social relations that give natural foods their meaning and thus are considered less safe and healthy than foods grown, gathered, and processed by friends and relatives. Natural foods, by contrast, are familiar, unadulterated, and close at hand, and for wary Russians they provide a safe alternative and an antidote to the dangers of commercial capitalism. In a very real sense, Russian consumers treat natural foods not just as comfort foods, but also as coping mechanisms that enable them to navigate the changes taking place in Russia today.

This sense that natural foods possess beneficial, and even restorative, qualities sheds light on the perplexing ambiguities that mark Russians' relationship to commercial foods. Despite the cultural value placed on noncommercial products, the reality is that many consumers find store-bought foods and commercial enterprises appealing. Grocery stores that stay open until late at night are far more convenient than the countryside for Russians who are constrained by the corporate clock. And for consumers who must watch their finances, buying fresh produce is cheaper than spending money on seeds, fertilizers, tools, canning equipment, and train fare.

None of my informants was comfortable with having to obtain natural foods in the commercial realm, and each person viewed this option as a last resort. Yet what these individuals shared was a commitment to reconciling the necessity of purchasing natural foods with the ideals of sociability and spirituality that underpin Russian natural foods philosophies. By emphasizing the origins of natural foods in Russian soil, and then by transforming store-bought products into home-cooked foods and circulating them through personal gift-giving networks, informants restored the ideals of naturalness to these commercial foods. Russian producers engage in similar tactics, such as by using advertising strategies that located products in peasant farms or dacha gardens or by packaging their products to resemble homemade goods.

The implications of recognizing and restoring the inherent qualities of naturalness to commercially produced natural foods are profound. For Russians who are discomfited by the larger social and economic changes that are sweeping their country, natural foods philosophies offer compelling means both to preserve older and more familiar cultural practices of social and spiritual intimacy and to reframe these activities and beliefs in terms that make sense in Russia's new economy. At the same time, Russians find reassurance in the notion that nature is a healing, purifying entity that cares and provides for the humans that inhabit it. Thus, even as the social world of Russia today changes dramatically, nature remains a trustworthy force that transcends the mundane and the commercial. Despite the threats to social relations, culture, and tradition that are associated with the postsocialist condition in Russia, even commercially produced natural foods reinforce those values and offer Russians a valuable alternative for preserving and reproducing their social world.

Natural foods are also the conduits through which Russians articulate their most personal feelings of intimacy with the natural realm, often in ways that convey a nature-centered form of spirituality. Russians such as the individuals described here who acknowledge this special intimacy treat nature as a dependable partner, trusted friend, and confidante. "Nature is always there," stated one person. The sense of intimacy that characterizes Russians' perceived relationship with nature reveals longstanding cultural ideas that the natural realm is the ultimate caretaker of humanity and always provides what its inhabitants need. This aspect emerged most poignantly as I was leaving the forest with Iuliia and Angela after a particularly fruitful excursion to pick mushrooms. Stopping at the edge of the forest, Iuliia turned around and shouted out several times, *"Les, spasibo!"*—"Thank you, forest!"

CHAPTER 5

Disappearing Dachniki

Landscape myths and memories share two common characteristics: their surprising endurance through the centuries and their
power to shape institutions that we still live with.

—Simon Schama (1995:15)

We [i.e., Russians] have a mindset [*mentalitet*], and it is
extremely difficult to change it.

—Konstantin, Nadezhda resident, reflecting on Russian nostalgia
    for dacha life

One intriguing trend within Russia's natural foods movement is that of
"peasant food." At relatively reasonable prices, brands such as "Little
House in the Village" and "Beloved Garden" promise consumers who
desire a taste of "the wild" not just healthy foods but also access to "tradition" in the form of association with an authentic peasant lifestyle. Pre-
packaged foods, however, offer little more than a vicarious and imagined engagement with this rural lifestyle. For consumers who long for a
more intimate and authentic experience, the peasant restaurant offers a
more viscerally satisfying option. Although the fare offered by peasant
restaurants generally resembles that available in other restaurants offering "Russian" food (e.g., vegetable-based soups, thick breads, meat-and-
potato dishes, blinis, and *pelmeni* [meat-filled dumplings]), it is the overall
experience that sets these peasant restaurants apart from their counterparts. Dining rooms decorated to resemble peasant farmhouses, complete
with vintage farm implements, taxidermied farm animals, and bales of
straw, as well as serving staff outfitted in pre-Soviet peasant uniforms
offering dishes described as "peasant" or named for historically significant
villages or figures from folklore, contribute to the illusion of an authentic

rural dining experience. The fusion of sensory experiences and cultural values suggestively transports diners to another place and time, where the benefits of natural foods and the agrarian lifestyle are intimately accessible through the body.[1]

Even as peasant restaurants are among the latest fads in culinary entertainment in Russia, they are also entangled in far more pressing national concerns about the death of the Russian countryside. The disappearance of Russia's villages and the waning of rural life more generally have concerned both Russians and their observers over the past century (see Ioffe and Nefedova 1998; Paxson 2005:39), but they have generated particular worry over the past decade as the effects of post-Soviet land and agricultural reforms have become increasingly visible in Russia's countryside. Such fears are captured by ominous headlines and stories in Russian media: "Who will the forest protect?" (Mart'yanova 2005), "Who is saving the peasant?" (Kiseleva 2005), "The shadow of catastrophe looms over Tver's forests" (Nesterova 2001), and, more starkly, "Death of the Russian Village" (Loginov 2005). Accounts in the popular press take on the quality of colonial expedition narratives about "lost tribes," as reporters describe venturing into remote, seemingly deserted villages where they find the last remaining two or three elderly residents who continue to eke out an existence. A drive down any road outside a major city center reveals old wooden houses sinking into their own ruins. In light of images such as these, it is not surprising that Russians have reached the discomforting conclusion that Russia's organic life is under attack and in danger of disappearing altogether.

Such fears represent the latest chapter in a longer history of attacks on Russia's villages and peasantry that was already underway in the second half of the nineteenth century with the push toward urbanization and industrialization.[2] By the beginning of the twentieth century, such processes had relocated many rural residents to urban centers, prompting an early wave of village decay. As cities expanded outward over the course of the twentieth century, they encroached on, and eventually encompassed, rural spaces. In some cases, rural spaces were fully subsumed as small houses and farms were torn down and replaced with factories and apartment buildings. In other cases, the edges of cities such as Moscow contain hybrid zones in which massive apartment buildings bump up next to farms, forests, and grasslands. In still other cases, villages were contained, but not subsumed, by their urban oppressors, so that public access ways through small cities such as Tver meander between apartment buildings and tiny wooden cottages where residents keep chickens, goats, and other animals.

Curiously, the urbanizing forces at work during the twentieth century were accompanied by a reprieve of sorts for the rural sector, although this reprieve itself reflected the state's conflicted, oftentimes ambivalent, and always paradoxical relationship to rural spaces. On the one hand, the countryside was, for the Soviet state, a dangerous place ripe for social disorder. Soviet leaders pursued the state's projects of forcible social leveling through attacks on the country's bourgeoisie. In the countryside, these efforts were implemented through the seizure, and very often the destruction, of farms, property, and livestock belonging to bourgeois peasants, or kulaks. Stripped of their property, kulaks were forcibly exiled from their farms, and often from their communities altogether. Physical brutality was a reality, and millions of kulaks died. Coinciding with these assaults on rural residents, and probably the more important factor underlying the Soviet Union's efforts to eliminate the kulaks, was the recognition of the strategic value of the countryside's agricultural resources to meet the food demands of the Soviet Union. Consequently, the removal of an entire population of peasants from the countryside facilitated the state's appropriation of farmland for the good of Soviet society and the establishment of state-employed laborers on those farms.[3] Ironically, the value of the Soviet countryside for the project of nation building was symbolized by a simultaneous celebration of the agrarian roots and traditions of the Soviet Union. A preservation campaign, waged primarily as a means to shore up the country's agricultural industry, involved applying the methods and approaches of urban industrialization to rural villages (Hann 2003:9–10), so that farming villages were transformed into state and collective farms. Thus, despite their geographic location in rural areas, collective farms were at the very center of the Soviet state. Not only was agriculture part of the state's industrial complex, but it was the very backbone on which the rest of the Soviet state's projects and goals depended.

In the post-Soviet period, assessments of the cultural and economic significance of Russia's rural sector are similarly conflicted. One of the consequences of Russia's new status in the global market economy and the breakup of the Soviet Union into independent countries is that Russia has become enmeshed in larger trade relationships with other agricultural countries. Consequently, it is not as urgent as it once was that Russian farms be able to feed the country's population. At the same time, however, the lack of state resources directed to Russia's agricultural industry, coupled with the privatization of state farms, signals the continued widespread devaluation of farming and rural life. A visit to one of Russia's most prestigious agricultural institutes in summer 2007 was indicative of this decline. Despite the tremendous knowledge and expertise of the institute's scholars and students, the facilities were in serious disrepair. The dormitory where members of our group stayed was falling apart; the floors were buckling and pulling away from the walls, the plumbing was in need of serious overhaul, and the electricity worked only erratically. More telling was the fact that the majority of the dormitory's residents were not students at the agricultural institute; enrollment at the institute had dropped, and to fill the empty spaces in the dormitory the institute was renting out rooms to low-income families from the region.[4] To support themselves and their research, scholars at the institute were forging research partnerships with colleagues in other countries in the hopes that these ventures might bring in funding.

Even the acquisition of farms by private companies has contributed to the symbolic degradation of the countryside since the industrial agricultural technologies that have been introduced require fewer workers and less knowledge of traditional farming techniques. Farmworkers are quitting their jobs in order to take up higher-paying and more secure employment elsewhere. Elderly villagers are forced to sell off or slaughter their livestock because they can no longer afford to keep them or no longer have the strength to maintain them, a tragic development that Margaret Paxson (2005) has poignantly documented in her work on the disappearance of a village in northern Russia. Most noticeable is the transformation among younger generations in rural areas, as young people abandon their families' agrarian lifestyles and move to the city in search of better jobs and a higher standard of living. Reality and other television programs have highlighted this trend, as many of the most eager participants on these programs are young people who have come to Moscow or St. Petersburg in the hopes of escaping their rural pasts. Consequently, although farming has not yet disappeared, the farmers themselves are noticeably disappearing from the rural landscape.

Paralleling these shifts are changes in land use and population composition in Russia's dacha communities. Although dacha communities are not necessarily disappearing per se, dachniki confess their fears that dacha life may be on the wane as the appeal of rural land drives Russia's thriving real estate market. Dacha plots owned by cash-strapped private companies or even more cash-strapped regional governments are at risk of being sold to developers who transform these areas into suburban bedroom communities for urban commuters. Elderly Russians with limited incomes sell their dachas in order to finance their retirement or medical expenses, and younger Russians who have inherited dachas from their parents sell them in order to buy property in more desirable locations where they can erect more modern, convenient residences. Among my own circle of acquaintances, my friend Irina sold her dacha to pay for her son's college education, including several years at a university in the United States, while a landlady in the late 1990s sold her dacha to pay for her husband's medical treatments. Margarita's elderly mother sold her dacha and gave the proceeds to her grandson so that he could purchase an apartment after his marriage.

Although some owners willingly elect to sell their property to pay off debts or for what seems to be for a greater family good—for instance, one woman who was not particularly enamored of the rustic life confided that she would be happy once she ridded herself of the burden of the family dacha—in general, respondents perceived such a move as highly undesirable, distressing, and a last resort. One couple contemplated selling their dacha after their sons had grown up and moved away because they no longer wanted the responsibility of maintaining the grounds and the cottage. Ultimately, however, they decided not to sell, and several years later they confessed that they were glad that they had decided to keep their dacha and were using it more frequently than they had before. Another woman who sold her dacha did so to a close friend, which meant that she could still visit frequently and enjoy the dacha as she had formerly. For her, this was an important decision because she associated her family life with the dacha and did not want to lose it entirely.

The unpleasant reality faced by many dachniki is that there may come a day when they must dispose of their dacha property. And when they do, the dacha life will disappear for them. Not surprisingly, there is a hesitation, and even unwillingness, to sell off dacha property. It is not, in most cases, a freely or easily made decision, but one at which people arrive only after prolonged debate and with great reluctance.

At the heart of this reluctance is an abiding and palpable wistfulness about the dacha life that proves difficult to conceal. Descriptions of dachas, gardens, and the natural life routinely turn into reminiscences, as dachniki fluidly move between past and present as they talk about and experience dacha life. In a conversation with my friend Ksenia I commented that it seemed to me that Russians were nostalgic for dachas, villages, and the countryside (derevnia) more generally. Ksenia considered the question for a moment and then replied that this assessment was probably accurate. Things were changing, she stated, because more villages were being abandoned (zabroshennoe). As Russians moved away from the villages, all that was left behind were a few elderly people who chose to remain.

Villages used to have cows and pigs, she reflected, but they do not even have those any more. Continuing, she asked if I knew who was buying up those abandoned villages. Answering the question herself, in a refrain that I heard repeatedly from other Russians lamenting the decay of rural life, Ksenia told me that the buyers were Muscovites and St. Petersburgers who enjoyed economic freedoms not shared by local residents in the Tver region. In particular, she complained, the villages between Moscow and St. Petersburg were being bought up by urbanites who wanted to live in the country but worked in the cities. Changes in the ownership and style of summer communities are part of much larger transformations that have been sweeping Russia in the post-Soviet period in the realms of housing, architecture, and social relations but are not always met with widespread public approval, especially in communities like Nadezhda, where residents have a strong sense of pride in their surroundings and their community. It is not just dacha communities, however, but every type of inhabited and uninhabited rural space—summer camps and resorts, health spas, villages, forests, and farmlands—that are sites for intensive redevelopment.

Narratives about change and transformation cohere around mythologies of "disappearing dachniki." Accounts, rumors, and innuendos about disappearing dachniki appear repeatedly in the media, public discourse, and even, I discovered, my own field notes, as Russians draw on themes of loss and nostalgia to make sense of rural change and what seems to be the fundamental transformation of dacha life. Recurring fears about the disappearance of dacha life frame critical issues informing how Russians navigate and experience the feelings of loss, disorientation, upheaval, and anxiety associated with the post-Soviet condition (Boym 2001; Oushakine 2000a; Yurchak 2006).

Landscapes are helpful for pondering these questions, and particularly for examining the subject of change itself. Although qualities of persistence, fixity, and "perduringness" are frequently attributed to landscapes (Casey 1996:26), especially when landscapes are apprehended through maps and boundaries, such spaces easily escape efforts to fix them spatially or temporally. In his natural history of Amazonia, Hugh Raffles cautions us that when it comes to landscapes, "It is the impression of stasis that beguiles. They may look secure, but landscapes are always in motion, always in process" (Raffles 2002:34). This reminder is particularly apt for Russian landscapes, which have a tendency to change size, shape, and even location.[5] Correlations of space and temporality are further complicated in Russia, as landscapes are not simply spaces where past temporalities have been sedimented, one on top of the other, but rather are locations where multiple temporalities coexist, infusing one another, struggling with one another. Post-Soviet spaces are, in some respects, "haunted" spaces where pasts are never fully past but always somewhere near at hand (Ladd 1997; Rosenberg 1996; Schama 1995; Tumarkin 1994; Verdery 1999). Russian landscapes are not, as we have seen, places to be observed from the perspective of a viewer, and they certainly are not entities whose primary characteristic is locational. Rather, landscapes are spaces to move through, to inhabit. It is by moving through and by inhabiting landscapes that people call them into existence and acknowledge their multiple temporal dimensions (de Certeau 1984; Paxson 2005; Richardson 2008).

BAD FENCES MAKE BAD NEIGHBORS

One afternoon as I was walking through the Nadezhda dacha community with a group of friends and neighbors, one of my companions stopped to draw my attention to a large cottage set back from the road in a spacious but overgrown yard. Architecturally, the cottage resembled the others in the community, although it appeared to be several times larger than most. As we stood there looking, the rest of our group caught up with us. The three older women—all in their fifties—began reminiscing about the cottage. This, they told me, was the original communal cottage where they had spent their first years in the dacha community. In the early years of the dacha settlement, before it had expanded to its present size, this building was one of several communal cottages in the community. For several years the women's families had shared this cottage with several other families. Each was assigned its own room, but everyone shared the dining room, living room, porches, and yard. Eventually, each family was allocated its own plot of land and built its own cottage. As the women took turns describing the layout of the cottage and the communal lifestyle they had enjoyed, they also reminisced about their childhoods and the joyful summers they had shared with one another. Clearly, what was important to these women was the sense of intimacy and camaraderie that they had enjoyed in that house and the collective lifestyle that it had fostered.

If the general feeling among longtime Nadezhda residents was that they were a tightly knit community, there was also significant dissatisfaction about the problems caused by outsiders who were intruding into their community. Although dachniki's comments about these "outsiders"—or "the Muscovites," as they were known in local parlance—often included commentaries on the vulgar architectural styles and home decorating that were presumably favored by these outsiders (and certainly evident on the exteriors of their houses), the single most problematic aspect of their new neighbors' lifestyle was the fences that they had erected around their properties.

In a community where most residents had known each other for their entire lives, and where the children who had once played in each other's yards were now the parents and grandparents of young people who moved freely throughout the community, fences demarcating property divisions within the community were largely symbolic. This was a collective enterprise where residents relied on personal interactions and an unspoken common moral code to identify members of the community and where they belonged, pass on information, and decide where the boundaries of one plot ended and the next began. Divisions between dacha plots belonging to older, longtime residents were typically marked by small, unobtrusive objects, such as stones or other decorations that were arranged as borders for flower beds. In some cases residents had installed small, flimsy wire fences that certainly posed no impediment to pedestrians or small animals. In many other yards property divisions were more simply demarcated by subtle changes in the flowers or by worn pathways between plots. Only the outside perimeter of the community was marked by formal, robust fencing.

During walks through the community, residents of Nadezhda frequently drew my attention to the lack of fencing between the properties of longtime residents as a sign of the intimate and trusting relationships they enjoyed with one another. Neighbors meandered through one another's yards to visit or borrow something, and family pets roamed freely on regular circuits to visit neighbors who fed them. Svetlana commented that one of the things she treasured most about dacha life was that "There are no fences. I can go anywhere I want—[and say to someone] give me a spoon, give me salt, oh, I would like some tea because I am out of tea. Do you understand?" By way of elaboration, Roman added, "It is that kind of community [obshchenie takoe]." Affirming Roman's point, Svetlana stated, "That is how it is here for me—it is still my collective [moi kollektiv]." In Svetlana and Roman's exchange, they emphasized not only the sense of freedom associated with a fenceless community, but also the nature of that community itself. This is a community where people can ask one another for help and know that that help will be forthcoming. Svetlana's choice of the term collective is revealing because it invokes the sense of a community formed through mutual assistance. In another part of our conversation, Irina continued these thoughts in equally poignant fashion: "In the city I am alone. There

FIGURE 10. Fences such as these are more symbolic than practical.

in the crowd, among everyone—I am alone. It does not matter that there are people all around me. But in the forest, I am not alone. You have to understand, in the forest, I do not have a feeling of being alone."

This dislike of fences did not mean that there were none in the community. In fact, in recent years a number of dacha properties had been enclosed by tall, sturdy fences made from wood and metal and secured with large padlocks. Residents' reactions to these fences were revealing. Although one family had installed a short fence around their property, their neighbors agreed this was an acceptable exception to community norms, as the couple's property was adjacent to a public pathway leading to the riverbank and because they spent much of the year living abroad. In this particular case, the fencing was an appropriate safeguard against outsiders. Public acceptance of this fence sharply contrasted with opinions about other fences in the neighborhood. Residents repeatedly and insistently impressed upon me that the other fences, which were typically tall ones made of solid concrete and metal with large doors, belonged to newcomers who had only recently moved into the community. In a few cases in which long-term residents had also erected their own fences, these acts were interpreted as evidence that these individuals had never truly belonged to the community. Fences were thus held up as a tangible marker of the social demarcation between authentic dachniki and interlopers.

Residents' discomfort with fences has escalated over the past several years as more residents, both long-term and newcomers, have added fences to their properties. By summer 2007 fences had become a significant point of contention within the community, as even longtime residents who had sworn that they would never put up fences had done so. Even as residents had begun resigning themselves to the fact that the feeling of community and mutual trust that they had previously enjoyed was changing, they were particularly incensed at the effects of these changes on longstanding ethics of communal access. One consequence was that fencing had changed the pathways leading through the community and into the forests, thereby disorienting residents within the landscapes that they had previously navigated without thinking or even seeing them. A second, even more problematic consequence was that the fences severely limited access to a common well that was situated in the middle of the community. By all accounts Ivan, the Nadezhda cooperative's president, was particularly incensed about this development and groused about it to anyone he encountered.

Residents in Nadezhda and other dacha communities, summer camps, and spas in the vicinity were also alarmed by the news that a private company had purchased a significant piece of property in the woods adjacent to these communities. No one seemed to know the specific details of the transaction, but judging by the activity of the local rumor mill, dachniki throughout the entire region were convinced, and horrified, that it was inevitable that the new owner would install fences around the property. Not only would access through the forest to the train station be curtailed, but so would access to several more distant fields and forests where dachniki went to gather mushrooms and blueberries.

Concerns about the ways in which fences were transforming communities both physically and socially were not unique to the Nadezhda cooperative but were shared by many dachniki in the Tver region and beyond. Outside Moscow, highway management practices have included the construction of concrete dividers to separate traffic moving in opposite directions, as well as efforts to reduce noise through the installation of tall soundproof walls around communities located along the highways. Although these efforts have improved traffic flow, they have impeded foot traffic, especially since pedestrian crosswalks have not always been added, and when they exist they are rarely recognized by drivers. As a result, local residents find that access to their communities has been curtailed. In even odder instances, residents' access to their own homes may be cut off, as was the case for people living alongside one section of the highway leading from Moscow to Tver, where soundproof walls had been erected directly in front of homes, blocking off the paths leading to their front doors. My personal observations and conversations with Russians confirmed that urbanites are losing ready access to the countryside. Rising transportation costs, the elimination of free transportation for pensioners, and the lack of handicapped access across Russia, including on public transit, keep elderly and disabled citizens at home. Longer working days and increased work responsibilities also severely curtail the amount of time that working-age Russians can devote to travel from home.

A revealing article titled "Behind Riabeev's Walls" documents changes that have taken place in the Riabeev summer community outside Tver. The article begins with two large illustrations that juxtapose summer life of the past with that of the present. The "before" photograph depicts a woman holding a bouquet of wildflowers and standing in front of a large wooden building. It is accompanied by the caption "A dacha resident standing near the Eighth 'Communal' Dacha." The "after" photograph depicts the same community but in a dramatically different way: it shows a sign for the community in front of two large houses (the first made from brick, the second from wood) and a small house, accompanied by the caption "Today's dacha residents strive for solitude" (Bushchev 2005:7). This juxtaposition of pictures effectively captures the simultaneously material and social transformations taking place across Russia's countryside, where architectural designs are powerful metaphors for personal relationships. At the same time, this striking visual comparison of "before" and "after"— or, as such temporal comparisons are most commonly rendered in Russian, "then [ran'she]" and "now [seichas]"—operates as a narrative frame for how Russians make sense of daily life, whether it is in rural or urban spaces. Although these deliberative invocations of comparative temporalities are often interlaced with a wistfulness, and even bitterness, about change, Boym has argued that they are in fact productive because "you can pick and choose your own here and now" (Boym 2001:96). This flexibility enables Russians to situate themselves selectively within a field of realities, or, perhaps more importantly, to inhabit multiple temporalities simultaneously. As a result, distinctions between past and present are not absolute but rather are points of engagement with the landscapes to which they are attached. As sensed, felt places (Basso 1996; Herzfeld 1991; Stewart 1996a), these landscapes draw Russians into a multitemporal reality where change is not necessarily unidirectional but rather a proliferation of possibilities of "then" and "now," "here" and "there."

THE PAST FOR SALE: DACHA REAL ESTATE

In summer 1995, while riding in a car to a dacha community, I noticed in the outskirts of the Moscow region what appeared to be a series of housing developments under construction. Unlike the massive generic apartment buildings that dominate the urban landscape in Russia, these structures appeared to be two- and three-story single-family brick houses, complete with porches, garages, and driveways and arranged around meandering streets and cul-de-sacs lined with light poles. On the porch of one finished home was a large barbecue grill. Noticing my interest in these developments, my companions snorted derisively that these were the homes of New Russians, Russia's nouveaux riches, and not those of ordinary people.[6] Such homes were, my companions suggested, the exception rather than the rule among Russians. When I returned to Moscow in fall 1997, I was intrigued to see that there were many more such housing developments both under construction and already completed in the Moscow suburbs. Glossy advertisements for these new subdivisions boasted about their lavish recreation facilities, security gates, food stores, and branches of local banks, among other amenities.

By summer 2005 these communities had become ubiquitous throughout the Moscow and Tver regions and were spreading into regions farther away. As my plane began its descent into Moscow's Sheremetyevo II Airport, I was able to see such communities spreading across the landscape. The highway leading from the airport into Moscow was a constant stream of billboards with advertisements for new suburban communities, construction companies, ready-made architectural designs, and plumbing services, among many other home-related items. A week later, during the first two hours of the drive from Moscow to Tver, we passed what seemed like a never-ending stream of new housing developments. On a boat ride along the Volga with Angela and Misha a few days later, we noticed that the formerly empty fields just outside the city were now filled with single-family detached homes and rows of attached, townhouse-style homes.

The prices for these new homes were not inconsequential, as revealed in the "For Sale" listings published in the regional weekly advertising newspapers that summer. Appearing in the newspaper *Iz Ruk v Ruki* (From Hand to Hand) for the week of July 15, 2005, were the following sample listings:

FIGURE 11. This new community of "McMansions" appeared in a small village across the river from Tver's historic district.

2 km from Tver (village of Pasynkovo), 3-story brick cottage *[kottedzh]*, 600 sq. m., first floor fully detached, gas, plumbing, radiotelephone, 24-*sotok*[7] yard, Volga River 300 m away, selling for $60,000 [US$]. Immediately!

4 km from Tver (village of Glazkovo), 2-story brick cottage *[kottedzh]*, 180 sq. m., precise, plastered, without separate interior work, exterior natural gas line, pipes, electricity, 12-*sotok* yard, on the bank of the Tvertsa River, next to the forest, year-round entrance, selling for $100,000 [US$].

Perhaps even more noteworthy was that even though in the mid- to late 1990s subdivisions such as these were primarily established as autonomous communities, separated from villages and dacha communities either by fences or by physical distance, by the early 2000s these distinctions were negligible. Small, ramshackle wooden dacha cottages, with their yards full of goats and a tangle of bushes, were now dwarfed by the new year-round brick mansions and swimming pools standing next to them. Yet when I asked friends and acquaintances about these new structures, I received the same terse reply that I had received previously: these were the homes of New Russians and foreigners and not those of ordinary people like themselves.

Despite avowals that these changes were representative of "New Russians," dachniki's cottages and gardens revealed something quite different. Dachniki did not deny that change could bring tremendous improvements in their lifestyles at the dacha, even though they might grumble about the change, as came out in the following exchange between Veronika and her mother, Zinaida. Describing their activities at the dacha, Zinaida said, "We have a little bit of potatoes, just two patches. Vera mows around them with a lawn mower." Veronika then responded, "She [i.e., her mother] still has not resigned herself to the lawnmower at the dacha."

Lawnmowers were a particularly visible marker of the changes taking place in dacha communities, as another couple explained. Margarita and her husband Iurii were amused by the disturbance caused by their purchase of a lawnmower. In the past, Margarita remembered, dachniki cut their grass by hand, either by using scythes and other hand tools or by picking the grasses. In the early 2000s, Margarita and Iurii decided to make their yard work easier by purchasing a motorized trimmer for cutting the grass around their dacha. The new tool piqued the interest and curiosity of their neighbors. Over time, several neighbors mustered up the courage to ask if they could borrow the trimmer and try it for themselves. After that, trimmers began appearing in the yards of their neighbors. More recently, Margarita and Iurii decided to upgrade and buy a lawnmower, the first in the dacha community. Not long after, they noticed lawnmowers in their neighbors' yards as well.

Another change that was welcomed was the introduction of cellular telephones, which became commonplace in Russia in the late 1990s, largely because many people still lacked regular and reliable landline telephone service in their homes. Even less common was landline telephone service in dacha cottages. Consequently, dachniki described cellular telephones as an essential innovation. Dachniki especially appreciated being able to know precisely which train a guest would be taking to the dacha or being able to call a family member still in the city with a list of grocery items to collect on the way.

For other dachniki, the changes facilitated by capital renovations to public utility lines in recent years have enabled residents to upgrade their heating systems and install running water inside their dacha kitchens, eliminating the need to draw water from a well and carry it to the kitchen for cooking or washing dishes. The availability of portable videocassette players and DVD players ensures that children can be entertained, particularly on cold and rainy days when they cannot play outside. Even laptop computers have been heralded for enabling students and other electronics-dependent professionals to bring their work with them to the dacha.[8] Most notable is the recent possibility of installing high-speed Internet service at the dacha, a feature heavily promoted by technology service providers on billboards lining the main highway between Moscow and Tver. Not everyone finds these developments beneficial, however, as dachniki complained that children no longer read or played outside.

Thus at the same time that dachniki find some aspects of modern technology advantageous, they also voice fears that changes are destroying the fabric of social life of their community and, more significantly, the very nature of the organic experience itself. Margarita and Angela described one permutation of these fears as the "babushka problem." The two women were comparing the generational conflicts they had suffered with their respective grandmothers. Angela stated that the conflicts between her and her grandmother arose because "we [i.e., Angela and her husband Misha] do not use the land *[my ne izpol'zuem zemliu]*." Her grandmother saw a large plot to be planted, but Angela and her husband preferred to plant a small plot with a few different things. Margarita agreed and added, "A grandmother needs to work until the very end *[babushka nado rabotat' do kontsa]*." Angela finished by stating that the changes occurring across Russia are apparent in the fact that for her grandfather, working the dacha was a duty, but now for her and her husband, these activities were hobbies *(khobbi)*.

Although longtime members of communities such as Nadezhda were certainly, and no doubt justifiably, frustrated with the physical and social changes taking place, especially the arrival of "outsiders" who refused to integrate themselves into the community, they were equally concerned with what these changes meant for the future of an authentic and cohesive organic lifestyle. Ultimately, the issue that was most fiercely debated and worried about was how and where a sense of authentic Russianness could be retained and identified in a quickly transforming society.

ORGANIC AUTHENTICITY

A theme that emerged repeatedly in conversations with friends and strangers was the conviction that a research project that treated dacha life as a contemporary phenomenon would not yield an accurate picture of an authentic dacha experience. Many people advised that I would need to take a step back into Russia's history, either by reading nineteenth-century writers such as Chekhov and Gorky or by visiting elderly peasants who still lived in rural settings that were presumed to be far outside the reach of post-

Soviet modernity. Consequently, friends and new acquaintances frequently took it upon themselves to locate "authentic" dachas and dachniki for me. One friend tried to set up an interview with a very elderly woman who was one of the last remaining residents of her tiny village, while other friends apologized for being dacha renters or visitors and not owners of their own cottages, as if this disqualified them from speaking authoritatively about the dacha experience. My friend Ksenia, who did not have access to a dacha but whose grandmother lived in a village outside Tver, repeatedly promised to take me to visit her grandmother's village for an authentic rural experience. When other obligations prevented her from keeping her vow before I left the field, she worried that I might be lacking important details for my research and would be unable to complete my book.

Some potential informants discouraged me from visiting them at their dachas because they were afraid that I would get the "wrong idea" about their homes. In other words, they were concerned that their cottages and gardens were not sufficiently "authentic." Particularly in areas where many dachas had been renovated and updated, residents were concerned that I would not get a "true" picture of a rustic cottage full of well-loved furnishings and clothing. Informants who proudly invited me to visit their beautifully renovated cottages and see their manicured lawns were nonetheless quick to point out the remaining touches of rusticity: an outhouse, a small storage shed, a rusty faucet in the yard, or a small bedraggled patch of berry bushes. Individuals who carefully recounted the histories of their dachas as we toured their cottages and lawns frequently added details about what used to exist in the place of indoor plumbing or a newly painted room. It was as much an accounting of what once was there but was no more as it was of what was there at the moment.

When it was apparent that informants' dachas were in fact the original buildings or retained elements of the original structures, their owners emphasized this fact in their accounts and tours. This was the case regardless of whether the dachas were small, rustic cabins or large, elegant cottages. To prove the age of her cottage, Anya's friend Tanya proudly peeled back the wallpaper to show the newspapers that had been stuffed into the walls as insulation, taking special care to point out the publication dates printed on the papers. Other dacha residents encouraged me to admire children's artwork hanging on the walls, only to reveal that the "children" were now in their thirties and forties. Antique samovars, in which water was heated by placing burning twigs or coals in a tube in the center of the pot, were pulled out of storage during dacha excursions, despite the fact that their owners typically used electric kettles in their daily practice.[9]

In cases where Russians either own nontraditional, albeit historic, dachas, or have updated their dachas, they take care to emphasize those aspects of the dwelling that are original or at least retain a semblance of historicity. For instance, Elizaveta inherited a spacious three-story cottage from her parents, who had been members of the local political elite. The cottage was significantly larger than other homes in Nadezhda, and it had been tastefully decorated with comfortable couches, reading chairs, and tables, as well as a huge bouquet of flowers that Elizaveta had received as part of her prize for winning a national competition for the most beautiful garden. As Elizaveta and her friends walked me through the house, they took care to emphasize that the large rooms, indoor plumbing, and furnishings were original features when the house was built in the 1940s. The indoor plumbing was singled out for special attention, and several people made sure that I peeked into the downstairs bathroom. Even today, indoor plumbing is unusual in dacha cottages; a faucet for cold water is most commonly placed inside the kitchen, if water is brought indoors at all. Elizaveta's cottage boasted a full downstairs bathroom with a spacious bathtub, toilet, and sink. More significantly, there was a gas water heater that instantly provided hot water for the sink and bath. Rather than acknowledging the privileged position that her parents had undoubtedly occupied, Elizaveta instead focused on the challenges that her family had faced in installing such a modern bathroom. Specifically, she recounted how state inspectors repeatedly battled her parents by attempting to remove the fixtures from the bathroom. Elizaveta thus neatly reframed her family's dacha narrative as a populist, antistate account that simultaneously positioned her as an authentic dachnik and her home as an authentic, historic building.

Another example of the challenges of authenticity facing dachniki was revealed to me in summer 2000, when Georgii and Anna, a married couple whom I had met at an academic conference, invited me to join them for a weekend at their family dacha. Located in one of the older and more prestigious dacha communities just north of Moscow, the dacha officially belonged to Anna's mother, a well-known intellectual who was nearing retirement. During the summer the older woman lived at her dacha full-time with her granddaughter, Georgii and Anna's eight-year-old daughter. My colleagues lived in Moscow during the week and made the ninety-minute drive to the dacha on the weekends to see their daughter and Anna's mother. A longtime friend of Anna's mother was also in residence for an extended period. Although Anna and Georgii had described their family's dacha in terms that suggested a typical cozy cottage, the home more closely

resembled a stand-alone house. The wooden cottage consisted of two stories, with at least three separate bedrooms and a sleeping loft, as well as a
large kitchen, dining area, study, and porches in both the front and back.
Two separate bathrooms were each equipped with hot and cold running
water. Given the comforts of the cottage, it was not surprising when my
hosts insisted that their dacha was not typical.

To compensate for the apparent shortcomings of their atypical dacha
for my research purposes, Georgii and Anna engaged in numerous lively
discussions with family members, friends, and neighbors who spontaneously dropped in or were encountered on the streets of the community,
asking where they might find authentic or real *(nastoiashchie)* dachniki for
me to meet and observe. Finally, after considerable discussion, my hosts
decided that the woman who lived in the house across the street was likely
our best option. In previous descriptions of their dacha community and
neighbors, my hosts had always referred to her simply as "the woman with
the goats." This elderly woman lived in a year-round house with her husband and kept a small flock of milking goats that was the source of fresh
milk and sour cream that she sold to neighbors in the community.

Rather than calling ahead of time to schedule an appointment, or even
to determine if the neighbor would be willing to speak with a visiting
anthropologist, my hosts decided simply to drop in unannounced, a move
that was in character with Anna's assertion that the unexpected visitor
was always expected at the dacha. Consequently, we caught the woman
and her family while they were eating supper. Despite the intrusion, they
invited us into their tiny, cramped kitchen and seated us at a small table
laden with plates, bowls of sour cream and jam, newspapers, gardening
implements, and cats. The woman was occupied with dropping spoon-
fuls of batter onto a hot skillet and turning blini onto a plate that she
presented to her husband and grandson. Although they invited us to join
them for supper, my colleagues politely refused. To explain the reason
for our visit, my colleagues introduced me and my project and expressed
their certainty that our hosts would be able to offer more authentic insight
into the dacha experience. Our hosts graciously accepted my colleagues'
assertions as a compliment and gamely agreed to answer my questions,
even as they insisted that they also were not experts on authentic dacha
life. The encounter was intriguing for what it revealed about the criteria
used for measuring authenticity. In this instance it was as if the goats, fresh
milk, and homemade sour cream determined that one were an authentic
dachnik. Yet at the same time, even the bearers of these legitimating criteria were hesitant to claim that title for themselves. Their disavowals con-

fused my hosts, who found themselves stymied in their efforts to produce an "authentic" dachnik for me.

If we return to the discussion of natural foods from the previous chapter, and to the discussion of peasant restaurants from the beginning of this chapter, it becomes clear that certain practices associated with peasant life stand in for "authentic" Russian culture. This association of "peasant" life with "authentic" Russianness also invokes an explicit temporal dimension. If contemporary Russian life is characterized by spacious cottages with running water, then clearly authentic Russian culture cannot be located in the "here and now" of the present moment, but rather must belong to the "there and then" of the past. During the course of my research, even as informants eagerly embraced the topic and offered their assistance, including generous invitations to visit and enjoy fruits and vegetables freshly picked from their gardens, many individuals nonetheless expressed their concern about the extent to which research conducted in the present could capture the realities of an authentically traditional cultural phenomenon such as the dacha experience.

Issues of authenticity are central to discussions about the changing nature of dacha life, and rural life more generally. Although the norms associated with this lifestyle are unwritten and vague, Russians consistently point to the persistence of certain practices. The presence of animals was another of these compelling features, as the example of "the woman with goats" illustrates. It is the presence and absence of animals, both domesticated livestock and wild creatures such as birds, hares, squirrels, and elk, that demarcate the natural world and its vitality. The declining numbers, or outright disappearance, of animals from dacha communities and rural settings raises concerns not just about habitat loss but also, and more significantly, about cultural loss.

Svetlana was particularly distressed by the disappearance of wild and domesticated animals from the area around Nadezhda. Svetlana had accompanied Iuliia, Angela, and me to my interview at Oksana's dacha. During our tour of Oksana's yard, Svetlana paused by the sunken pond that Oksana had created as the centerpiece of her backyard. When I asked if there were frogs in the area, Svetlana turned mournful as she recalled that in the past, frogs had been plentiful and had filled the area with their songs. Summer was a wonderful time because of the constant singing of the frogs and their beautiful music. Now the absence of the frogs was apparent by the silence, she lamented. She speculated that the disappearance of the frogs was likely due to the increased cat population in the community, in combination with general changes related to housing construction. Svetlana's distress was obvious, and during the course of the afternoon she repeatedly returned to the subject of the disappearing frogs.

Veronika also mentioned the disappearance of animals in her family's dacha community as evidence of unwelcome changes:

> Earlier, as you know, our neighbors at the dacha kept pigs and chickens. All kinds of animals. We had rabbits . . . as well as a goat. [The goat] stayed there all summer. Oh, fu [i.e., what am I saying?], he lived there all winter. That goat was there, but that was all earlier. Now no one keeps animals anymore. They bring their dog [to the dacha]—that's the extent of the animals.

Later that afternoon, as Iuliia, Svetlana, Oksana, Angela, and I strolled along the paths leading from Oksana's dacha toward Iuliia's dacha, Svetlana entertained us with a running commentary on how the community had changed over the past several decades. After pointing out which houses were new and which had been substantially altered, she recalled that previously the community had been alive with animals. Some dacha owners kept farm animals such as cows, goats, and chickens; in the colder months these animals lived on the first floors of their owners' homes and provided a natural source of heating. These animals, however, no longer existed. Yet in a departure from her earlier comments about how structural changes had brought about the decline in frogs, Svetlana did not cite the changing occupational habits and economic lifestyles of local property owners as factors in the disappearance of farm animals. Svetlana instead blamed the livestock decline directly on outsiders who had moved into the area. Specifically, she blamed a man from the Caucasus who had moved into the area several years earlier. According to local gossip, the man went around the community and bought up all of the livestock, which he subsequently slaughtered and cooked for *shashlyk* (shish kebabs).

By blaming this man, Svetlana did not merely suggest that outsiders were socially disruptive, but she linked these outsiders with Russian discourses blaming minorities, especially individuals from the Caucasus and Central Asia, for negative changes, chaos, and decline in Russia. Although Svetlana did not invoke explicitly racial elements, instead emphasizing the culinary practices of Caucasian culture as the catalyst for this transformation, the underlying message was clear.[10] Moreover, by invoking disruptive Others as a factor contributing to the disappearance of animals in the area, Svetlana made a strong statement about the disappearance of authenticity in the community.

Such concerns with identifying and locating an authentic dacha lifestyle, and also with lamenting the absence of this lifestyle, manifest themselves in various ways, revealing that local ideas about authenticity and tradition are highly subjective and relative. Yet fusing these differing views on where and how to locate authenticity is a pervasive cultural conviction that an authentic dacha experience can be concretely situated in spatial and temporal terms, even if those spatial and temporal terms are flexible, or even imaginary. This reality raises a perplexing question about how dachniki accommodate the changes they make in their own lives.

Given the seemingly constant views about authenticity and change that have been articulated by my friends and acquaintances since 1995, I was surprised when, in summer 2004, close friends offered to show me pictures of the renovations they had recently completed on their dacha. Evgenii and Olga were middle-aged, middle-class Muscovites who had bought their dacha plot in a region less than two hours outside Moscow in the mid-1990s. When they had first purchased the plot it was completely uncultivated. They cleared the plot and then planted fruit trees, berry bushes, and an extensive garden that they irrigated with water that was collected in a cistern. On one side of the plot they erected a crude but functional shed in which they kept their tools, a few pieces of furniture, work clothes, a hot plate, and a few cooking utensils. Despite their busy work schedules in the city, Evgenii and Olga visited their dacha as often as they could in order to work in the garden and perform maintenance on the building. Evgenii and Olga took great pride not just in their dacha plot, but also in their ability to live an appropriate dacha life. Fresh fruits and vegetables gathered from their garden and from the forest behind their property, and afternoons spent in the rustic *banya* (steam bath) they later built, took center stage in their personal accounts of their dacha.

Although Evgenii and Olga had periodically voiced their desire to replace their shed with a slightly larger and more comfortable cottage that would be conducive for overnight stays and for hosting guests, neither had given any indication that this sort of project would be forthcoming in the near future. Nor had they ever expressed approval of the more grandiose styles of dacha architecture. Thus I expected that their newly renovated dacha structure, when it eventually appeared, would be a simple, although slightly larger, structure that resembled a traditional cottage. I was surprised, then, to see pictures of a three-story plank-and-beam wooden structure that boasted three separate bedrooms, a kitchen, living room, and family room, as well as porches on the front and back of the house. As their one concession to rusticity, they had elected to leave the toilet outside in a separate structure. Evgenii and Olga matter-of-factly informed me that this was their new dacha and that they hoped to move into it permanently once their children had graduated from university and they were closer to retirement.

Even as individuals like Evgenii and Olga hold onto the romantic ideals of dacha life, they also acknowledge that now they face other challenges and wish to pursue other interests. As children they were free from the responsibilities of the dacha, but as adults they are confronted on a daily basis by the complications and challenges of managing property. Among middle-class dacha owners who either rented or owned small dachas and plots of land, a common sentiment was that property ownership brought with it a special set of headaches. During the group interview that took place on my first night in Nadezhda, Masha commented, "When you have your own home, you spend all of your time doing repairs. It is depressing [menia eto ugnetaet]." Her comments sparked a wave of sympathetic murmurs and agreement, with Valentina saying, "Yes, it is a sad state of affairs." Masha continued by listing the constant problems of being a property owner: "The roof is falling in, the refrigerator is breaking down, you need to winterize the water pipes, but they are already broken, too." At that point Iuliia interjected, "You really need to have a man stationed at the dacha!" Masha agreed and added, "Of course! You cannot do anything without a man, or without a lot of money!" Masha and Iuliia's companions quickly picked up the thread and added their own comments. Svetlana asked, "Which is better: men or money?" Veronika responded, "The best is to have them both." When Roman added, "There is never very much money," his wife quickly interjected, "and men never have any money!"

Despite the gales of laughter and lighthearted banter elicited by Iuliia's and Masha's comments, these remarks could not disguise an unpleasant truth: dacha cottages and gardens require considerable amounts of labor and resources that are sometimes beyond the means of their owners. Even as this group of friends continued to joke about the value of men and of money, their conversation shifted to the more serious topic of the hardships of maintaining a dacha. For Masha the difficulties included running out of gas and suffering short circuits of the electrical system. For others, the problems entailed finding the necessary financial resources to pay for general maintenance or upkeep. Others had suffered material losses when thieves had broken into their cottages over the winter and stolen furniture and gas tanks.

Assertions of authenticity, then, are as much about imagining the persistence of an idyllic past located in an idyllic space far removed from the realities of urban life as they are about making sense of the choices that one must make in the "real world." Change is discomforting, but it is a reality that cannot be avoided. It is how people make these choices and justify them that reveal whether they are part of an "authentic" organic lifestyle or not.

THE INVASION OF "THE MUSCOVITES"

Mirroring events that were occurring in dacha communities across Russia, dramatic changes were visibly affecting both the appearance and atmosphere of the Nadezhda dacha cooperative by summer 2005. Over the preceding several years many residents had begun transforming their small, rustic cabins into larger, more modern dwellings. Changes ranged from the modest to the grandiose. Some residents had modified and enhanced their outdated utility systems, added insulation and heating to winterize their cottages, and replaced old, faded, and worn furniture and appliances with newer items. Aesthetic improvements generally did not involve the purchase of brand-new items but rather the recycling of gently used but still serviceable pieces from people's apartments. Other residents had expanded their existing cabins by adding new rooms, attics, or outbuildings. In still other cases, residents had dismantled their old cabins and built new cottages that were larger, more durable, and more conducive to living and working for extended periods of time. Although most people retained a vegetable garden, the spaces devoted to food had steadily decreased as residents devoted more attention to flowers, grass, and other lawn decorations. Because these improvements were made by long-term community residents, they were seen by others as relatively minor, unremarkable, and part of a normal cycle of change.

What did generate considerable discussion and critique, however, were the changes introduced by a different set of residents. Called simply "the Muscovites," without any indication or certainty that these individuals were in fact from Moscow, these residents comprised a distinct subgroup within the Nadezhda community. These "Muscovites" consisted of several families who had bought dacha properties in the community, replaced the older cottages with elaborate brick houses, and erected tall metal fences around their grounds. Longtime residents grumbled that these individuals kept to themselves and socialized only with other "Muscovites" who came to visit on the weekends.

One "Muscovite" residence was repeatedly singled out for particular disdain for not fitting the image and values of the Nadezhda community. Although residents were quick to point out the aesthetic flaws of this dwelling, especially its brick façade and elaborate decorations, they were most distressed about the antisocial behavior of its owners, a young married couple who rarely interacted with their neighbors and regularly engaged in weekend behavior that violated the social norms that residents emphasized were core principles of their community. Their most recent indiscretion was a birthday party for their child that they had organized prior to my arrival, an event that was described to me repeatedly over the course of my summer in Nadezhda. According to the various accounts that I heard from numerous individuals, the couple had invited a large group of friends to their dacha for the weekend celebration. The festivities included a performance by a pop singer who was brought in from Moscow. Loud noise from the concert and the party blasted through the quiet dacha community until the wee hours of the morning, disturbing the other, and obviously uninvited, residents of the community.

Residents complained loudly about the noise and how the cars of visiting guests had disrupted the peace and quiet of the community, but they reserved their harshest criticisms for the aesthetic tastes and morality of the couple. The singer was, by all accounts, of limited talent and had primarily performed songs about criminal life. Residents saw this as fitting, given that the previous owners of the dacha had reputedly been involved in criminal activities in Moscow. The current owners had purchased the house from the widow of the previous owner, who had allegedly been murdered as a result of his business dealings. Not surprisingly, the new owners were suspected of being just as shady, if not more so. The stories related by my informants differed as to the age of the child: initial accounts described him as two years old, while later accounts described him as two months. Over the course of the summer, most versions of the story used the younger age, which was interpreted as even more compelling evidence of the profligacy and ostentatiousness of the couple and their friends. Angela reported that her father had joked that the new owners should hang up a banner that read, "We are not good enough to invite Alla Pugacheva [one of Russia's most famous and flamboyant pop singers]," a sarcastic suggestion that although the new owners possessed money, they did not have enough money—or, more importantly, enough taste or class—to stage a higher-quality performance.[11] Embedded within the scathing, albeit humorous, comments of Angela's father Sergei and other Nadezhda residents was a statement about the intrinsic traits of authentic dachniki. It was not just the lifestyle choices made by "Muscovites" that distinguished them from their neighbors but also their morals.

As much as these differences in morals and character were associated with outsiders who moved into existing dacha communities, dachniki acknowledged that they belonged more to a post-Soviet identity that was believed to be developing in Russians. Hence parents and grandparents were vigilant in monitoring their children and grandchildren in an effort to stamp out these traits before it was too late. The first difference was one identified as a hyperaggressive personality, a trait that correlates with the accusations of criminality and violence attributed to "Muscovites" like the newcomers to Nadezhda. When reflecting on why she valued going to her dacha, and to the countryside more generally, Irina informed me, "I do not like all this aggression in our society today . . . [Here at the dacha] there is a different life, it is a different planet. With a very different population."

Oksana made a strikingly similar point on a separate occasion. Echoing Konstantin's notion of a distinctively Russian *mentalitet,* Oksana first invoked geographer Lev Gumilev's theory about genetically derived "ethnoses," usually understood as a distinctive worldview unique and intrinsic to a specific ethnic population, and particularly his work on connections between ethnoses and landscapes. According to Oksana's interpretation, Gumilev's argument proposed that each ethnos had a natural cycle of about 1,500 years, which would mean that Russia's ethnos emerged in the ninth to tenth centuries. Because ethnoses take shape during the human developmental stages, they are formed in each individual during childhood. Oksana noted that various factors shape this ethnos—territory, national composition, and the history of Russia, among other influences—which result in the obvious differences between populations, such as between Russians and Germans. Applying Gumilev's theory, Oksana asserted that Russia has acquired an aggressive character, even a primitive character, that has been shaped by numerous changes and events during the Soviet period, including housing practices and architectural styles. She claimed that these features now exist in the unconscious parts of Russians today, before mentioning her grandson and why she finds it important, even necessary, to bring him to the dacha with her: "When a child is born, he grows, and he grows up in this aggressive architectural environment. He is uncomfortable, he is aggressive. But when he is in nature he begins to relax [*relaksirovat'*]." In Oksana's view, although these aggressive tendencies are nascent in Russians, particularly those of the younger generations, they can be staved off, and perhaps even neutralized, with exposure to nature.

The second quality associated with "Muscovites" is more problematic, but it is also a compelling indicator of the negative consequences of change. What dachniki fear most of all, it seems, is the loss of a particular type of sociality that is presumed to accompany the natural life. One component of this fear is a perceived disinterest in spending time at the dacha among younger generations. This was the issue that Angela identified as part of the "babushka problem" that pitted her against her grandmother in their views on proper gardening practices. Iuliia also noted this difference when describing the characteristics that define Russia's younger generations:

> They go somewhere else to rest. They want to see the world and to see it themselves. It used to be that we spent all of our time here trying to see each other. Right? Someone might have small children coming here, but then when they are teenagers, of course, they are trying to go somewhere for rest . . . There really are not family ties these days, because everyone has scattered all over the place . . . In the Soviet period it was easier living. Much easier.

Iuliia's comments become even more illuminating when we include her response to my question about why living in the Soviet period was easier: "It used to be that everyone was together. People gathered to eat dinner together."

Gathering together, sharing a meal—these are themes that resonate with Svetlana's assertion that she loved the fenceless dacha life because of the ethics of sharing and mutual support it engendered. An absence of fences meant not only unhindered access to space but, more importantly, unhindered access to one's neighbors. This sense of a shared experience came through clearly in the following statement by Irina about why she was nostalgic for the dacha life:

> There, it is a dacha village [dachnaia derevnia]. Everyone there knows everything about one another. Who has arrived, who has arrived with someone, whose lover has built a home here, and so on. Do you understand, it is a bit . . . amusing. If you hold yourself apart from everyone, then of course you will find it all a bit suspicious: [for example,] what on earth is she doing here? In general, these are all your own relationships here. It is a very specific kind [of relationship] . . . There, you understand, there is some piece of an ancient village foundation, a community [obshchina], that kind of community. Everyone knows everything about you, where you were born, how you were brought up . . . Oh, [it is] amusing!

What upsets an authentic, natural lifestyle is not simply the arrival of outsiders, the anonymous, generic "Muscovites," but rather perceived changes in a presumably traditional Russian system of values that privilege community, responsible personal behavior, and an ethic of mutual support—in other words, the feeling of a shared insiderness.[12] As commentaries on changes enacted in the contemporary moment and associated with a post-Soviet condition, these concerns are part of a broader Russian enactment of post-Soviet nostalgia in which Russians struggle to locate themselves in time, space, and community (Boym 2001; Yurchak 2006).

FIGURE 12. Dacha neighbors visit one another to show off the first potatoes of the season.

When inflected through the dacha life, and the organic life more generally, nostalgia is not simply about a relationship with the past so much as it is an effort to grapple with the present and the future. Dachniki such as Iuliia, Oksana, Irina, and their friends and neighbors, much like their predecessors, both real and fictional from a century before, recognize that there is something special about the organic life, and they are struggling mightily to protect and preserve not just this essential quality but also their place within it before passing it on to subsequent generations.

DISPLACING AND EMPLACING THE ORGANIC LIFE

How do people become aware that they are strangers in their own lands?
Someone must make them so. Sometimes they are forcibly removed.
Sometimes they are just reclassified.
—Anna Tsing (1993:154)

Tsing uses the above statement to explain how the codification and implementation of official standards for appropriate living conditions effectively displaced Meratus from a reality that was, for them, normal and ordinary into an existence outside normally sanctioned society. There seems to be a fitting analogy here for contemplating the future of an organic lifestyle in Russia, at least as Russians themselves understand these possibilities.

As I was leaving Tver at the end of the summer in 2005, my driver guided us through a part of the city marked by massive high-rise apartment blocks standing alongside small wooden cottages. Workers were haying in the fields next to these residences, using scythes and other handheld farming implements. The image was striking, primarily because the juxtaposition of "old," perhaps even "traditional," farming techniques against "new," and even "modern," housing developments seemed to underscore the fragility of a rural lifestyle in the face of the inevitable encroaching forces of post-Soviet capitalist development. It was as if residents of the apartment blocks could step back in time to a simpler organic life just by walking out their front doors.

Irina's comments capture this sense of stepping back into a better moment in time most vividly:

> I do not know, how was it before? We had it all at the dacha . . . Listen, Lissa, it is terrible at home, it is terrible in the city, but there [at the dacha] it was good. Do you understand? There are people who do not like going to the dacha. There are people who live for themselves in the city . . . they are urbanites. They get bored at the dacha, they do not like it there. They [need to be] there where there are skyscrapers and huge civilization. But I, for example, especially once I became an adult and started getting older, the more I moved away from civilization, the easier it became. I became some kind of country bumpkin *[derevenshchina]*—oh my! And the longer it went on, the easier it became. And I think that here . . . there is a note of intimacy in relation to the dacha—it is simply that people feel good here. [Being at the dacha] relieves stress. In the forest, I am calm!

The visual juxtaposition of apartment blocks, cottages, and "traditional" farming techniques was also striking precisely because the mixing of multiple temporalities suggested that persistence and continuity might be possible after all. If Russians are nostalgic for both real and imagined pasts, there are ways for them to bring back those remembered times and to enjoy them again in the here and now. Loving grandmothers treat their grown children to their favorite childhood foods, children's artwork hangs proudly on walls long after the children have grown up and moved away, and old quilts on lumpy mattresses re-create the physical sensations of dacha life from one's youth. Ancient television sets and refrigerators, with their temperamental settings, offer a direct link to a material past that is fading away in modernized apartments in the city. And the worn paths between people's cottages that have been marked by countless feet over the years stand as far more effective physical markers that link, not separate, old friends far more effectively than iron fencing.

Nostalgia, then, is not so much a looking back as it is a means of bridging the past and the present. Nostalgia can also represent a step back into personal pasts as well as national pasts. The organic world is an archive of material, social, and sensory artifacts that are otherwise disappearing in the world at large. Nostalgia is thus both a commentary on social change and a form of social change itself, just as the organic life is as much a state of mind as it is a lifestyle. In its own way, change is a form of stasis, permanence, and continuity. The simultaneous strands of past and present, change and stasis, appear vividly in the comments of Svetlana and Roman:

> *Svetlana:* Many dachas have lost their owners, and there they are, falling apart. Right next to a dacha, there is one that has been let go and is falling apart. Dachas are being sold and bought more and more often, so that people can build their own . . . Villages are falling into the ground [*rushat'sia*], and forests are becoming fewer.
>
> *Roman:* But everyone says that everywhere there are not any more good spots.

As Roman suggests, it may be that both change and complaints about change endure, so that we hear in the laments of today's dachniki echoes of Gorky's and Chekhov's dachniki, complaining about their vanishing lifestyle and the trash produced and left behind by summer visitors.

CHAPTER 6

Dacha Democracy

Building Civil Society in Out-of-the-Way Places

Toward the end of my stay in Tver in summer 2005, Larisa and Pavel, a married couple who were friends with Angela's mother, invited Angela and me to visit them at their dacha northwest of the city. Through Angela's mother, Larisa passed on instructions about which minibus to take. Fortunately, because Larisa and Pavel's dacha community was located at the end of the minibus line, we did not have to worry about knowing where to get off along an unfamiliar road. When we exited the minibus, Angela called Larisa on her mobile telephone to let her know that we had arrived. Larisa told us that she would start walking and meet us in about ten minutes. While waiting for Larisa to arrive, we explored our surroundings. A rusted metal shed served as the dispatch office and break room for the minibus drivers. Next to this stood an equally rusted metal building that apparently served as a minimarket where dachniki could pick up a few food staples and other necessities. Several stray dogs lounged in the dirt under the porch of the minimarket. Arranged around the tiny square of dirt were three sets of metal archways that led to the three separate dacha communities that all converged at the minimarket/bus stop.

When Larisa arrived, she greeted us and then informed us that she would take us on a tour of the community on our way to her dacha. A more recently established dacha development, this community had established dirt lanes that were wide enough to accommodate cars, neatly demarcated "streets" named after various species of trees (beginning with fruit trees), and tidy, small fences encircling yards filled with neat but riotous profusions of flowering plants and blooming fruit trees. As we walked, Larisa pointed out certain houses for their style or for what was growing in the yard. She then took us down a path leading to the outside of the dacha community so that we could see the pond.

Because the warm day was a weekday, there were only a few families with small children splashing in the pond or sunbathing on the small beach. Several men stood in the tall reeds lining the banks of the pond and fished. Larisa told us that the pond was one of her favorite places at the dacha but that pollution and litter were taking their toll on the water quality and the condition of the beach. Indeed, we had to step around piles of refuse on our way to and from the edge of the pond. Even more distressing was that the pond was shrinking. Larisa told us that she was not sure if this was because of overuse of the water supply, environmental degradation, or some other unknown reason. Over the course of that summer in Russia, there had been several reports of ponds and lakes that had mysteriously vanished overnight. We continued on our way, encountering an elderly man who was pulling a bundle of reeds that he had collected from the pond, before arriving at Larisa and Pavel's dacha.

During the several hours that Angela and I spent with Larisa and Pavel that afternoon, our host and hostess repeatedly impressed upon me the pleasure and satisfaction that they received from their dacha. It was clear that the couple took great pride in the location of their dacha community, as well as the flower and vegetable gardens they had planted and the *banya* they had built themselves. Much of our visit revolved around tours of their yard to inspect the newest flowers that were blooming, and to ooh and ahh over the mutant cucumber that had somehow taken up residence in a cistern and grown to the size of a large squash. Our formal interview session quickly gave way to an extremely large lunch and an informal tasting of homemade wines brewed from my host's homegrown berries.

Despite the pride that my hosts took in their dacha, their garden, and the fruits of their labors, it was apparent that the single most important quality of the dacha was that it provided a quick and easy escape from the city. My hosts repeatedly mentioned that because the community was conveniently located near the train platform and at the terminus of two separate minibus lines that went directly to the center of Tver, they could reach their dacha easily at virtually any time of the day or night. Larisa and Pavel particularly relished the fact that the late evening bus schedule meant that they could leave work in the city and go to the dacha to spend the night. They lamented the fact that in the winter the dacha community was inaccessible except by private car.

The importance of their dacha as an escape became more apparent a week later, when Larisa and Pavel invited Angela and me to visit them at their apartment in Tver. Located in a newer section on the outskirts of the city, their apartment was approximately a twenty-minute tram ride or a thirty-minute walk from the city center. Constructed in the late 1960s and early 1970s, the apartment buildings in this section of town were primarily medium-sized blocks of five to six stories, with multiple entrances and no special aesthetic appeal. Our hosts' apartment, on the top floor of a five-story walk-up, was a tiny two-bedroom flat that had housed four people (Larisa, Pavel, and their son and daughter) for almost twenty years. Only recently had the son married and moved into an apartment with his new wife. Despite the son's departure, the apartment was cramped for its three remaining occupants. During our visit, the four of us perched awkwardly around the kitchen table, elbowing each other as we tried to reach our plates. Whenever our hostess needed to get something from the stove, two of us stood so that she could reach around us. When their apartment was seen in this context, it was obvious why the family valued their dacha as an escape. More than that, however, their dacha afforded them a very different life than the one they had in the city.

In another case, my elderly Muscovite friend Aleksandra enjoyed her son's dacha as an escape from the physical and emotional abuse that she suffered in the city at the hands of her estranged husband. Over the past several years Aleksandra had grown extremely concerned about her well-being as she continued to share a small two-bedroom apartment with her husband—one of the unfortunate realities of the continuing shortage of affordable and accessible housing in Russia. Aleksandra was excited about the renovations that her son and his wife were making to their dacha just outside Moscow, primarily because her son had told her that once the dacha renovations were concluded, she could move there for the summer and avoid her husband. For Aleksandra, the dacha and the countryside represented safety, even if it was only temporary, from the emotional and occasional physical abuse by her husband.[1]

Since Russia's urbanization drive in the late nineteenth century, cities have been simultaneously heralded as both the means and the pinnacle of the country's move toward modernization and civilization. City planners carefully designed parks, public squares, apartment blocks, and other city spaces to represent the greatness of the country. Urban spaces themselves were to monumentalize Russia's heritage and future. Yet at the same time, cities have also been places of great danger and violence, both real and imagined. Urban apartment dwellers effectively barricade themselves in their apartments with the ubiquitous double-door system, coupled with a complex series of locks and deadbolts. It is not uncommon to see fights break out among men along city streets, in the markets, or near train stations. The constant presence of armed police and security guards furthers the sense that the city is a dangerous space.

As the comments by both Oksana and Irina in the previous chapter reveal, cities are associated with aggression and violence, a view shared by my friend Paulina, an unmarried schoolteacher in her thirties who lives in a studio apartment on the southern outskirts of Moscow. The two neighboring apartments are occupied by families who seem to spend most of their time yelling and hitting one another when they are not yelling at Paulina and other neighbors and vandalizing their property. Paulina despairs of ever being able to move to a better apartment, but she also recognizes that even if she moved she would likely still have to live among aggressive neighbors.

The pathology of urban settings is experienced and expressed by urban residents like Paulina, Oksana, and Irina as breathing disorders, nausea, headaches, hypertension, insomnia, disorientation, and panic attacks. Larisa revealed that when she lives in the city she suffers from high blood pressure. When she is at the dacha, however, she rarely takes her medication and her blood pressure is normal, a fact confirmed by the home blood pressure monitor that she uses. This perception that urban settings are intrusive and destructive helps contextualize the pervasive sentiment that the natural world compensates for the shortcomings inherent in Russians' everyday, primarily urban, lives.

In the words of Irina, the dacha was an alternate reality, a different planet where she was no longer confined by space and enforced intimacy. Nature's resemblance to "another planet," however, does not mean that the organic world lacks rules or order, nor that it exists as a separate realm in isolation from the rest of Russian life, a point that speaks to Latour's admonishment that we should be skeptical of setting up Nature and Society as distinct entities (Latour 1993). Despite the natural world's image as a socially, economically, and geographically "out-of-the-way" place, nature as both place and lifestyle is very much integrated as a regular, necessary, and ordinary part of the rest of Russian life. In fact, as we have seen repeatedly and in many different ways throughout the preceding chapters, "out-of-the-way" places often turn out to be the places where people find life and work to be easiest and most meaningful. By contrast, it is Russia's hypermodern urban settings that are the most "in-the-way" sites of Russians' social worlds today.

Too often, however, the value of such out-of-the-way spaces is misrecognized because of persistent assumptions that meaningful activity happens only in the center, not in the periphery, a dichotomy that has persistently remained lodged in city/countryside binarisms (Williams 1973). A simple core/periphery or city/countryside distinction is problematic in Russia, not only because of the physical, geographic realities in which the two domains intersect and intrude upon one another, but also because the very concepts of city and country exist only in relationship to one another. Perhaps most important, however, is that core/periphery and city/countryside dichotomies rest on a presumption about where to locate "meaningful life."[2] As Kathleen Stewart reminds us, the "periphery" is oftentimes the place where the most significant work is done, if only we could remove our blinders and see it. As she notes, "it is in these most marginalized, out-of-the-way places that place seems to matter most while the places lodged firmly in the center of things grow vague and interchangeable" (Stewart 1996b:42). Stewart's point resonates with Herzfeld's (1997) notion of "cultural intimacy," in which spaces that are distanced geographically and symbolically from the gaze and reach of the state are in fact those sites where the most meaningful activities of the state's citizens take place. In both thought and practice, Russians treat the natural realm as a center, not the periphery, and by extension as the ordinary and not the extraordinary, of the post-Soviet world they inhabit. In many ways throughout Russia's history, it is in the natural world of dachas, gardens, and forests where the work of nation building and state building has taken place.

Studies of civil society in post-Soviet societies, as elsewhere, have been predicated on the proposition that civil society is a marker or manifestation of democracy rather than a quality of daily life that may take different forms in different societies. Hence the primary question posed by political scientists and development experts concerned with the nature of post-Soviet societies has typically focused on the question of whether countries like Russia possess anything approximating a civil society, and whether they can be classified as a democratic, or more typically democratizing, society.[3] The presumed lack of a civil society, and by extension the absence of democracy, has been interpreted as a consequence of the controlling and monolithic nature of a Soviet state that did not allow independent and spontaneous civic associations to emerge (see critiques of these perspectives in Hann 1996; Hann and Dunn 1996; Wedel 1998).[4]

Such perspectives are misleading, however, especially when broader perspectives of civil society, public sphere, and civic association are considered. William M. Reisinger's definition of democracy as "a system of rule by 'the people'" (Reisinger, Miller, and Hesli 1995:943) seems to describe what happens in natural spaces such as dacha communities and forests, where Russians create communities, make up their own rules, and develop a sense of order and justice, which they then monitor and regulate.

Reorienting the focus to the natural world as a material and symbolic center of Russian social practice that is linked to an imagined urban periphery productively introduces a new vantage point for observing and understanding the transitions of democracy and civic engagement that are taking place in Russia today. Rather than thinking of natural spaces as existing at an unfortunate and disadvantaged distance from the urban center, it is important to consider how they make possible the activities that take place in cities, especially global cities such as Moscow. By following political movements as they emerge organically, we can rethink where and how we locate Russia's "center" or "core" in ways that take seriously how seemingly out-of-the-way places like forests, villages, and dacha communities are essential settings for the enactment of the micro- and macro-processes of Russian daily life. Russia's new democratic values of freedom, autonomy, liberty, and civil association emerge vividly and with tremendous effect in these settings, and the organic life emerges as a form of civil society that shapes everyday life.

COMMUNITY ORGANIZING AT THE DACHA

Although dacha communities generally lack the official institutional settings, such as town halls, schools, or public auditoriums, that have been associated by some political theorists (e.g., Putnam 2000) as formal markers of a viable and permanent community life, these summer communities are nonetheless still marked by a lively civic sector where residents gather to discuss and implement the public work of the community. In dacha districts such as Nadezhda, the community's civic landscape exists wherever its residents congregate and engage in activities oriented toward supporting the goals of the community: gardens, porches, pathways between cottages, clumps of berry bushes in the forest, and even secluded patches of grass along the riverbanks.

Dacha communities are typically a hybrid of formal and informal bureaucratic organization. During the Soviet period, the Nadezhda community was organized into a formal cooperative whose members shared the responsibility for the general maintenance and safety of public spaces as well as for the general conduct of residents and visitors. Officers were elected from among the residents, and these individuals were charged with such tasks as enforcing safety rules, ensuring that public utilities such as water and electricity were operating properly, and that members paid their rent and dues on time and in full.[5] The activities and accounts of the cooperative's members were carefully maintained by co-op officers and municipal officials. Although dacha cooperatives were primarily summer communities, residents enjoyed the same types of formal community events that were available in Soviet cities, such as sporting events, concerts, and even dances.

Nadezhda is rather unique in that the community has maintained this organizational structure into the present. One consequence of the privatization of dacha property in many areas is a change in population, as dacha owners sell their cottages to newcomers. As a result, the formal institutional structure of dacha cooperatives has disappeared in many areas. Although the Nadezhda community has also experienced a recent influx of newcomers, the community has largely retained its formal institutional structure. Ivan, the current president of the Nadezhda cooperative, runs a tight but congenial ship. He approaches his role seriously, and during the summer he visits frequently with his neighbors to listen to their requests for assistance or repairs, pass on information, collect rent, and keep an eye on the community's business. While on the train and during the walk from the train platform to the community, Ivan takes advantage of his relatively captive audience and solicits volunteers to engage in activities such as litter collection and community maintenance.

Despite the natural setting, Nadezhda is full of signs attesting to the organizing activities of its members. Throughout the woods, handwritten announcements tacked onto trees notify residents of community news. Warnings about prowlers and the current level of fire threat jostle for space with announcements for the upcoming children's pageant, updates on public utility services, sign-up sheets for the litter brigade, and advertisements from residents who have something for sale or a litter of kittens to give away.

In many ways the socializing that takes place in settings such as these has a feeling of genuineness. Spontaneity and infectious joy characterize this form of socializing, as it is perfectly normal to meet other people in the woods and to fall into conversation with them. At the same time, camaraderie and mutually constituted personal investment are more intense in natural spaces than they are in the cities. In the privacy of public settings such as the woods and along the riverbanks, friends enjoy greater intimacy than they do within their own homes in the cities. Even strangers can lose their strangeness and quickly become absorbed into the community in natural spaces, provided they adhere to community norms.

In the Soviet period it was not uncommon for apartments to be allocated through workplaces, so that apartments in the same building or in buildings in the same neighborhood were often assigned to workers from the same workplace. For instance, the apartment blocks in Aleksandra's Moscow neighborhood were assigned to high-ranking party officials and KGB officers, and Aleksandra's neighbors were also her husband's coworkers at the KGB headquarters. Similarly, Angela's parents were both professors at the regional university, and their apartment was located in a building reserved for university staff and other intellectuals. Dacha allocations also followed this pattern, and employees of the same firm or agency were given plots in the same dacha community. Thus dacha communities were typically a satellite location for citizens' preexisting social worlds; Soviet citizens never fully left behind their workplaces and neighborhood communities, but rather they transferred them from the city to the countryside.

This multisited and easily transferable sociality typifies the experience of most residents of the Nadezhda dacha community, since most make their personal and professional homes in Tver and have long moved in intersecting and overlapping social circles. When the Nadezhda community was originally founded, plots were allocated primarily to local party officials, high-ranking workers in the city's factories, and faculty at one of Tver's universities. Many Nadezhda residents live in apartment buildings in the same downtown district of the city, a relatively small area bordered by the river and an automobile-free zone. In addition, most residents have had their dachas in the Nadezhda community for forty to fifty years, and sometimes longer; and they, their children, and their grandchildren have spent most of their lives with and beside each other.

Given the multiply overlapping circles in which these individuals move, it would seem logical that residents of the Nadezhda dacha community would encounter each other regularly throughout the year. Intriguingly, however, close physical and social proximity in the city and at work does not translate into socializing or even chance encounters among residents in the city. Rather, Nadezhda residents are most likely to run into each other in rural spaces outside the city. In other words, actual social interaction and engagement among Tver residents typically happens in the countryside during the relatively short summer season, and more commonly during spurts of several days over weekends and holidays.

The short duration of these social encounters, however, does not minimize their intensity. If anything, the experience and performance of sociality and community is heightened in the countryside. Despite the fact that this socializing is temporally compressed into a few summer months, it takes on the sense that it happens year-round. In just a few minutes neighbors who have not seen each other for months in the city are able to reestablish a sense of intimacy that makes it seem as if the months that have passed have been mere moments, an experience that evokes dachniki's comments about the expansive and contractive qualities of dacha time.

Perhaps the most important place where people meet and greet each other is the train. Nadezhda is conveniently located just five stops away from Tver along one of the main railway lines connecting Tver with St. Petersburg and Moscow. Suburban trains make the twenty-five minute run from Tver several times a day. Despite the frequency of trains, however, Nadezhda residents often end up taking the same train. Though this is likely a result of their similar vacation schedules, they often describe the event as a coincidence. Neighbors and family members first meet each other, often unexpectedly, on the Tver platform and then find themselves sharing the same compartment. Relatives who board the train at different stations arrange in advance to meet each other in a particular compartment. Angela and Misha, who taught at the local university, frequently encountered their former students on the train, a situation that provoked whispered discussions about whether it was appropriate to acknowledge students who had rarely come to class or had failed a course miserably. Judging by the nervous behavior displayed by some students when they spotted Angela and Misha, it seemed likely that they were wondering the same thing.

Train rides to dacha communities quickly become festive social gatherings, as residents visit with one another over a couple of bottles of beer or a snack of melting ice cream. Nadezhda's president, Ivan, spends his time during the commute strolling through the train cars in order to greet his fellow dachniki, meet their visitors, and conduct community business. My first introduction to Ivan, and to many other residents of the Nadezhda community as well, occurred on the train. Ivan and I had already heard of each other through mutual acquaintances, but even though his cottage was only several houses away from that of Angela's family, several weeks passed before we were formally introduced one afternoon on the train. On that occasion Ivan was taking his usual walk through the train when he spied my friends and me. In keeping with the highly social and intimate feeling of the dacha-bound train, no invitation was needed—or expected—for him to sit and join us. After we were introduced, Ivan, a fellow academic, quickly began grilling me about my academic credentials and research project until he was apparently satisfied. He then began telling me about the community and his role as cooperative president. After I apparently passed muster with him in that encounter, Ivan frequently dropped by my friends' cottage to give me the latest news or to elaborate more fully on a point we had been discussing earlier.

Trains have been an especially important means for disseminating information in Russia. Until recently, automobiles were relatively rare. Even now, many people who own cars use them only for special occasions. Of the few families of my acquaintance who own cars, most leave them parked in secure garages and only remove them for trips to the dacha. In some cases the trip to the garage can be longer than the trip to the dacha. Iurii and Margarita's car is parked in a garage across the city from their home, a journey that takes approximately forty-five minutes by public transportation. Although many dacha communities are located near highways, access from the highway to the community itself may be difficult by car. That is certainly the case for Nadezhda, as car owners must drive several miles off-road over difficult terrain (and hope that the rickety bridge over the river is operational). Hence trains, as well as subways and buses, are often the most efficient, if not always the most convenient, means of traveling to dachas. Russians take their lives with them on public transportation, as dogs, cats, and other household animals ride along for the trip. Russia's culture of reading (Brooks 1985) is reinforced by the reliable vendors who enter train cars and buses to sell newspapers and magazines. These vendors are followed by other enterprising individuals peddling ice cream, pens, balloons, batteries, and fertilizer, among many other items.

The forced physical intimacy and shared experience of traveling by public transportation encourages an environment in which riders, often complete strangers, pass on news either by sharing their reading materials or by engaging in conversation. The communicative aspect of public transit has acquired special significance during moments of political crisis, when more formal avenues of dissemination have been curtailed. As Alaina Lemon has described for the events of the 1991 putsch, Muscovites who lived in the suburbs gathered outside the subway stations to hear the latest news as it was brought from the center by commuters (Lemon 2000).

The following conversation from a group interview that I conducted in Nadezhda illustrates the importance of train rides as social events:

> *Roman:* Here is the situation. It used to be in the past that we would go to the dacha by *elektrichka* [suburban train] because there weren't any cars. And everyone who was traveling was familiar! Everyone would sit practically in the same compartment. And then the socializing would begin, and the con-

versations . . . everything got simpler and simpler and simpler . . . And then suddenly we would be in Nadezhda. That is, we had already arrived at the station.

Iuliia: You would be talking so much that sometimes you would even miss your stop!

[Everyone laughs]

Roman: It was not like on the metro, where you just sat down and rode. You would come a little bit earlier and sit while the places filled up. By the time you started moving, you were already talking.

Valentina: You would be talking and talking, and suddenly, bam! You were at Sosnova [the station after Nadezhda; i.e., you had missed your stop].

Roman: You see, the *elektrichka,* it was a place for socializing.

In response, another person joked that one would not want to travel with a neighbor who was well known in the community for his incessant chatter, a comment that provoked further peals of laughter.

Typically, after residents disembark from the train or the minibus, they continue on foot, sometimes for several kilometers, thereby allowing neighbors to continue their conversations along the way. The main path that links the train station to the dacha community resembles a rush-hour thoroughfare, as residents, their guests and pets, and other day visitors make the trek through the woods and on to the community. Groups expand and contract as people catch sight of friends and neighbors, introduce guests, and pass on gifts or supplies that they have brought with them. Children and adults alike use the walk to make plans to visit each other over the weekend or to pass on weather reports or other information.

The sense that social relationships are constituted in and through natural spaces was brought home repeatedly during dacha visits. Wherever my friends and I walked in what seemed to be a secluded part of the forest or along the riverbank, we quickly discovered that these seemingly deserted spaces were illusions. Instead, we often found other friends and neighbors close by among the leafy trees, green grass, raspberry bushes, and small hollows. One afternoon during my stay in Nadezhda, Angela, Misha, and I went to the nearby river for a swim. After looking for a quiet place away from the families with small children and dogs, we placed our towels on a small hillock that was sheltered from the main beach area by tall grasses. Almost immediately a head popped out of the nearby grasses—it was a neighbor and colleague of Angela's aunt. Even though the other woman worked in the same office as Iuliia, she had been traveling abroad for work, and so no one at work had seen her for several months. It was only at the dacha that she was able to catch up with her friends and co-workers.

THE FREEDOMS OF AN ORGANIC CIVIL SOCIETY

Dachas, forests, and meadows are the very sites where Russians socialize, feel safe, and engage in collective responsibility. These common spaces are also marked by a striking civic life, most notably citizens' attention to the ideals of freedom that have become prominent in the postcommunist period. As informants repeatedly told me, it is in natural spaces that they feel most free and where they experience the effects of the changes taking place in today's Russia most profoundly. It is also where individuals seem to feel most able to express their opinions and to criticize the forces that otherwise structure their lives.

One arena in which these new freedoms are most visible is the economic realm, a reflection of the ways in which Russia's experiment with market capitalism has produced new practices of private property and ownership. To a great extent, the notion of formal, private ownership has not applied to dacha plots, nature, or other rural spaces until recently, so that, as Lovell notes for the case of dachas, "the boundary between state and personal property became conveniently blurred" (2003:173–74).[6] Historically, dachniki have paid only nominal fees for rent, utilities, and other municipal services in their dacha communities. In Nadezhda, rental prices were so low that residents called them "symbolic rents." Even in 2005, for instance, the average rent for Nadezhda cooperative members was only four or five rubles per year (the exchange rate at the time was twenty-nine rubles to US$1). These low prices contributed to the idea that residents had been "given" their plots by the state as both gifts and entitlements. Over the past decade, however, Russian privatization efforts, coupled with changes to property rights, have led to new understandings and possibilities for ordinary citizens to own land, housing, and other forms of private property. Despite these trends toward increasing private ownership, the rules and regulations governing private property, property taxes, and title claims are so vague, imprecise, and fluid that they prove confusing to both ordinary Russians and officials.

Moreover, the ambiguities of these policies make them difficult to implement or enforce, further encouraging popular suspicion and apathy. These changes are compounded by the dramatic shift in dacha populations as long-term residents give up their property and move out and outsiders move in. Both these changes in local communities, as well as the shift from rental property to privately owned property, have affected the organization and function of dacha cooperatives. In Nadezhda, whereas long-term residents maintain their dues-paying membership in the cooperative association, newcomers who have moved into the community after purchasing their dachas have typically elected not to join the cooperative. These changes in the ways that people own and use physical property, as well as whether they formally join the community's institutional structure, have had profound effects on the social dynamics within such communities. Longtime residents share a concern that the newcomers are not as invested—socially and materially—in the welfare of the community. Additionally, by not joining the cooperative association, these neighbors inhabit a space outside the moral authority of the community, a status that invites criticisms of their behavior as deviant and dangerous to social norms.

While the politics of formal membership in dacha cooperatives reveal significant concerns and disagreements about the presumed degree of commitment to the community by residents, they also crystallize a more profound set of debates about the nature of freedom as a personal right and the limits of this personal freedom within society. Concepts and practices of personal freedom and individual choice were associated with natural spaces long before the postsocialist transition, but they are acquiring new relevance in today's Russia. Russian philosophies of geography-based nationalism are fundamental to these formulations of freedom, so that one of the most important traits attributed to Russia's natural settings is the capacity to encourage personal development and the attainment of self-fulfillment. The correlation of place, nation, freedom, and existential fulfillment emerged in the following conversation around Iuliia's kitchen table:

> Viktoriia (who lives and works in the United States during the year): Melissa, I want to compare what it is like at the dacha with life in America. In America, whenever we go somewhere out in nature or go to a park, there is not that kind of feeling that you are free [vot net takogo oshchushcheniia, chto ty svoboden].

> Valentina: I wanted to say that there is not any freedom [at the dacha].

> [Laughter]

> Svetlana: America is a different civilization.

> Viktoriia: No, it is not that America is a different civilization. It is that there [i.e., in America], there are all these roads, where everything is planned out, totally organized . . . Where to go, where to park your car, where to eat.

> Masha: So everything is already decided for you.

Viktoriia: There are regulations everywhere. That is, you cannot simply go to a place where you want, like go take a dip in the lake. There the general feeling is that everything is impossible, constrained.

Valentina: Everything is forbidden.

Viktoriia: And here it is not that way.

The point that Valentina and her friends were trying to impress upon me was that unlike rule-bound countries such as the United States (or Germany, added another person), where regulations and formal plans are imposed everywhere, in Russia there was a sharp distinction between the hyperordered reality of planned settings, whether they were cities or villages, and the unregulated spaces of nature.[7] Whether within dacha communities, with their institutional and rule-bound organizational structures, or within forests, wooded parks, or other rural spaces, informants claimed not to feel the effects of these regulations on their behavior and feelings. Informants repeatedly related that being in nature—in their gardens, in the forests, or in the thickets of city parks—allowed them to be completely unfettered. Nothing was forbidden and everything was possible. Strikingly similar themes emerged in a chance encounter with a Russian immigrant living in California. My simple inquiry about the last time the woman had returned to Russia for a visit prompted a lengthy philosophical commentary on the number of years that had passed since her last visit and how she could not wait to return to enjoy the freedom and openness of Russian nature. Although she was quick to assure me that she enjoyed the many state and national parks, forests, and beaches in the United States, and especially in Northern California where she lived (and where access to the outdoors is easy), she reflected that American nature did not feel as free, familiar, and safe as Russian nature. Even the smells in Russian forests conveyed a greater sense of freedom and expansiveness—freedom of movement, ease of breathing, a greater openness of self—than she found in American forests.

This insistence that natural spaces feel completely free disguises the fact that these settings are very much subject to both formal and informal rules and restrictions. In addition to the building codes and fees imposed on dacha cooperative residents, legal and moral codes govern proper behavior in wild spaces. Rules and regulations posted at the edges of forests and in dacha communities detail what one can and cannot do while in these areas. For instance, signs posted at the entrance to Filevskii Park, in west-central Moscow, inform visitors that they are forbidden from setting fires, letting their dogs run free, driving cars, camping, picking flowers, and chopping down trees. Further in the park, along the river, another set of signs forbids swimming. Despite these warnings, however, on any given day the park is filled with people tending campfires, running their dogs, wading, fishing, swimming, and even riding Jet Skis. The situation is similar in the ecological park in Vorob'evy Hills, in Moscow's south-central district, where signs reading "No cars" are routinely ignored. In the summer months, Russia frequently experiences cholera outbreaks, prompting local authorities to ban swimming and fishing in rivers and streams, a move that does little to deter beachgoers and anglers. I was perhaps most startled at the deliberate evasion of official rules when I was walking through the Bytsovskii Nature Forest with my acquaintance Maxim, an ecology professor. Although Maxim had called my attention to the rules posted at the entrance to the forest, including a prohibition against picking plants, he repeatedly broke off leaves, branches, and flowers so that he could describe them to me.

These sorts of actions reveal that there are rules, and then there are rules.[8] What this creative circumvention and sometimes outright dismissal of rules exposes is the extent to which Russians envision and experience natural spaces as intensely private and personal settings that are outside and thus immune to formal order. In nature, one feels free to indulge in behaviors that one might not normally risk. In public settings such as the flower market, Russians are keenly aware and observant of the regulations set out in *The Red Book,* Russia's handbook to endangered flowers and wildlife. They submit to the rigid physicals required for public hygiene purposes before they are allowed to dip their toes in the municipal swimming pool, and they chastise friends and neighbors for smoking in their cars or on the public bus. Yet such rules, and the compulsion to honor them, seem to recede with distance from the public sphere and public view.

By distinguishing which behaviors are acceptable in nature and which are not, Russians complicate distinctions between public and private. At the same time that they treat nature as their private living quarters, they do so publicly and in full view of their neighbors and the state but with little concern for regulation by others. This is a form of privacy in which there is no secrecy and little oversight. Privacy exists only in public view. Reconfigurations of the distinctions between public and private, and between civic and domestic, were important components of the Soviet project. Commentators have frequently noted that the lack of private space and the lack of a private sphere were key features of Russian daily life during the Soviet period. In many ways, private spaces were dangerous sites where the seeds of discontent and actions antithetical to the state could be germinated and nurtured.

Housing practices were one of the primary settings for the reordering of public and private, personal and collective. As Victor Buchli describes for the case of Soviet housing, "radical proposals existed that called for the complete obliteration of the domestic sphere" (Buchli 2000:29). Katerina Gerasimova makes a similar point in her observation that "It might seem that the inhabitants of communal apartments were unaware that they lacked privacy, but the concept of privacy has never been a feature of Russian and Soviet culture and, in fact, the term itself is hard to translate into Russian" (Gerasimova 2002:207). Accounts of life in communal apartments during the Soviet period repeatedly emphasize this sense of a lack of privacy at home. In her account of life in a communal apartment in Leningrad during the Soviet period, Svetlana Boym describes how even the most intimate and ordinary parts of one's day—such as bathing and using the toilet—were always done in recognition of the audience waiting just outside the door (Boym 1994).

Yet it was not that the domestic and private were completely obliterated, but that these spheres were reformulated in different physical, symbolic, and emotional ways. As the public became interiorized in people's domestic lives, their private lives moved out into public settings. In particular, Soviet citizens learned to compartmentalize their lives and their relationships with other people, so that "private" aspects existed out of sight of neighbors. As Svetlana Boym (1994) notes, people without access to physical spaces of privacy retreated to spaces of emotional or psychological privacy. For the case of dachas, Stephen Lovell writes that in contrast to the *kommunalka* (communal apartment), with its "public privacy," dacha communities were "characterized by an altogether more benign 'private publicness'" (Lovell 2002:119). What observers like Boym, Buchli, Gerasimova, and Lovell have noted are the ways in which the public and the private not only became intertwined but were also inverted. That is, as the spaces of people's dwellings came to be seen as publicly controlled spaces, or at least as spaces regulated and monitored by the state, outside spaces came to acquire significance as safe places for private conversations, personal errands, and self-renewal. Walking was important not just as a form of exercise but also as a forum for socializing. Strolls through the park with friends provided a safe opportunity for conversations on potentially dangerous topics as well as perfunctory catching-up. Forests and particularly dachas emerged as oases of "one's own."

Active reconfigurations of public and private continue in the post-Soviet period, even as their parameters shift in response to new forms of personal and public behavior. One consequence of marketization is the emergence and growth of public spaces for more private sorts of activities. Sidewalk cafés, coffeehouses, restaurants, and bars have become places for local residents to gather for both public events and private encounters. Young people sit in coffeeshops and do their homework, while local politicians conduct business meetings with colleagues and constituents. Local community groups organize art shows and borrow wall space from proprietors to hang their art.

Not all of the ramifications of these changes have been met with widespread approval. In some places the increasing appropriation of spaces for public activities has been accompanied by dismay over how those spaces are being used. A new morality of space has recently emerged, especially in response to the very visible colonization of public spaces by young people, vendors, and the homeless. In both Moscow and Tver, summer evenings find city sidewalks, benches, and parks filled with teenagers and young adults who have gathered to talk, smoke, drink, and play music. Older residents complain about the resulting noise, smell, and behavior. Public drunkenness—and especially the apparent increase in the numbers of younger and younger children who are becoming intoxicated and disorderly in public—has increasingly become a topic of debate.[9] Such trends are evident in the countryside as well, as groups of young people gather in the forests and along the riverbanks for drinking parties and campfires. Thus, there continues to be a widespread ambivalence and disagreement about the moral order associated with private and public spaces. But where these disagreements seem most profound and problematic is at the intersection of personal freedom and the presumed unstructured, unregulated spaces of the countryside.

THE DARK SIDE OF DACHA DEMOCRACY

The freedom of wild spaces sometimes comes at a cost. As Russians have quickly discovered, not only can the utopian dreams of freedom and independence associated with nature quickly disappear, but dacha democracy and the organic civil society it produces can also have adverse effects on Russian social life. In the case of land ownership, Russian regulations concerning the rights of individuals to move more freely throughout the country and to buy and own property have not been matched with similar developments in land protection and conservation. Increasingly, land is being bought up by wealthy individuals and developers, even when that land has not legally been available for sale. Such developments, as well as the lack of oversight over land sales, have prompted concerns not just about the fate of Russia's forests and meadows, but also about the fate and disposition of dacha communities and the ability of other nature enthusiasts to access these lands. Dachniki who possess longstanding rights of tenancy fear that their property will be sold out from under them without warning. Such fears are stoked by rumors about unnamed "friends of friends" to whom this has happened. In other cases, the forests and fields around dacha communities have been suddenly sold to developers. Nadezhda residents recall the morning they woke up several years ago to discover that a forested area had been stripped of its trees overnight. Such appropriations of land and their transformation into "private property" are worrisome because they call into question established norms, both legal and cultural, that classify these lands as "public," as well as local ideologies about how these public lands are to be used and by whom.

Within dacha communities, tensions between the public and the private characterize dachniki's efforts to manage carefully the intimacy and sociality of dacha life. Despite avowals of the delights and benefits of living in such close quarters with neighbors, an uncomfortable reality is that constant surveillance is the result when people live in full view of one another. Even when neighbors have been close friends for many years, too much familiarity can become problematic. Neighbors in dacha communities keep close tabs on each other and what people are doing to and in their plots. Although others' awareness of one's activities can be gratifying, such as when neighbors notice how well one's garden is doing, there are risks as well. Dachniki who neglect their vegetable gardens or fruit trees run the risk of being criticized. One elderly woman who had been unable to visit her garden for an entire summer because she had remained in the city to care for her dying husband was distraught about having abandoned her plot, and even more so about her neighbors' opinions of this neglect. Margarita and Iurii reported that their dacha neighbors frequently called them at their apartment in the city to complain about how they were letting their grass grow too tall. After the couple decided to replace their long grass with a short-growing American variety, like the kind found on American golf courses, their neighbors called again to complain about the appearance and appropriateness of that style of lawn.

Another problem related to intrusions by others into one's personal domain is the need to protect one's cottage and equipment shed from theft and vandalism. Dacha cottages are particularly vulnerable over the winter, as thieves target shuttered dachas in order to steal tools, furniture, and other valuables and frequently vandalize the property. Homeless persons and other vagrants take shelter from the winter weather in closed-up cottages, sometimes turning them into long-term squats. One family reported that over the winter vandals had broken into their dacha community and stolen their gas canisters. Another family whose dacha had been burgled and vandalized rescinded an invitation for me to visit them because they had not yet been able to refurbish their cottage and clean up the mess. As a mutual friend explained, the family was too ashamed of their wrecked dacha to allow an outsider to see it.

During summer 2005, several spectacular acts of dacha violence were widely reported on Russian television news programs and circulated through community gossip channels for several weeks. Even though the events described in these accounts took place far outside the Tver region, their impact was felt in Tver's dacha communities. The crimes became a constant topic of conversation around Tver, and within the Nadezhda community neighbors made a point to relay the latest updates to one another. One evening, when Viktoriia and Roman were walking me back from a visit to their dacha, we stopped to talk to a group of women who lived in the neighboring cottages. The women were discussing the most recent incident of dacha violence that had been reported on the national news, but it soon became apparent that the women were previously discussing acts of violence closer to home. One woman urged another to share with us her own experience. The neighbor recounted that several days earlier she had come out of her dacha and discovered several youths trying to break into her yard. Fortunately, she scared them off. Although it did not appear as if the young men had caused any physical damage to her property, they had clearly caused significant emotional distress to both her and her friends.

One response to this upsurge in dacha violence is the growing use of private insurance. In the mid-1990s my Russian friends voiced their skepticism about insurance and laughed at Americans who bought private insurance for their automobiles or homes. As friends told me, it was ludicrous to expect that one could be reimbursed by an institution such as a bank or insurance company. If one were involved in a car accident, it was easier to swap names with the other driver and follow up privately, or simply expect not to be reimbursed at all. By the early 2000s, however, private insurance was becoming more significant, and insurance companies were advertising not just in Moscow but in other parts of the country as well. Even more telling were the insurance success stories that were being recounted. One friend related that a family member had been able to recover some of the cost of valuables that had been stolen during a robbery at her dacha.

Ultimately, whether they are threatened by vandals, dishonest developers, or nosy neighbors, both natural spaces and the forms of sociality they cultivate are in danger from the very freedoms and liberties they promote. In multiple ways, it is through the natural world that Russian citizens are getting important lessons in market capitalism and democracy. Ideals such as privacy, security, and ownership come at a price, and often their consequences are less desirable than imagined. At the same time, the increasing use of insurance policies, coupled with increased trust in the reliability of insurance payments, suggests that these new realities of personal property are accompanied by new ethics of responsibility and accountability. While there may still be limited protections against the intrusions of others, there is growing awareness of possible compensation for those intrusions.

"DACHNIKI, DON'T BE PIGS": TRASH AND THE POSTSOCIALIST LANDSCAPE

Despite the guarantees of security promised by proponents of Western-style democracy, the practices of individualism and personal responsibility associated with these ideals often fail miserably in contributing to a well-mannered world in today's Russia. Fires and trash have emerged as particularly vexing threats to the safety and security of the countryside.

Fire is one of the greatest concerns facing rural areas during the hot, dry summer months. Signs posted along highways that pass through forested regions warn travelers about the dangers of campfires, and similar advisories appear at the entrances to dacha communities and public parks. In heavily forested communities where the vast majority of cottages, outbuildings, fences, and other structures are made of wood, one small spark can quickly turn into a raging fire that could devastate a dacha community, the surrounding forest, and nearby villages. Although many dacha communities are located near lakes or small rivers, and although most dacha plots have at least a well or cistern of water, community water reserves are limited. Typically they are either inadequate for the size of the community or are not located close enough to be effective in fire fighting. Several fires that had taken place in the Tver region over the past several years were still fresh in residents' minds and evident in the scarred landscape. To remind Nadezhda residents of the threat posed to the community by fire, cooperative leaders posted warnings on public notice boards and trees both inside the community and along the paths running through the forest.

Despite these constant warnings and heightened public vigilance about fire danger, it was not uncommon for residents walking through the forest to discover fires that had been set to burn trash or leftover construction materials. On two separate occasions over the course of several weeks,

Angela, Misha, and I discovered blazing fires that had been set without adequate trenching or away from overhanging branches and then abandoned. On one occasion, during the several hours we spent putting out the flames and then monitoring the ashes for stray sparks, no one came by to check on the fire. Back at Angela's family's dacha, conversations over the next several days frequently circled back to these particular fires as well as to other untended fires that had recently been discovered. A general consensus emerged among my friends and their neighbors about the presumed perpetrators: irresponsible new "Muscovite" neighbors who had recently bought a dacha plot in the community. Although this couple was not the same one known throughout the community for the noisy birthday party and concert, they were similarly blamed for their irresponsibility and apparent lack of commitment to the overall well-being of the community.

Trash was also a serious issue, both in terms of the practical management of waste disposal and in terms of the image of the community as seen by outsiders. Although dacha residents often carry home small sacks of trash when they return to the city, it is not until the end of the season that most are able to dispose of their rubbish in its entirety. Many residents comment that the process of closing up their dachas at the end of the season is complicated by the fact that they have to hire a car or taxi not just to transport their belongings, but also to carry out the rubbish that has accumulated over the summer. Occasionally there are designated places in the forest where residents can deposit metal or other items. Once these pits become filled, they are covered with dirt and become part of the natural landscape.

In general, dumping in the woods is discouraged. Signs nailed to trees throughout the forests remind residents that dumping is forbidden and warn them about the fines for disobeying the rules, although the fines listed are typically so low—ten to a hundred rubles (about 50 cents to $3 dollars in 2005)—as to be laughable. Ironically, the locations of the signs forbidding dumping frequently become the very sites where rubbish accumulates. And, despite the posted restrictions stipulating that "only metal" or "only wood" be left, trash pits contain a broad variety of discarded items: cookware, plastic buckets, old clothing, children's toys, small and large home appliances, cars, and the other sad detritus of people's everyday lives. Dachniki found trash pits such as these or those in city spaces embarrassing because they felt they portrayed a negative image.

Desecration of natural spaces carries both social and financial penalties. The author of an article published in a regional newspaper warned local residents that "in the summer these days, going out to nature is pos-

FIGURE 13. Trash heaps like these become part of the natural landscape.

sible, but dangerous" because of the risk that a stroll through the forest might now include a talk with the local police. The subject of the article was the increased fines imposed by the State Duma for destruction of forests. The new code regulated not only cutting down trees, but also taking home branches or cuttings, with fines ranging from 1,000 to 1,500 rubles. Corporations could face fines of twenty to thirty thousand rubles for such infractions (Skliarova 2005:4).

Trash emerged as a significant point of contention in both Moscow and Tver during summer 2005. Although attention to trash, pollution, contamination, and other environmental issues emerged in the Soviet Union and Eastern Europe during the late 1980s and early 1990s in the wake of the Chernobyl disaster (Gille 2007; Petryna 2002) and amidst a growing connection to global green political movements (Harper 2006), issues of trash, recycling, and environmental responsibility were certainly not prominent among the concerns voiced by my Russian friends and informants until very recently. Looking back at my field notes since 1995, I found only a very few, very brief mentions of these issues. Conversations about recycling generally concerned how Muscovites reused and rehabilitated old and worn-out goods for new purposes. Any extended conversations on this subject were primarily with North American colleagues in Moscow who were stymied by the lack of trash cans and recycling bins in the city.

Despite the lack of extensive public discussion about trash, civic hygiene has long been a critical issue for Russian, and previously Soviet, leadership. Public cleanliness was promoted as a public issue, but one that was instituted from the top down by state or city officials as part of a long-standing public relations campaign to promote Russia to foreign tourists and businesses. Most commonly, these public cleaning efforts were beautification efforts in highly visible public areas, such as the extensive landscaping campaign that Moscow city officials pursued in the city center in 1997 for the 850th anniversary of the founding of Moscow. The following year, in preparation for hosting the World Youth Games, Moscow officials planted new flowerbeds, repainted public buildings, and removed "unsightly" elements—including members of the homeless population—from the cityscape. Such civic landscaping projects are not inspired primarily by environmental concerns but are entangled with larger processes of "spatial cleansing" (Herzfeld 2006) in which public authorities and private citizens alike engage in a collective exercise of disguising, but not necessarily solving, social problems that threaten the state's public image.[10]

By summer 2005 public rhetorics of trash removal and recycling had shifted registers and were becoming more conspicuous in public consciousness. Throughout Moscow, vividly painted bins for paper, bottles, and other litter were prominently placed at regular intervals along city sidewalks. Billboards and posters encouraged citizens to place their refuse in the proper receptacles. In Tver, a campaign to combat littering and promote responsible trash collection used a series of posters that depicted a small boy, attired to resemble a Young Pioneer, brandishing a broom as he performed his civic duty for public hygiene. Ironically, these posters were often accompanied by tall heaps of refuse at their base. As the efforts of municipal authorities in both Moscow and Tver revealed, ethics of public hygiene now included notions of public stewardship of the environment as part of its project of civic beautification, a shift in orientation about the proper agents of responsible action. Unlike natural foods philosophies that depicted the environment as the caretaker of the citizen, thereby relieving individuals of full responsibility and autonomy, these civic hygiene initiatives placed responsibility squarely on the shoulders of the population.

In Tver, problems with trash as a social and visual disruption escalated so severely that a series of articles appeared in local newspapers describing the epidemic. One reporter called Tver "Trash City" (Musornyi Gorod) and wrote that although trash is a year-round problem, "April is the most

FIGURE 14. Dachniki in this community posted signs throughout the neighborhood reading "Dachniki, do not be pigs. Dumping trash is categorically prohibited." These sites subsequently became the largest dumping areas for trash.

terrifying month for Tver," because that is when the melting snows reveal the trash that has been kept hidden throughout the winter (Burilov 2005:5). The mayor of Tver stated that in his opinion the city should not simply control trash removal, but it should also inspire every resident to take action with their own rakes and shovels ("Chinovniki" 2005:2). To this end, city officials were reviving "traditional all-city Subbotniki" as part of a municipal plan to promote "cleanness and order" *(chistota i poriadka)* through "voluntary work" in which "employees of the city administration will clean the streets of Tver" ("Chinovniki" 2005:2).

Intriguingly, this increased public attention to trash, littering, and responsible stewardship of public spaces was met with ambivalence, and outright hostility in some cases, by Russian citizens. In their disgruntled reactions to the imposition of civic hygiene efforts, both Misha and Paulina distinguished between being responsible for one's own actions and being responsible for the irresponsible actions of others. This perspective represents not just a departure from the ethics of collectivism, especially collective responsibility, that have shaped many social practices in Russia, but also a critical awareness that ideals of unlimited and unconstrained freedom may be socially destructive. During a visit with Paulina, we took a walk in the forest near her apartment on the outskirts of Moscow. While sharing stories about our respective dogs, Paulina turned the conversation to the issue of public hygiene and asked if it was true that Americans were required to clean up after their dogs. When I replied that this was certainly a practice in urban areas such as San Francisco or Boston, Paulina responded with a look of disbelief. She commented that supporters of such a policy were trying to implement it in Moscow, but that she did not think that the proposal was very popular. She certainly would not mind cleaning up after her own dog, especially because her dog was a small terrier, she said, but she did not see why people should be required to clean up after their pets when there was so much other trash on the street. She pointed out that people just throw their trash on the ground, which was much worse in her opinion.

Misha, a professor in Tver, expressed similar misgivings when he described his frustration with the recent efforts of university officials to revive the Soviet-era practice of coerced "voluntary" labor known as Subbotniki, or Saturday workers. During the Soviet period, citizens' collective investment in and stewardship of the state, and of public spaces in particular, was cultivated in a variety of spheres, but perhaps most notably with the practice of Subbotniki. Although this service was notionally voluntary, in reality, workers, students, and soldiers were forcibly mobilized to spend their weekends and holidays engaged in public service activities such as trash collection, janitorial work in apartments and workplaces, yard work around apartment buildings, and even helping with harvests at state farms (see also Shlapentokh 1989:100–101). Although commonly seen as a feature of the socialist period in Russia, these practices have continued into the present in the form of both formal workplace projects and informal grassroots community groups. According to Misha, the Subbotniki plan implemented by his university strongly urged faculty and staff to spend one weekend each month picking up litter around the university campus. Misha refused to do so, however, on the grounds that because he himself did not litter, it was not his responsibility to remove the trash discarded by others.

Littering and other acts of vandalism have become critical issues with significant consequences in contemporary Russia. It is unclear why there is so much more trash clogging the natural landscape and public spaces than before, although some informants linked the increase in trash to changing understandings of civic responsibility. Informants specifically blamed new understandings of freedom that have seeped into Russia in the post-Soviet period. Middle-aged and older Russians often commented that young people had embraced the idea that "freedom" meant that they were free to do anything they wanted. According to this interpretation, "freedom" was an individual-focused notion that suggested freedom from constraints and freedom to act; it was not a community-focused notion that entailed freedom from the actions of others. Like Paulina and Misha, critics of trash suggested that certain forms of freedom could be antithetical, and in some cases downright dangerous, to ordinary, law-abiding citizens. The author of the article describing Tver as "Trash City" wrote, "Freedom [svoboda], which our party and government proclaimed for many years, has one negative nuance: many people seem to think that it means that freedom liberates them from obligations. Therefore even youth now have one hundred times more rights than obligations, never mind what the older people have" (Burilov 2005:5).

DACHAGATE:
RUSSIAN DEMOCRACY IN THE RURAL SECTOR

The organic civil society that emerges in and through natural spaces plays out on more than just the microlevel of the everyday lives of ordinary citizens but is also deeply embedded in the very highest levels of the Russian state. In summer 2005 Russians were riveted by a highly publicized and convoluted scandal involving the dacha belonging to a high-ranking Russian politician. In what was called "Dachagate" in the Western press ("Dachagate" 2005; Stephen 2005) and, more benignly, "The Kasyanov Affair" in the Russian press (Pankin 2005b), Mikhail Kasyanov, who was prime minister under President Vladimir Putin between 2000 and 2004, came under investigation by federal prosecutors for the allegedly fraudulent sale of an elite government dacha. According to news reports, State Duma deputy and journalist Alexander Khinshtein initiated the proceedings against Kasyanov by reporting that Kasyanov had used his position as prime minister to privatize and then purchase the government dacha he had been allocated at a price that was considerably below its market value and without placing it for sale on the public market ("Case Opened" 2005; Monastyrskaya 2005).

According to Khinshtein's reports, a private company bought the villa for eleven million rubles (approximately US$370,000) in January 2004, and then sold the villa to Kasyanov for the same price in August 2004, six months after Kasyanov had been fired by President Putin. Meanwhile, a private company that had appraised the villa before the January sale claimed that the villa was in fact worth US$27 million (Abdullaev 2005:4). The story became even stranger and more complicated by allegations that the rights to the villa had been transferred from an oil company that had brokered a forty-nine-year lease for the villa in 1996 to two other companies, one of which had been acquired by Kasyanov in early 2004 ("Federal Guard Service" 2005:3).

To many observers, Dachagate was just one more example of the ironies and problems that have plagued Russia's political and economic transformations since the collapse of the Soviet Union in 1991. The fact that the house at the center of the Dachagate scandal was worth millions of dollars highlighted the sharp and escalating divide between the outrageous lifestyles and entitlements of Russia's elite and the more modest, and even impoverished, circumstances of ordinary citizens. Even though Kasyanov received the lion's share of attention in summer 2005, the dachas of other elites also attracted considerable scrutiny during that period. In a full-page article titled "Whose Dacha Is Better," the Russian daily newspaper *Argumenty i Fakty* presented a photomontage of dacha compounds in the Moscow region belonging to wealthy and famous Russians, including that of singer Alla Pugacheva ("Ch'ia Dacha Luchshe?" 2005:7). News programs regularly featured articles and fly-by glimpses of the lifestyles of Russia's wealthiest and most famous dachniki. Knowing of my interests, acquaintances frequently asked me if I had seen the latest article or heard the latest gossip about the dachas of the elite.

Although it was clear that Russians appreciated the entertainment value of the lurid, tabloidesque accounts of Dachagate, what was more revealing was the extent to which Dachagate emerged as a serious and sustained topic of discussion among the Russian public. Russian citizens used the trials and tribulations of Kasyanov as an entry point for discussing the larger and far more serious political battles that were underway in Russia. Observers downplayed media reports that focused primarily on the legal and financial aspects of Kasyanov's dacha purchase and instead identified the real issue as Kasyanov's viability as a candidate in the next presidential campaign. Although Kasyanov had previously served as President Putin's prime minister, he had subsequently become a vocal critic of the Kremlin and its policies. There was intense speculation that he would be a serious challenger to the Kremlin's candidate in the next election. Members of the press and ordinary Russians alike thus interpreted the investigation of Kasyanov's dacha affair as evidence that the Kremlin was trying to discredit Kasyanov and force him out of the election (Abdullaev 2005). A representative headline from the time, on the front page of the daily newspaper *Versiia,* screamed "Dachas for the Ambitious! Because of the scandal surrounding 'Sosnovki' [the dacha], Mikhail Kasyanov has no chance of becoming president" (Orlovskii 2005:6).

In spite of the relentless personal attacks against him, Kasyanov maintained he still intended to run for president. In an interview with Ekho Moskvy radio in mid-September, Kasyanov promoted himself as an advocate for democracy and accused President Putin of retreating from the democratic ideals and freedoms he had pursued during his first term in office. Kasyanov elaborated his critical stance on President Putin's policies, arguing, "The democratic freedoms that the country had then are now being taken back—first and foremost, the independence of the judicial system, of the media, the changes to legislative law—and with the fact that things are continuing along this path. And, of course, this affects the country's economic development, and we are already seeing the negative effects in this sphere" (Ekho Moskvy 2005).

That a dacha was at the center of national debates about democracy, capitalism, and the political fortunes of Russia's leaders was neither coincidental nor surprising to Russian observers. Throughout Russia's history, dachas and the lifestyles associated with them, especially the extravagant lifestyles of elites, have served as powerful markers of the nature of political life in Russia. Today they offer visual markers of Russia's postsocialist transition and the often conflicting and confusing directions this transition has taken. The scrutiny of elite dachas that was sparked by Dachagate offered a window onto the ever-changing and bewildering circumstances of privatization, private property, and economic mobility that face all Russians. Privatization is an increasingly common and significant concern for many people, and Kasyanov's problems are emblematic of the issues they face. Banking conditions and regulations concerning private property and taxation have changed frequently and unpredictably in Russia over the past fifteen years, stymieing the efforts of both ordinary and elite citizens who need to follow these policies, as well as the officials whose task it is to enforce them. These dizzying changes have been exacerbated by the uneven enforcement of standards, thereby contributing to widespread ignorance and outright distrust of economic and legal institutions. Thus, even as Russians found humor in Kasyanov's plight, many were also sympathetic to his circumstances.

At the same time, the political brawling that took place between Kasyanov and the Kremlin revealed deeper and more significant debates about the nature of democracy and the characteristics of the new political leadership in Russia today. By targeting Kasyanov's dacha, the Kremlin threatened Kasyanov's political platform and his potential as Russia's next leader. As subsequent accounts revealed, Kasyanov's alleged activities of buying low and selling high were not isolated occurrences but were in fact common tactics among Russia's political elite. Writing in response to the Kasyanov Affair, *Izvestiia* journalist Aleksei Pankin pointed out that since the early 1990s, "fighting over dachas among the ruling elite has been a major driving force behind the social development of the country in recent times" (Pankin 2005a). In what he called his "Dacha Theory of History" (Pankin 2005a), Pankin described the political battles that have shaped Russia's political landscape from the late Soviet period to the present as they played out through dachas.[11] In Pankin's historical narrative, the events of the 1990–91 period took on special resonance as outgoing Soviet leaders took with them parting gifts of newly privatized government dachas. The new leadership challenged these "retirement packages," prompting further complications. Pankin wrote that "the *nomenklatura* might have been prepared to surrender the Soviet state without a fight, but not their dachas" (2005a).

Journalists covering subsequent battles between political foes have deliberately used politicians' dachas as backdrops for their news reports. Not only do dachas make good visuals, but journalists and political activists have reframed discussions of architectural styles and locations into commentaries on politicians' presumed sympathies and agendas (Pankin 2005a, 2005b). As news accounts hinted, whether politicians chose classical or modern design styles seemed to be a good indication of their political inclinations.

Perhaps what was most intriguing about the Dachagate scandal was that even as citizens were troubled by what the Kasyanov Affair revealed about the state of Russian politics, there was also a pervasive sense among members of the general public that these events were completely normal. For many Russians, the political strife that was at the core of Dachagate and attacks against other elite dacha owners confirmed what they already knew: that dachas are logical, and even natural, sites of heightened political activity. This sentiment was expressed repeatedly during interviews and informal conversations with friends and acquaintances. The significance of dachas as sites of political expression and resistance was not limited to political and economic elites but applied to ordinary Russians as well. As one acquaintance succinctly stated, dachas have always been the physical spaces where acts of struggle and resistance have taken place.

Numerous informants pointed out that during the Soviet period dachas were often the front line of state-citizen negotiations over privacy, autonomy, and personal property. From the perspective of the state, dachas and dacha gardens represented efficient and lucrative channels for monitoring and controlling the country's population. In a context where urban housing was at a premium and many citizens were forced to live in cramped quarters with other residents, dacha cottages represented an enticing option for private space outside the social gaze. Similarly, the foods available in personal dacha gardens, rivers, and forested areas were compelling alternatives to industrially produced foods, when the latter were available. Yet even as the Soviet state encouraged the use of natural spaces such as dachas and the countryside for the physical and emotional well-being of its citizens, state officials did not want dacha gardens to replace the state as the center of its citizens' lives. Through such measures as restrictions on how dacha cottages could be constructed and furnished and taxation on garden produce, the state reminded citizens of their place, responsibilities, and rights in the social order.

Not surprisingly, Soviet citizens actively resisted the state's efforts to control how they used their dachas and their gardens. In a society where bribes often greased the wheels of bureaucracy and made the impossible possible, it was not uncommon for dacha owners to compensate building inspectors for looking the other way. Like many informants, Maya remembered how her family circumvented building codes that made it illegal to insulate dacha cottages for year-round habitation. Over the years Maya's father engaged in a protracted cat-and-mouse game with the local building inspector. As quickly as her father could install insulation or enlarge the cottage, the building inspector could tear it down; just as quickly, her father would rebuild. Other informants recalled how their families under-reported the amount of food they grew on their land to evade the taxes levied by the state on harvests exceeding "personal use."[12]

This tradition of resistance at the dacha has continued into the post-Soviet period. Several informants pointed out that much like Kasyanov, even ordinary people turn to their dachas to resist the changes in allocation and privatization laws currently taking place in Russia. Even as building codes have eased and taxes on produce have been eliminated, post-Soviet citizens find other ways to articulate their views on the state of their new society. Like many apartment dwellers across the country, many dacha owners choose not to pay their utility bills. Others sneak into the fields of private farms to harvest fresh produce or "borrow" building materials for their own personal use.

Finally, dachas have been key commodities in the process of privatization sweeping Russia. Even as Russian officials and their Western advisers have promoted the benefits of privatizing public property, many ordinary people remain skeptical that they will personally reap long-term benefits from these changes. The most common consequence has been that apartments and dachas that were originally allocated to citizens for their personal use at minimal rent are now being offered to their residents for purchase at significantly higher prices. Although the idea of being able to buy the property they have been renting for years is appealing, many people cannot afford the purchase price. Consequently, many individuals who are supposed to give up their allocated dachas are refusing to relinquish them and continuing to inhabit them and carry on with their lives. A segment on a television news program focused on one such situation, in which long-term residents who had refused to leave their rented properties were detained by the police as they exited the train that stopped near their dacha community. The incident turned ugly; the television cameras showed elderly men and women being roughly shoved into makeshift holding cells by officials, and the struggles between residents and officials turned into physically and verbally violent brawls.

As incidents such as these illustrate, dachas have served both as symbolic mediums for political currents and as practical sites for the enactment of political activities. More than just providing a living commentary on the rise and fall of Russia's political and financial elite, however, dachas are powerful symbols and vehicles for Russia's "democratic transition" as it is being experienced and contested by Russians from all walks of life. In very real and compelling ways, dachas serve a dual purpose as both channels and sites of political activity.

Even as dachas, forests, and the countryside offer compelling and profound commentaries on Russian political and economic development, they are not related only to national political and economic transformations, which have too often been the preoccupation of civil society analyses. Instead, natural spaces are the sites where ordinary people engage in the small-scale political activities that constitute their daily lives. Public debate and commentary—as well as efforts to create distinctions between public and private, carve out spaces of safety and well-being, and form associational groups, among many other practices—constitute the smaller and more personal, but no less significant, activities of civil society work that take place in the natural sector.

CHAPTER 7

The Daily Dacha Soap Opera

Let's drink to the dacha! To the way it is with us right now!
—Iuliia, in a group interview with her friends in Nadezhda,
   summer 2005

Television has consistently played a significant role in the dacha lives of my friends and acquaintances over the past two decades. In the mid-1990s, at the beginning of the consumption revolution that swept the postsocialist world, Russians' television-viewing habits changed dramatically as the privatization of Russian media, the arrival of cable and satellite television, and widespread public interest in Western trends fostered a veritable explosion of foreign television programs, especially Western movies and serials, on Russia's airwaves. Foreign soap operas such as the American show *Santa Barbara* and the Mexican telenovela *The Rich Cry Too* were particularly popular, especially among female viewers. At that time, although videocassette recorders were becoming more readily available, they were used primarily for viewing pirated videotapes of American movies and rarely to record television shows for watching later. Consequently, rather than miss the broadcast of the latest episode of their favorite programs, many devout viewers planned their schedules accordingly. In the mid- to late 1990s, when my landlady Anya (like many of her friends) collected her local weekly newspaper, the first thing she did was check the television schedule and mark the times for all of her favorite programs. Every day she consulted the schedule and planned her activities so that she would be home in time for her shows.

   The coordination of daily routines with television schedules did not end when Russians left the city for their dachas. During our visits to the dacha of Anya's friend Tanya, our daily routine of berry picking was punctuated by regular viewing of Tanya's soap operas. For those brief periods, all work ceased and the television was brought out from under the pile of newspapers and gardening implements that ordinarily rested upon it, placed in front of the chairs in the main room, plugged in, and turned on. When Tanya's shows had concluded, the television was returned to its spot in the corner. Similar activities were repeated multiple times, at multiple dachas, over the course of this research. In the past several years, evidence of the widespread availability of cable and satellite television networks has been visible both in the profusion of advertisements along the roadways leading to housing communities, including dacha communities, the proliferation of antennas and satellite dishes mounted on dacha cottages, and the diversity of television-related magazines for sale by vendors on dacha-bound trains and buses.

During my stay in Nadezhda during summer 2005, television was frequently a catalyst for socializing among residents. Friends and neighbors chatted about the latest episodes of their favorite programs and reminded one another of the schedules for several popular crime dramas, particularly a series of updated versions of classic Agatha Christie mysteries and a new serial based on the popular mystery novels by Alexandra Marinina featuring the feminist detective Anastasiia Kamenskaia. Sketch comedy shows were another popular genre, and residents amused one another by retelling the jokes and skits that had been performed. For several weeks there was growing agitation in the community when several television broadcasting antennas in the vicinity were damaged, limiting the ability of some residents to use their televisions. During that period residents' conversations focused largely on the lack of television and the various efforts employed by residents and the cooperative's administrators to convince public utility workers to fix the problem.

Angela's father, Sergei, would make analogies to television themes in his often-sarcastic commentaries on the goings-on of his neighbors in Nadezhda. The various high jinks of one neighboring family in particular proved too delicious to escape Sergei's wry humor. The parents of the family were the same age as Sergei and his wife, and the daughter and son-in-law were the same age as Angela and her husband. In fact, Angela and the daughter had gone to school together, and the families had known one another for many years. In the post-Soviet period the entire family had reinvented themselves as "new businesspeople" after one family member had secured a position in an international cosmetics company that requires employees to recruit new employees. The family member had parlayed the position and the connections it afforded into additional job opportunities for the rest of the family, as well as investments from the proceeds garnered by recruiting other people into the company. It was rumored that the family had been so successful in this enterprise that they were running an exceptionally lucrative pyramid scheme. Sergei, a professor, teased Angela, also an academic, about the significant difference between her lifestyle and that of her former classmate, who traveled the world as a high-powered businesswoman. By all accounts, the family was loud and boisterous, and family members frequently yelled and argued with each other. Sergei joked that watching the events next door was like watching his own private soap opera.

The relations between Sergei's family and his other neighbors were much more congenial. On one side of his dacha lived Valentina, and she and Iuliia often visited back and forth to inspect each other's gardens and chat. On another side lived Konstantin and his wife. Konstantin and Sergei had been friends for many years, and the two men constantly engaged in banter and affectionate teasing. Their properties were adjacent to one another along the length of their respective gardens, and it was only a subtle change in the rows of the gardens that indicated the end of one property and the beginning of the other. Given that both families spent most of their time outside in their gardens, they had lived in full sight of one another for many years. From the comfort of the chairs on the porch of his dacha, Konstantin sat and talked with Sergei while the latter worked in his yard. In the afternoon it was not uncommon for the two men to sit down at one or the other's table with a bottle of beer and a snack.

In spring 2007, when I made a quick trip to Russia, Angela visited me in Moscow. Among the news she passed on was a message from her father that he was looking forward to hosting me at the dacha again that summer. When I returned to Russia several months later Sergei had a new story for me to include in my book: he wanted me to write that life at the dacha now included the return of the radio.

During the several months between my trips to Russia, Konstantin had suddenly and unexpectedly built a fence around his property, effectively separating his yard from that of Sergei's family. Sergei was upset by the development, primarily because of what the fence meant for the long-standing relationship between the two families. Sergei interpreted the fence not simply as a violation of a friendship, but even an indication that Konstantin had never been a true friend in the first place. This rude awakening prompted Sergei to question whether any part of the relationship between the two families had been genuine. To express his disgust and distress at this turn of events, Sergei began to describe the fence as a beneficial change in the close quarters of the dacha community. Sergei commented that before the fence, when the neighboring families lived in full view of one another, dacha life was like a television program in which he observed firsthand all of the unpleasantness taking place in neighboring yards. Now, since the placement of the fence, hearing the squabbles and troubles over the fence was like listening to the radio, which was less intrusive and hence preferable to the prior situation.

The tensions between the two neighbors did not end with Sergei's caustic comment about preferring to listen to the "radio" but continued throughout that summer. Sergei decided that he would no longer treat Konstantin as a friend but rather as a neighbor who must be tolerated because of proximity. When I visited Angela's family at their dacha that summer it was the height of blueberry season, and Angela's aunt Iuliia prepared her famous blueberry pies. As word (and perhaps the aroma) of the pastries spread in the dacha community, Iuliia's friends popped by for a quick visit and to enjoy a fresh pastry. As Angela and I were returning to the dacha from a walk in the forest, we met Konstantin on the path. Konstantin greeted us and then said that he had heard that Iuliia had made her delicious blueberry pies. By his manner, it was evident what Konstantin was hinting at. Back at the cottage, Angela related to her aunt what had transpired. Iuliia responded, not surprisingly, that Konstantin was not worthy of receiving one of her pies and that he had shown remarkable audacity in making the suggestion.

By summer 2009, as this book was being completed, the "fence wars" in Nadezhda had taken a new turn. My friends reported that residents in the community were no longer simply erecting fences between their properties, but they were also relocating the fences on the perimeter of their properties, moving them beyond their existing plot lines and into the community spaces of the forest. For residents who lived on the edges of the dacha community, these tactics were a means of expanding their properties by force rather than through legal or financial means. Such developments prompted complaints among those residents whose dachas were in the interior of the community and thus unable to enjoy the same liberty to expand their properties. These events aggravated simmering tensions within the community as those residents with dachas in the interior were effectively "stranded" and further distanced, both materially and socially, from their neighbors who were enjoying both larger yards and the social and material benefits that might accrue to these expanded spaces.

The soap-operatic qualities of the events sparked by the construction of something as seemingly innocuous as a fence are revealing on multiple levels. Certainly they reveal the sensitivity and fragility of relationships and the passions underlying social relations in such a small, tightly connected community. At the same time, these "soap operas" also operate as microcosms of larger trends taking place across Russia. In particular, such tales of the consequences wrought by fences crystallize the larger changes unfolding in Russia's economic system, not just in terms of how property rights and ownership practices are enacted and interpreted by ordinary citizens, but also in terms of how these new property regimes are affecting ethics of sociality and civility. The decisions by Nadezhda residents about how and where to build fences, and the social consequences that are touched off by these decisions, are not isolated occurrences but rather ones that are happening in dacha communities across Russia. It is not difficult to see how fences—and the perceived threats they pose both to a sense of community and to representations of national solidarity—lend themselves to allegories about the nature and consequences of post-Soviet transformation in Russia.

To focus on the peculiarities of fences, the fundamental changes they represent, and the hostilities they incite merely as inevitable markers of post-Soviet transformation, however, is to overlook something much more profound and enduring about dacha life. Even though these "fence tales" are products of contemporary times, they are not necessarily exclusive to these times. We hear in the laments of Sergei, Iuliia, their neighbors in Nadezhda, and dachniki elsewhere in Russia echoes of similar laments from Gorky's and Chekhov's dachniki more than one hundred years earlier. In a prescient foreshadowing of Nadezhda's fence troubles, Chekhov's story "The New Dacha" focuses on how the construction of a new bridge in a rural community upsets the local sense of social harmony and tradition (Chekhov 1999). As Chekhov describes, construction of the new bridge and the accompanying arrival of an upper-class supervisor and his family disrupted both the physical order and the social order of the community. Local residents articulate their displeasure at the changes symbolized and actualized by the new bridge through hostility toward the outsiders, eventually leading to the rapid departure of the newcomers. Yet despite their efforts to stop these changes, time moves on, the bridge is built, and new upper-class neighbors move into the area. As the local residents learn, change is inevitable, thus calling into question the ethos of timelessness that characterizes the dacha world.

What is perhaps most significant about Sergei's soap opera analogy is the reminder that the world of the dacha is profoundly paradoxical. Like soap operas, dachas are settings where emotional, social, economic, and political extremes are manifested, heightened, juxtaposed, and perhaps even reconciled. For instance, the allure, both sentimental and mystical, that dachas, forests, and the organic life more generally hold for Russians such as the people described in this book becomes particularly meaningful within a larger cultural context in which many Russians feel alienated within and from their own country. The qualities of hyperurbanization, hyperconsumerism, and hypertemporality that are perceived by many to characterize everyday life in today's global, capitalist Russia has led many citizens to claim feelings of dislocation, disorientation, uprootedness, and homelessness (see Boym 2001; Oushakine 2000a). These issues of alienation and dislocation raise critical questions about where the "real" Russia might be located, both spatially and temporally, in today's world. As Russia becomes more deeply entangled in the consumer flows of global capitalism, urban settings such as Moscow and St. Petersburg, and even smaller cities such as Tver and Ekaterinburg, increasingly come to resemble generic global cities (Sassen 1991) more than they do anything that might be recognizable as a "quintessentially" Russian city. Both ordinary Russians and their analysts seem to agree that authentic Russianness is to be found outside such urbanized, consumerist settings, preferably in stereotypically rural settings such as dacha communities and villages. Rural spaces, then, are held up as potential sources of authentic, primordial Russianness, with all that such claims about geographic primordialness imply about indigenousness, heritage, familiarity, and comfortable sociality.

Yet the fact remains that although villages, forests, rivers, and other natural spaces may be celebrated as the places where Russianness is most intensely and authentically experienced and expressed, these same spaces have themselves long been under attack, and their claims to authenticity have been questioned. The Soviet-era trend toward industrialization that propelled workers from the countryside to the cities has continued into the post-Soviet period, as the privatization of state farms and the growth of Russia's new economy centered in the metropoles of Moscow and St. Petersburg has further prompted young people to flee to the cities for work and a chance to join the global economy. Villages are dying, both literally and figuratively, as the elderly occupants who have been left behind pass away and as the rickety wooden structures that once housed the community slip away from their foundations and sink into the earth. In some cases villages exist only by virtue of the one or two ancient residents who have been left as symbolic markers meant to preserve these spaces. At the same time, upper- and upper-middle-class Russians are transforming themselves into "rural" settlers who buy up abandoned properties and rural plots and transform them into ostentatious luxury villas and recreational compounds. The value of these new buildings is apparently measured more by their design styles—a style that one Moscow architect described as "palaces of monsters"—than by their capacity to inspire tranquil and comfortable living, as a new trend in Russian architecture is the redesign of these new "palaces of monsters" for the realities of everyday living. As this Moscow architect revealed, he and his colleagues are busy with requests for help from owners of modern dachas who have discovered that their spacious brick dachas are not only impossible to keep warm, and thus require new heating and insulation systems, but are also plagued by strange internal spatial configurations that make the placement of furniture and other home furnishings—and thus the enjoyment of daily life—difficult. While such cottages may look beautiful from the outside, appearances are deceiving and merely disguise, and even exacerbate, the many problems contained within.

Consequently, as the discussions throughout this book have documented, even as dachas and the natural spaces in which they are located are compelling precisely because of the qualities of familiarity, intimacy, and comfort that Russians associate with them, they are also spaces that are increasingly fraught with anxiety and danger. In sharp contrast to national mythologies of Russian nature as a paradise, this is no longer a pristine landscape, but one that has continually been ravaged by industrialization, environmental destruction, and human occupation. The "good life," as it is imagined to exist in these romanticized natural settings, is in very real danger of slipping away with every felled tree, every decaying village, and every commercial colonization of the wilderness.

Thus, dacha stories—whether they are about fences, bridges, litter, or uninvited relatives—are far more significant than simple narratives of ruptured friendships. Instead, these stories have consistently provided the grist for powerful commentaries about the nature of Russian life and the issues that have preoccupied Russians, and perhaps their counterparts elsewhere, across several centuries. As Gorky's watchman Pustobaika so succinctly states, "Dachniki—they're all identical" (Gorky 1906:45–47).

DACHA EXCEPTIONALISM

In this book I have sought to balance a detailed accounting of dacha life as it has been idealized and enjoyed by Russians—not just over the past two decades, but also over the past century—against the realities of this world as they play out in everyday lives. In so doing, I have been concerned with what this interplay between dacha mystique and dacha reality might reveal not just about the nature of the dacha world itself, but also about the nature of the larger social realm that dachas inhabit. At the same time, I have been committed to correcting what seems, at times, to be the marginalization of dachas to the periphery in accounts of Russian social life. It remains a perplexing question as to why dachas have for so long eluded sustained scholarly analysis. Part of the answer, I suspect, lies in analytical confusion as to the precise place of dachas in Russian life and uncertainty about whether the vantage point of the dacha can tell us anything important beyond that immediate world. Both popular and academic discourses perpetuate the difference and distance of the dacha world by situating dachas at the geographic and cultural edges of ordinary Russians' lives and by highlighting the peculiarities of traditional dacha life and its distinctness from modern urban living. Yet analytical paradigms that continue to reify distinctions between "traditional" and "modern" are not just outdated, but they are also insufficient for considering seriously the significance of dachas, both for studies of Russia and for social analysis.

Over the past several decades, anthropology has increasingly moved away from Malinowski's injunction to search for "the inponderabilia of actual life" (1961:18) and has instead become preoccupied with the extraordinary and the exceptional. With this shift has come a shift in the settings where anthropologists do their research: cities, institutions, and virtual communities, among many other locations. Village ethnography, long the hallmark of anthropology, now competes for attention with ethnographies conducted within the more abstract, less geographically located worlds of transnational virtual markets, global ideas, and human imagination. Anthropologists have been at the forefront of reinventing the very boundaries of what constitutes human social life and where these social lives exist. At first glance, Russian's dacha world would certainly seem to fit the bill of the exceptional and the extraordinary, particularly if we take at face value the recurring emphasis in my informants' statements that dachas, forests, and nature more broadly constitute alternate spaces, alternate realities, and even alternate "planets," far removed from ordinary life.

Yet even as dachas are something special, perhaps even extraordinary, the reality is that dachas and the organic life are also not so out of the ordinary. Dachas and nature refract a host of persistent and unequivocally mundane issues in today's Russia: economics, urbanization, housing, family dynamics, the centrality of political life, and even the reach of the state. As the Dachagate scandal revealed, presidential politics become recognizable and personal when they are removed from Moscow and instead play out through negotiations over dacha property laws—issues that are immediately familiar to ordinary citizens, who are themselves dealing with new laws governing real estate and ownership. At the same time, the policies and folly of the state and the workplace and even national ideals of healthfulness gain different currency and import when viewed through tree limbs and potato bushes at the dacha, where one decides how to spend one's own time and turns one's labor into an activity that is personally fulfilling. The annoyances brought on by the forced sociality of densely populated urban spaces are transformed by the rustic and natural setting of dacha communities, where neighbors live in full view and hearing of one another but find ways to circumvent and ignore but also treasure one another.

So long as dacha life and its attendant philosophy of organic living are relegated to the category of the exceptional and the marginal, it is difficult to imagine what these practices might contribute either to an understanding of Russian life more generally or to anthropology's project of critical cultural comparison. Yet restoring the ordinariness to dacha life enables us, first, to see how dachas refract and illuminate larger themes in Russian life, and, second, to put everyday Russian life in comparative conversation with studies of everyday life elsewhere in the world. By thinking about dachas as an ordinary aspect of Russian life, we can reflect on diverse issues of broader ethnographic importance such as the dynamics of family intimacy, the ways in which national politics intersect with local realities, the place of nature in the lives of urbanites and rural residents who are living through urbanization projects, and the economics of nostalgia, among many other topics of contemporary interest.

For instance, although Russia's dacha tradition comes out of different historical circumstances than those that spawned European and North American allotment gardens in the first half of the twentieth century, and their more recent incarnations in the form of personal and community gardens of the Slow Food, sustainable agriculture, and "back-to-the-land" movements of the past two decades, Russian dacha culture offers the possibility to understand the value of summer cottages not simply as recreational and leisure settings but as spaces of personal agency and control, and for understanding the appeal of personal gardens not only as a tool for stocking for family pantries but also for their role in personal self-worth and pleasure. At the same time, the values that Russians attach to the foods that they grow in their gardens and harvest from the forest complicate prevailing analyses and popular wisdom about what makes these foods healthy, meaningful, and even safe.

Similarly, while Russians' philosophies about organic living are perhaps most apparent at the dacha and in the rural, natural settings in which they are situated, they also transcend these spaces. As I have argued in this book, at the heart of Russians' philosophies of organic living is an idealized natural world that is not tied to actual rural spaces but may, in fact, exist anywhere, including in urban or suburban spaces. The ideals of organic living—nostalgia for cultural heritage, preference for the taste of "ecologically clean" produce, and a deliberate attempt to escape the rat race of daily life by slowing down and putting one's own interests and needs above those of an employer or the state—are, to a great extent, portable, and Russians take these ideals with them and use them to help deal with the anxieties and aggravations of daily life. Attention to these ideals of organic living, as well as the ways in which they move between realms, raises important questions about the boundaries that distinguish rural, urban, and even suburban spaces on the one hand and work and leisure on the other; the relationships that exist among these domains; and even the nature of centers and peripheries, their relationship to one another, and the forces that simultaneously tie them together and set them apart.

The "back-to-nature" ethic embodied in both Russian ideals about the organic life and dachniki's activities contributes an important comparative example to understandings of environmental and nature movements in other parts of the world. Russians' ideas about environmental stewardship invert the expected relationship between person and land, so that nature is understood to care for and protect people. Yet this does not absolve individuals from responsible behavior, even though what constitutes "responsible" action might seem at odds with the goals of environmental conservation. As a result, while popular opinion in Russia might hold that litter and fires in forests are undesirable, the perpetuation of such practices is understandable within the logic of a philosophy that sees nature as the one space where the normal rules and structures do not apply.

Finally, the themes of displacement and disappearance that infuse the processes of change playing out in Russian dacha traditions help contextualize other narratives of moving borders and vanishing cultures. In many respects, Russians' narratives of "disappearing dachniki" are not new, but rather part of a much longer conversation about change, how people respond to those changes, and the analytical politics that underpin ideals of pristine, unchanging cultures and efforts to preserve them. Although it is unlikely that the very ideals of a distinct and recognizable Russian "nation," as embodied by "Russian identity" and "Russian culture," are in danger of disappearing entirely, at least in the foreseeable future, it is evident that aspects of this national culture are undergoing transformation. Certainly Russia's rural communities are being transformed as resident populations and architectural styles change, even as the underlying values, perspectives, and mythologies persist. These changes in Russia's dacha world, and the anxieties touched off by these changes, mirror larger national concerns about demographic change. What makes the "Muscovites" who have arrived in dacha communities over the past two centuries so problematic and disruptive is their outsiderness, their foreignness, which prompts an anxiety that is mirrored at national levels as Russians make sense of demographic shifts with a declining Russian population and a growing population of non-Russians.

If dachas are productive for rethinking paradigms of space and cross-cultural comparison, they are perhaps even more inspiring for rethinking the temporal dimensions of today's Russia. Ever since the events of 1989 (the fall of the Berlin Wall) and 1991 (the Soviet putsch), Russia and the rest of the former Soviet world have been identified by both analysts and local residents as societies undergoing constant, rapid, and profound change, a perspective that has inspired an entire field of "transitology" studies. Although the "shock therapy" methods touted by economic development experts in the early 1990s promised that the actual period of transformation would be short-lived (Sachs 2005:109–47), the reality is that twenty years later scholars and other observers continue to refer to this region as inhabiting a "transitional" period. The curious reluctance of scholars to relinquish transition paradigms as explanatory frameworks reveals an enduring preoccupation with change as the reality of everyday life in this region (Caldwell 2005).

How to conceptualize "transition" in ways that do not perpetuate and reify transition as both paradigm and social phenomenon remains a thorny issue for analysts. Even as ethnographers have made compelling cases for moving beyond singularizing narratives to consider the multiple permutations of "socialisms" and "postsocialisms" in this region (Berdahl 2000; Burawoy and Verdery 1999; Dudwick and De Soto 2000), productive alternatives have proved equally elusive. Katherine Verdery's (2002) call for critical comparisons between postsocialism and postcolonialism as a way out of a geopolitically delimited theoretical mode has received little traction within this field, a point that Yurchak (2006) raises in his critical interrogation of historicizing paradigms in accounts of Soviet society and echoed by Manduhai Buyandelgeriyn's (2008) call for "post-post-transition theories." A curious artifact of these historicizing paradigms is their reification of particular historical moments, an issue raised by Chris Hann (2007) in his critique of the "presentism" of much postsocialist ethnography. Hann writes that "As the second decade of 'transition' draws to a close it is time that the anthropologists working in this region begin to take up temporalities other than the postsocialist present. . . . This expansion of the temporal framework will raise crucial theoretical issues that have not yet been adequately faced by the ethnographers of transformation" (Hann 2007:2). Chakrabarty (2000) makes a similar point for European scholarship more generally and its resistance to considering, much less engaging, ideas from non-European societies and intellectual traditions. As these observers note, critical ethnography always takes history seriously, but more in terms of identifying and engaging broader historical trends and processes rather than by subjecting or shoehorning societies into a predetermined historical framework, as "transition" paradigms often do. Thus, by allowing ourselves to free social worlds such as Russia, and Russia's dacha world in particular, from specific temporal moments, we not only reposition these communities within other cross-cultural conversations, but we also consider the extent to which they can be understood on their own terms and with attention to their own internal consistencies, inconsistencies, rhythms, and directionalities.

Dacha worlds offer fruitful possibilities for productively disrupting "transition" paradigms in multiple ways. As the discussions of alternative temporal realities, including nostalgia, that were raised earlier in this book illuminate, the everydayness of the dacha world is deeply embedded within an entanglement of multiple pasts, presents, and futures that are both personal and public. Thus accessing and understanding the experiences and concerns of today's dachniki requires a consideration of their predecessors and their successors, both literary and real, thereby illustrating that the travails and joys of Chekhov's and Gorky's dachniki are not so very different from those of today's dachniki. By calling into question the boundaries of temporal moments, dacha worlds also challenge us to rethink the qualities of timelessness associated with these realms. Even as the outward trappings of dacha life—architecture, garden design, fences—change, the basic routines, interests, values, and bodily rhythms of the dacha world possess a perduringness that draws dachniki back, year after year—or at the very least occupies their musings year after year—and that makes their experiences translatable and solid across time.

It is this quality of perduringness that emphasizes the significance of dacha worlds as distinct place-worlds that are constantly made and remade through mutual processes of animation between people and the natural world. As long as dachas and nature attract dachniki, and as long as dachniki inhabit these spaces, this world will persist, even as the parameters of this world wobble, shift, and become transformed. And because of the mutual enervation of place and person, it is precisely here, in the shadows of the nation-state and the global marketplace, where Russians enjoy and exercise the greatest potential to live their lives as they see fit. It is at the dacha where Russians can comment critically on the state, the market, and their neighbors; where they can reclaim hard labor for their own benefit and pleasure; and where they can not only create meaningful social relationships but also experience them fully, in both their positive and negative forms. It is here at the dacha where the work of the nation-state proceeds vibrantly, as made obvious by the fact that even Russia's political leaders retreat to dachas to conduct their business and wage political battle with one another. It is here, at the dacha—in the quiet of the garden, in the dark of the forest, and within the walls of a rustic cottage held together by outdated calendars, the drawings of children who long ago reached adulthood, and baskets of berries and mushrooms—where an alternative, but no less real, place-world exists.

Thus as the setting for the extraordinarily ordinary and ordinarily extraordinary, the dacha occupies a space that is both intrinsic to and generative of Russians' everyday worlds. Even if dachas and other natural settings are not the physical locations where Russians spend the majority of their time, they are the places that Russians identify as where life is lived most intensely and meaningfully. It is this ordinariness of dachas that invites a reorientation of the relational and spatial logics underlying Russia's social order so that we can reconsider whether the true center of Russia might in fact lie at the dacha and in these rural spaces, while the margins and peripheries lie in urban spaces such as cities and in institutional settings such as the Kremlin itself.

Notes

1. DACHA ENCHANTMENTS

1. The word *dacha* is also used in other parts of Europe, most notably Berlin, where small urban plots of land with gardens and sheds are known as *datcha* (Heide Castañeda, personal communication).

2. Although dachas are not entirely absent in accounts of pre-Soviet, Soviet, and post-Soviet life (e.g., Pesmen 2000; Ries 1997), accounts focus primarily on the self-provisioning activities and social relationships that take place at dachas, so that the larger "dacha life" remains peripheral.

3. Although Lovell identifies a need for the anthropological study of dacha gardens as a way to understand Russian society (2003:229), my own work on this topic and my own sense that this was an important topic to explore precedes Lovell's call.

4. Lovell also notes that *dacha* became synonymous with *villa* in nineteenth-century accounts (Lovell 2003:30), a connection that appears in English translations of Russian dacha literature.

5. Distinctions between "us" and "them," where "us" refers to the population and "them" to the state, as well as more fluid distinctions between "ours" and "not ours," are common tropes of self-making in Russian daily life. See also Caldwell 2002.

6. Caroline Humphrey has argued that the name *villa* used for these structures designates their status as "private property and a demonstration of wealth," markers of Russia's new economic, rather than political, elites (Humphrey 2002:186).

7. Lovell links the emergence of Russia's twentieth-century garden culture to the revival of the "garden plot movement" in the 1950s, when the Soviet state actively organized garden collectives (2003:191). Lovell also observes that his informants trace the use of the word *dacha* to indicate both cottage and garden simultaneously to the 1960s (2003:199).

8. See also Ries's discussion (1997:27–28) of the various meanings associated with *narod*.

9. In a subsequent discussion of the significance of land for these ideas of biological relationships, Paxson writes, "Rodina, the land of the rod [i.e., genus, lineage], is kin and rodina is earth. When it is of the earth, a rodina can nearly smell with local soils; when it is Mother Russia, it is a vast expanse that one loves. . . . Being rodnoi is a special form of being svoi [i.e., one's own, part of a collective], with an emphasis on the fact that the soil and kin are shared" (Paxson 2005:84).

10. See Skultans 1998 for a fascinating treatment of partisans who lived and fought in the Latvian forests during World War II.

11. For a chillingly normal account of neofascist youths who gather at dachas in the countryside to roast *shashlyk* and eat berries while honing their skill at violence, see Ross Kemp's account of the National Socialist Party in Russia in the episode on Russia in his series *Ross Kemp on Gangs,* available at www.youtube .com/watch?v=LI4Q4RhvGNk (accessed September 4, 2008). I thank Madeleine Reeves for directing me to this documentary series. I thank Zachary Bowden for the information about Russian punks who retreat to their dachas for drinking fests *(zapoi)* and squat with European friends on vegan dacha retreats (personal communication, spring 2007).

12. The *nomenklatura* was a system of appointments to all decision-making positions throughout the Soviet party-state and whose unparalleled importance made it colloquially synonymous with the elite or ruling class itself.

13. My orientation to the perspectives and experiences of "middle-class" Russians resembles that of Naomi Galtz in her dissertation research on Russian dachas (Galtz 2000). Her work, like mine, presents an important departure from studies that have emphasized dacha culture among elites (for example, Lovell 2003, or Humphrey 1998 on New Russian "villas"). Like Galtz, I also recognize the challenges posed by using labels such as "middle class" and seek to find a more appropriate way to capture the diverse experiences of ordinary Russians.

14. The lifestyles and building practices of upper-class dachniki have been addressed elsewhere (e.g., Humphrey 1998).

2. INTIMATE IRRITATIONS:
LIVING WITH CHEKHOV AT THE DACHA

1. By many accounts, the estate of Abramtsevo was the inspiration for Chekhov's play *The Cherry Orchard.* For a fascinating and comprehensive account of Russian estate life among Russia's artists and intellectuals, complete with beautiful illustrations, see Roosevelt 1995.

2. Translations of Gorky's *Dachniki* are mine.

3. For an excellent historical discussion of the literary and political context of Gorky's *Dachniki,* as well as an illuminating interpretation of the play's significance, see Frank Dwyer's afterword to his English-language translation and stage arrangement of the play (Gorky 1995:165–215).

4. Accessed through the Public Electronic Library (Publichnaia Elektronnaia Biblioteka), available at http://public-library.narod.ru/Chekhov.Anton/dachniki .html (accessed August 6, 2008).

5. All translations of this story are mine.

6. For an account of how Soviet authorities also used tourism to the USSR as a way to spread national values abroad, see Salmon 2006.

7. For more detailed discussions of presocialist and socialist forms of "medicalized leisure" in natural settings, see McReynolds (2006:32–36) and Koenker (2006:127).

8. See especially Maurer's article on Soviet alpinism (2006).

9. In her article on Czech *chata* (i.e., dacha) culture, Bren (2002) suggests that Czech officials found *chatas* useful because they enabled a particular type of freedom among citizens.

10. Over the past several years, the popularity of fishing has noticeably increased. Stores catering to outdoors activities, and sometimes exclusively to fishing, are now more visible in cities like Tver and Moscow. It is also more common to see people carrying fishing gear on public transportation. Lastly, there are now numerous television programs devoted to fishing, as well as fishing expeditions that one can take to the lake and river regions in Russia, such as in Siberia.

11. Compare with Herzfeld's observations (1997:120) about the relationship between distance and enchantment.

3. THE PLEASURE OF PAIN: GARDENING FOR THE SOUL

1. See Caldwell 2004b for an extended treatment of the economic constraints facing Russians in the late 1990s and the everyday survival strategies that people employed, including using their dachas.

2. See also the statement by one of Margaret Paxson's informants in rural Russia during a walk in the forest: "'Breathe in the air,' Iuliia told me, 'it's good for your health and good for the soul'" (Paxson 2005:88).

3. Compare with Jung 2006, which describes Bulgarian consumers' laments and complaints.

4. It is also worth noting that bread and salt are the quintessential national symbols of Russian traditions of hospitality.

5. See also Verdery's discussion of etatization (1996).

6. In August 1998, Russia was hit by an economic "crisis" *(krizis)* when the government freed Russia's currency from its artificial conversion rate to hard currency and instead allowed the rate of the Russian currency to be set by the dynamics of the international market. The value of Russia's currency plummeted (within a matter of days, the exchange rate between the ruble and the U.S. dollar went from 6 rubles = $1 to 15 rubles = $1), and the government, banking sectors, and commercial enterprises defaulted. Russian consumers saw the value of their earnings—and their savings—evaporate as prices shot up without the simultaneous readjustment of their salaries and pensions.

7. I must confess that even though I was probably forty years younger than my hostesses, and a regular exerciser, I found it difficult to keep up with them and frequently crawled off to bed hours before they did.

8. My suspicion was that Ksenia and her son coordinated the meeting via mobile telephone, although she never mentioned this possibility, and I was not in a position to verify it. Regardless, the important point remains that her confidence that her son

would know when she would appear suggests a different notion of time and when her son would expect her.

9. In a departure from the Soviet three-queue shopping system (the first queue to decide what to buy, the second to pay and receive a receipt, and the third to exchange the receipt for the goods purchased), in which customers often had to demand service from cashiers, McDonald's introduced a single-queue system in which cashiers waited on customers and advertised when they were available to serve the next customer with the words "*Svobodnaia kassa.*" For more discussion of the nature and impact of McDonald's in post-Soviet Russia, see Caldwell 2004a.

4. NATURAL FOODS:
FEEDING THE BODY AND NOURISHING THE SOUL

1. Markova (2005) notes that the average price for blueberries in Tver in the summer of 2005 was thirteen to fifteen rubles per cup (approximately US$.50–.55).

2. During the height of mushroom season, Russian newspapers publish frequent advisories about mushrooms, as well as reports about illnesses and deaths from poisonous mushrooms (see, for instance, Toohey 2007). At the same time, newspapers and magazines also provide information about which varieties of mushrooms are available in city markets and in which location (e.g., Morozov 1998). Some magazines devote much, if not most, of an entire issue to mushrooms. The September–October 1998 issue of *Gurman* and the August 1998 issue of *Restorannye Vedemosti* are largely dedicated to mushrooms.

3. See also the website for the Food Democracy program at the Small Planet Institute at www.smallplanetinstitute.org/learning_action/food-democracy/.

4. Although Darra Goldstein writes that one factor contributing to the emergence of the vegetarian movement at the end of the imperial period in Russia was the "green city movement" (Goldstein 1997:107), vegetarianism is not widespread in Russia today, nor do Russian consumers necessarily link vegetarianism with natural foods. An official Green Party has only recently emerged in Russian politics, and it is marginal and not exclusively focused on environmental and other progressive social causes.

5. See Caldwell 2002 and 2004a for fuller discussions of these trends. See also Jung 2009, Klumbytė 2009, and Mincyte 2009.

6. A recent *New York Times* article reported that Russia's collective farms have emerged as the latest investment target for large agribusinesses (Kramer 2008).

7. Azhgikhina and Goscilo write that during the Soviet period, women's preferences for "natural" cosmetics derived from the lower cost and greater availability of natural food products (1996:105).

8. *Krapiva* occupies a fascinating place in Russian mythology of World War II survival, and it has recently reemerged in the popular imagination—and cuisine—as a form of nostalgia food.

9. This was especially true for the low-income pensioners who are the subject of my earlier research (see especially Caldwell 2004b).

10. In a revealing comparative example, Yuson Jung also reports that her Bulgarian informants frequently found debris in factory foods. One informant who

worked in a food factory described the amusement among co-workers who deliberately placed debris in foods (Jung 2005).

11. About the earliest days of the Soviet state, Borrero writes that "Although Lenin complained of the excessively negative descriptions of state cafeterias in the Soviet press, the truth was that few cafeterias actually lived up to basic health and culinary standards" (1997:168).

12. For a very different case study of postsocialist attitudes about foreign food technologies, see Maris Gillette's study of factory foods in China (Gillette 2000).

13. The June 2004 issue of the women's health magazine *Zdorov'e ot Prirody* (Health from Nature) carries a full-page ad (p. 87) for the store Dikaia Tykva (Wild Pumpkin), which claimed to carry "organic food products, certified in Europe."

14. *"Beri nash—Liubimii Sad."* For a more extensive discussion of the nationalizing rhetoric of "ours" and "not ours" in Russian food practices, see Caldwell 2002.

15. Hervouet (2003) makes a similar point for the case of Belarus, as does Smith (2003) for Hungary.

16. See Caldwell (2004b:118–22) for a more detailed discussion.

17. In her work on Lithuanian dairy practices, Diana Mincyte has made a similar observation about the continuing demand for raw milk and farm-fresh milk and suspicions, or at least dislike, of dairy products from commercial farms and sold in shops. The introduction of EU certification requirements, which in principle seek to do away with raw milk, is especially problematic. See Mincyte 2009.

18. See Shevchenko 2002b for a discussion of how Russians also invest their money in food appliances like refrigerators.

19. This notion that national landscapes produce bio-national qualities appears elsewhere in post-Soviet contexts, including Lithuania, as Neringa Klumbytė (2009) has described for the politics of sausage.

20. In her study of Russian dachas, Naomi Galtz writes that a key mantra of gardening during the Soviet period was "the need for both 'usefulness and beauty' (*pol'za i krasota*)" (2000:314).

21. In his study of summer gardens in Ukraine, Taylor Terry found that even the presence of industrial runoff in the fields did not deter local gardeners from eating the products planted there (personal communication).

22. The "ecologically clean" designation is also commonly found on Russian foods produced and sold outside Russia, such as on Russian-style dairy products that I have bought in Russian grocery stores in the United States.

23. As part of its investment holdings the Russian Orthodox Church operates a number of commercial enterprises, including banks, oil companies, and a bottling plant. Individual churches and monasteries also operate smaller-scale food and water ventures.

24. The details on the label not only clearly testify to the importance of showing the natural sources of products, but they also resonate with other cultural concerns about the healthful properties of natural food products. The full description on the label reads: "In the quiet secret corners of nature, located in the transparent lakes of the Valdai National Preserve, at depths of more than 130 meters, was born this unique, rich, satisfying mineral water 'Reserve.' The water absorbs into itself all the cleanliness and primordialness *[pervozdannost']* of the nature of this

region, as well as healthy *[poleznii]* properties. Fluorine, which enters the composition of 'Reserve' water, helps make up for a deficit of this healthy mineral, 70% of which enters in our organism chiefly through water."

25. I found out much later that after Katerina had arrived home that evening she became extremely ill for several days. From her description of her symptoms, it sounded as if she had suffered from severe heat stroke that was probably brought on or exacerbated by dehydration, although she did not consider this a possible explanation for her illness.

26. See Kormina (2010) for a description of Russians using natural springs during Orthodox religious tours. Techniques for accessing water and natural springs also appear in dacha and gardening magazines, such as the June 2004 issue of *Sad svoimi rukami* (A Garden by Your Own Hands) (Kovaleva and Kovalev 2004).

27. The theme of nature as a gift giver is further reproduced in publications focusing on gardening and natural foods. One such newspaper features a section called "Gifts of Nature" and subtitled "Earth—the one who feeds" *(zemlia— kormilets)*. In it are recipes made from in-season produce, such as a section in the August 2005 issue of *Toloka v Rossii* (p. 23) that focused on recipes for tomatoes, cucumbers, squash, and red currants. The feminine form of *kormilets* is *kormilitsa,* which also means "wet nurse," thereby suggesting an even more intimate relationship between nature and people.

28. The Hare Krishna complex has been closed for a few years and is in the process of relocating to a community just outside Moscow.

29. Similarly, two cooking magazines, *Kulinar* and *Restorannye Vedemosti,* each provide a gastronomic horoscope at the end of every issue. The caption in *Restorannye Vedemosti* announces that this "gastronomic prognosis" will provide readers with advice on how to help their bodies and lives through food. Finally, the motto listed on the front page of *Priiatnogo Appetita!* is *"gotovit' s dushoi, est' s udovol'stviem* (cook with soul, eat with pleasure)."

30. The emphasis on creating harmony through ordering gardens also appears in non–feng shui garden designs, such as an article titled *"Put' k garmonii* (Path to Harmony)" (anonymous article in *Sad svoimi rukami* 2004, volume 6).

31. This information came from the August 2005 issue of *Toloka v Rossii* (p. 188). There are no authors attributed to the articles from which this information is taken.

32. For an interesting comparative case of the moral and spiritual values that are ascribed to soil in Denmark, see Kaltoft 1999.

5. DISAPPEARING DACHNIKI

1. The popularity of peasant restaurants is part of a larger phenomenon of culinary tourism that has swept Russia in recent years. Restaurants, food magazines, and the travel industry more generally provide a wide range of possibilities for consumers who want to use food as a means to experience the world, whether vicariously or through actual travel. I discuss this phenomenon more fully in Caldwell 2006.

2. They also are not unique to Russia. See Raffles 2002:152.

3. These tragic events also coincided with a horrific famine in which an esti-

mated seven million peasants died. For a particularly gripping analysis of the violence of Soviet collectivization and the famine, see Conquest's *The Harvest of Sorrow: Soviet Collectivization and the Terror-Famine* (Conquest 1986).

4. In her book on homelessness in Russia, Svetlana Stephenson (2006:83) writes that collective farms were often dumping grounds for "social waste"—i.e., homeless persons, the unemployed, and other undesirables—during the Soviet period and continuing into the post-Soviet period.

5. See also Boym's discussion (2001:88–89) of the ways in which spatial markers—statues and monuments, in particular—wander around Russia, thereby reorienting the very dimensions of space.

6. See Caroline Humphrey's essay on these new housing trends and Russia's emerging middle and upper classes in Humphrey 1998 (also reprinted in Humphrey 2002).

7. One *sotka* is equivalent to one centihectare. The most common allotment size for dacha plots was six *sotki*.

8. I was frequently encouraged to bring my laptop to the dacha, although my friends said that they understood when I declined. A friend who was trying heroically to finish his dissertation was often forced to listen to the well-meaning comments of his relatives that it was too bad that his computer was a desktop model. If only he had a laptop, they lamented, he would be able to bring his dissertation to the dacha and finish more quickly.

9. In discussions about "authentic" dacha life informants repeatedly asked if I had ever seen or used a real samovar. One of the historical museums in Tver has an extensive collection of antique samovars, and for an extra charge visitors can participate in a tea ceremony in which a museum guide details the history of the Russian samovar and tea drinking. The presentation reaches its climax with the pouring of tea made in an authentic samovar. Acquaintances who were concerned that my research would suffer if I had never used an authentic samovar were relieved when they learned that I had visited the museum and participated in the tea ceremony.

10. For a more extended treatment of racialized inflections of blame and consumption in Russia, see Caldwell 2003.

11. Coincidentally, during summer 2005 Alla Pugacheva was one of many prominent celebrities who came under tabloid and public scrutiny for the size and flamboyance of her dacha compound.

12. Yurchak notes that *obshchenie* (society or community) "is both a process and a sociality that emerges in that process, and both an exchange of ideas and information as well as a space of affect and togetherness" (2006:149).

6. DACHA DEMOCRACY:
BUILDING CIVIL SOCIETY IN OUT-OF-THE-WAY PLACES

1. This theme of natural spaces, and dachas in particular, as spaces of safety and escape for both victims and criminals appears frequently in contemporary Russian crime dramas and detective novels.

2. The privileging of an urban/rural divide is also present in academic studies, including of post-Soviet societies, where "urban anthropology" is set apart as

something different from other types of ethnographic inquiry and methodology. Although Russian ethnographies are typically grounded in either urban settings (e.g., Caldwell 2004b; Ries 1997; Patico 2008) or rural settings, including villages and nomadic groups (e.g., Paxson 2005; Ssorin-Chaikov 2003), the work of ethnographers of Russia reveals that these distinctions are not absolute or even productive.

3. At a recent series of workshops titled "Development in Post-Soviet Societies" convened at the Kennan Institute for Russian Studies (April and December 2007), this perspective was apparent in the discussions that took place among the participants. While the political scientists, legal scholars, and development professionals insisted on linking "democracy" and "civil society," the anthropologists and sociologists insisted on more expansive notions of civil society as qualities and spaces of life that were not necessarily political or even civic in scope.

4. Chris Hann's essay on civil society models, the anthropology of civil society, and civil society studies in the postsocialist world (and elsewhere) is particularly useful for understanding these approaches (Hann 1996).

5. It is important to recognize that in some cases, the organizational structures of dacha cooperatives were part of the state's techniques for monitoring and regulating its citizens. It was not uncommon for dacha cooperative officials and other residents to engage in acts of surveillance of their fellow residents. Certainly the president of the Nadezhda cooperative was observant of newcomers to the community—including the visiting ethnographer. Nevertheless, this issue rarely came up in conversations with residents about their dacha experiences, and in fact most people emphasized their dachas as safe places in contrast to their apartments or workplaces.

6. Lovell (2003) also reports that private ownership of dachas did exist during the Soviet period, but this was not the norm.

7. When I related this idea to colleagues in Germany, they burst into laughter and explained that German gardens are so constrained by rules governing every little aspect that they are a nuisance.

8. Within Russian social practice there is a long history of finding creative ways to circumvent official rules and unfortunate circumstances. As ethnographers have repeatedly documented, the creative "making do" strategies of Russians and other socialist citizens effectively meant that the possibilities were endless given the proper resources, connections, and attitudes. In the case of Romania, Steven Sampson has described the country as "a society where all things were possible and nothing was certain" (Sampson 1995:126).

9. I address these issues more fully in Caldwell 2009.

10. For further discussion of similar efforts at civic relandscaping, see Caldwell 2004b:180–82.

11. This was the title used in the English-language version of this article, which appeared several days after the original Russian-language text. In the original *Izvestiia* article Pankin used a slightly different title—"History in Dachas"—that was just as revealing but emphasized a more natural historical progression rather than a historiographic interpretation of that history (Pankin 2005b).

12. In a personal communication, Taylor Terry reported that a Ukrainian dachnik he interviewed showed off the secret ceiling trapdoor and ladder that he had installed in his dacha. The ladder led to an insulated and furnished attic. None of this was permissible according to local ordinances.

Bibliography

Abdullaev, Nabi. 2005. "New Details Emerge about Kasyanov Villa Sale." *Moscow Times* 3215: 4.

Acheson, Julianna. 2007. "Household Exchange Networks in Post-Socialist Slovakia." *Human Organization* 66(4): 405–13.

Aleksandrova, Vera. 2005. "Pervye gektary kartofelia." *Tverskaia Zhizn'* 79(25, 690): 1.

Argumenty i Fakty. 2005. "Ch'ia Dacha Luchshe?" July 29(1290): 7.

Azhgikhina, Nadezhda, and Helena Goscilo. 1996. "Getting under Their Skin: The Beauty Salon in Russian Women's Lives." In *Russia, Women, Culture,* edited by Helena Goscilo and Beth Holmgren, 94–121. Bloomington: Indiana University Press.

Baehr, Stephen L. 1999. "The Machine in Chekhov's Garden: Progress and Pastoral in the Cherry Orchard." *Slavic and East European Journal* 43(1): 99–121.

Barber, Benjamin R. 1995. *Jihad vs. McWorld: How Globalism and Tribalism Are Reshaping the World.* New York: Ballantine Books.

Basso, Keith H. 1996. *Wisdom Sits in Places: Landscape and Language among the Western Apache.* Albuquerque: University of New Mexico Press.

Belasco, Warren. 1999. "Food and the Counterculture: A Story of Bread and Politics." In *Food in Global History,* edited by Raymond Grew, 273–92. Boulder, CO: Westview Press.

Bellows, Anne C. 2004. "One Hundred Years of Allotment Gardens in Poland." *Food and Foodways* 12: 247–76.

Bentley, Amy. 1998. *Eating for Victory: Food Rationing and the Politics of Domesticity.* Urbana: University of Illinois Press.

Berdahl, Daphne. 2000. "Introduction: An Anthropology of Postsocialism." *In Altering States: Ethnographies of Transition in Eastern Europe and the Former*

Soviet Union, edited by Daphne Berdahl, Matti Bunzl, and Martha Lampland, 1–13. Ann Arbor: University of Michigan Press.

Bessière, Jacinthe. 1998. "Local Development and Heritage: Traditional Food and Cuisine as Tourist Attractions in Rural Areas." *Sociologia Ruralis* 38(1): 21–34.

Bhatti, Mark, and Andrew Church. 2000. "'I Never Promised You a Rose Garden': Gender, Leisure and Home-Making." *Leisure Studies* 19: 183–97.

Blavascunas, Eunice. 2008. "The Peasant and Communist Past in the Making of an Ecological Region: Podlasie, Poland." PhD diss., University of California, Santa Cruz.

Borrero, Mauricio. 1997. "Communal Dining and State Cafeterias in Moscow and Petrograd, 1917–1921." In *Food in Russian History and Culture,* edited by Musya Glants and Joyce Toomre, 162–76. Bloomington: Indiana University Press.

———. 2002. "Food and the Politics of Scarcity in Urban Soviet Russia, 1917–1941." In *Food Nations: Selling Taste in Consumer Societies,* edited by Warren Belasco and Philip Scranton, 258–76. New York: Routledge.

Boym, Svetlana. 1994. *Common Places: Mythologies of Everyday Life in Russia.* Cambridge, MA: Harvard University Press.

———. 2001. *The Future of Nostalgia.* New York: Basic Books.

Bren, Paulina. 2002. "Weekend Getaways: The *Chata,* the *Tramp,* and the Politics of Private Life in Post-1968 Czechoslovakia." In *Socialist Spaces: Sites of Everyday Life in the Eastern Bloc,* edited by David Crowley and Susan E. Reid, 123–40. Oxford: Berg.

Brooks, Jeffrey. 1985. *When Russia Learned to Read: Literacy and Popular Literature.* Princeton, NJ: Princeton University Press.

Brownell, Susan. 1995. *Training the Body for China: Sports in the Moral Order of the People's Republic.* Chicago: University of Chicago Press.

Buchli, Victor. 2000. *An Archaeology of Socialism.* Oxford: Berg.

Burawoy, Michael, and Katherine Verdery. 1999. "Introduction." In *Uncertain Transition: Ethnographies of Change in the Postsocialist World,* edited by Michael Burawoy and Katherine Verdery, 1–17. Lanham, MD: Rowman & Littlefield.

Burilov, Valerii. 2005. "Musornyi Gorod." *Veche Tveri,* April 14, 50(3632): 5.

Bushchev, Aleksandr. 2005. "Za riabeevskim zaborom." *Tverskaia Zhizn'* 132(25, 743): 7.

Bushnell, John. 1990. *Moscow Graffiti: Language and Subculture.* Boston: Unwin Hyman.

Buyandelgeriyn, Manduhai. 2008. "Post-post-transition Theories: Walking on Multiple Paths." *Annual Review of Anthropology* 37: 235–50.

Caldwell, Melissa L. 2002. "The Taste of Nationalism: Food Politics in Postsocialist Moscow." *Ethnos* 67(3): 295–319.

———. 2003. "Race and Social Relations: Crossing Borders in a Moscow Food Aid Program." In *Social Networks in Movement: Time, Interaction and Interethnic Spaces in Central Eastern Eurasia,* edited by Davide G. Torsello and Maria Pappová, 255–73. Dunajská Streda, Slovakia: Lilium Aurum.

———. 2004a. "Domesticating the French Fry: McDonald's and Consumerism in Moscow." *Journal of Consumer Culture* 4(1): 5–26.

———. 2004b. *Not by Bread Alone: Social Support in the New Russia.* Berkeley: University of California Press.

———. 2005. "Newness and Loss in Moscow: Rethinking Transformation in the Postsocialist Field." *Journal for the Society of the Anthropology of Europe* 5(1): 2–7.

———. 2006. "Tasting the Worlds of Yesterday and Today: Culinary Tourism and Nostalgia Foods in Post-Soviet Russia." In *Fast Food/Slow Food: The Cultural Economy of the Global Food System,* edited by Richard Wilk, 97–112. Lanham, MD: Altamira Press.

———. 2009. "Tempest in a Coffee Pot: Brewing Incivility in Russia's Public Sphere." In *Food and Everyday Life in the Postsocialist World,* edited by Melissa L. Caldwell, 101–29. Bloomington: Indiana University Press.

Caldwell, Melissa L., ed. 2009. *Food and Everyday Life in the Postsocialist World.* Bloomington: Indiana University Press.

"Case Opened Against Official Who Sold Property to Kasyanov." 2005. Interfax News Agency, July 11.

Casey, Edward S. 1996. "How to Get from Space to Place in a Fairly Short Stretch of Time: Phenomenological Prolegomena." In *Senses of Place,* edited by Steven Feld and Keith H. Basso, 13–52. Santa Fe, NM: School of American Research Press.

Chakrabarty, Dipesh. 2000. *Provincializing Europe: Postcolonial Thought and Historical Difference.* Princeton, NJ: Princeton University Press.

Chekhov, Anton. 1885 [1996]. "Dachniki." Publichnaia Elektronnaia Biblioteka (Public Electronic Library). Available at http://public-library.narod.ru/Chekhov .Anton/dachniki.html (accessed August 6, 2008).

———. 1999. *Later Short Stories: 1888–1903.* Edited by Shelby Foote, translated by Constance Garnett. New York: The Modern Library.

———. 2004. *A Journey to the End of the Russian Empire.* Translated by Rosamund Bartlett, Anthony Phillips, Luba Terpak, and Michael Terpak. London: Penguin Books Great Journeys.

———. 2007. "At a Summer Villa." In *Love and Other Stories,* 157–61. Champaign, IL: Book Jungle.

Chen, Nancy N. 2003. *Breathing Spaces: Qigong, Psychiatry, and Healing in China.* New York: Columbia University Press.

"Chinovniki vykhodiat na subbotnik." 2005. *Veche Tveri,* April 14, 50(3632): 2.

Clarke, Simon. 2002. *Making Ends Meet in Contemporary Russia: Secondary Employment, Subsidiary Agriculture and Social Networks.* Cheltenham, England: Edward Elgar.

Cleveland, David A., and Daniela Soleri. 1987. "Household Gardens as a Development Strategy." *Human Organization* 46(3): 259–70.

Conquest, Robert. 1986. *The Harvest of Sorrow: Soviet Collectivization and the Terror-Famine.* New York: Oxford University Press.

Cooper, David E. 2006. *A Philosophy of Gardens.* Oxford: Clarendon Press.

Costlow, Jane. 2003. "Imaginations of Destruction: The 'Forest Question' in Nineteenth-Century Russian Culture." *Russian Review* 62(1): 91–118.

Cox, Randi. 2003. "All This Can Be Yours! Soviet Commercial Advertising and the Social Construction of Space, 1928–1956." In *The Landscape of Stalinism: The Art and Ideology of Soviet Space,* edited by Evgeny Dobrenko and Eric Naiman, 125–62. Seattle: University of Washington Press.

Cross, Samuel H. 1945. "Nineteenth Century Russian Painting." *American Slavic and East European Review* 4(3/4): 35–53.

Crowley, David, and Susan E. Reid. 2002. "Socialist Spaces: Sites of Everyday Life in the Eastern Bloc." In *Socialist Spaces: Sites of Everyday Life in the Eastern Bloc,* edited by David Crowley and Susan E. Reid, 1–22. Oxford: Berg.

"Dachagate: The Kremlin Goes after Mikhail Kasyanov." 2005. *The Economist,* July 16.

De Certeau, Michel. 1984. *The Practice of Everyday Life.* Translated by Steven Rendall. Berkeley: University of California Press.

Dudwick, Nora, and Hermine G. De Soto. 2000. "Introduction." In *Fieldwork Dilemmas: Anthropologists in Postsocialist States,* edited by Hermine G. De Soto and Nora Dudwick, 3–8. Madison: University of Wisconsin Press.

Dunn, Elizabeth Cullen. 2008. "Postsocialist Spores: Disease, Bodies, and the State in the Republic of Georgia." *American Ethnologist* 35(2): 243–58.

Ekho Moskvy. 2005. "Former Russian Premier Starts Race for the Presidency." English transcript of Russian-language interview with Mikhail Kasyanov. September 14, 2005, 16:15 GMT, supplied by BBC Worldwide Monitoring.

Ely, Christopher. 2000. "Critics in the Native Soil: Landscape and Conflicting Ideals of Nationality in Imperial Russia." *Ecumene* 7(3): 253–70.

———. 2002. *This Meager Nature: Landscape and National Identity in Imperial Russia.* DeKalb: Northern Illinois University Press.

———. 2003. "The Origins of Russian Scenery: Volga River Tourism and Russian Landscape Aesthetics." *Slavic Review* 62(4): 666–82.

Engel, Barbara Alpern. 1993. "Russian Peasant Views of City Life, 1861–1914." *Slavic Review* 52(3): 446–59.

Epshtein, Mikhail. 1990. *Priroda, Mir, Tainik Vselennoi: Sistema peizazhnykh obrazov v russkoi poezii.* Moscow: Vysshaia Shkola.

Evdokimova, Svetlana. 2000. "What's So Funny about Losing One's Estate, or Infantilism in *The Cherry Orchard.*" *Slavic and East European Journal* 44(4): 623–48.

"Federal Guard Service Linked to Kasyanov Case." 2005. *Moscow Times,* August 2(3221): 3.

Fehérváry, Krisztina. 2002. "American Kitchens, Luxury Bathrooms, and the Search for a 'Normal' Life in Postsocialist Hungary." *Ethnos* 67(3): 369–400.

Fitzpatrick, Sheila. 1999. *Everyday Stalinism: Ordinary Life in Extraordinary Times: Soviet Russia in the 1930s.* New York: Oxford University Press.

———. 2003. "The Good Old Days." *London Review of Books,* October 9, 2003. Available at www.lrb.co.uk/v25/n19/print/fitz03_.html.

Floryan, Margrethe. 1996. *Gardens of the Tsars: A Study of the Aesthetics, Semantics and Uses of Late 18th Century Russian Gardens.* Aarhus, Denmark: Aarhus University Press.

Frierson, Cathy A. 1997. "Forced Hunger and Rational Restraint in the Russian Peasant Diet: One Populist's Vision." In *Food in Russian History and Culture,* edited by Musya Glants and Joyce Toomre, 49–66. Bloomington: Indiana University Press.

Gabriel, Cynthia. 2005. "Healthy Russian Food Is Not-for-Profit." *Subsistence and Sustenance,* special issue of *Michigan Discussions in Anthropology* 15: 183–222.

Galtz, Naomi. 2000. "Space and the Everyday: An Historical Sociology of the Moscow Dacha." PhD diss., University of Michigan.

Gambold Miller, Leisel L., and Patrick Heady. 2004. "Cooperation, Power, and Community Economy and Ideology in the Russian Countryside." In *The Postsocialist Agrarian Question: Property Relations and the Rural Condition,* edited by Chris Hann and the "Property Relations" Group, 257–92. Münster, Germany: Lit Verlag.

Gerasimova, Katerina. 2002. "Public Privacy in the Soviet Communal Apartment." In *Socialist Spaces: Sites of Everyday Life in the Eastern Bloc,* edited by David Crowley and Susan E. Reid, 207–30. Oxford: Berg.

Gille, Zsuzsa. 2007. *From the Cult of Waste to the Trash Heap of History: The Politics of Waste in Socialist and Postsocialist Hungary.* Bloomington: Indiana University Press.

Gillette, Maris Boyd. 2000. "Children's Food and Islamic Dietary Restrictions in Xi'an." In *Feeding China's Little Emperors: Food, Children, and Social Change,* edited by Jun Jing, 71–93. Stanford, CA: Stanford University Press.

Gleason, Abbott. 2000. "*Russkii Inok:* The Spiritual Landscape of Mikhail Nesterov." *Ecumene* 7(3): 299–312.

Goldstein, Darra. 1997. "Is Hay Only for Horses? Highlights of Russian Vegetarianism at the Turn of the Century." In *Food in Russian History and Culture,* edited by Musya Glants and Joyce Toomre, 103–23. Bloomington: Indiana University Press.

Gorky, Maxim. 1906. *Dachniki: Stseny, Chetyre Akta.* Berlin: Verlag Snanije.

———. 1995. *The Summer People.* Translated by Nicholas Saunders and Frank Dwyer. Lyme, NH: A Smith and Kraus Book.

Gorsuch, Anne E. 2006. "Time Travelers: Soviet Tourists to Eastern Europe." In *Turizm: The Russian and East European Tourist under Capitalism and Socialism,* edited by Anne E. Gorsuch and Diane P. Koenker, 205–26. Ithaca, NY: Cornell University Press.

Gorsuch, Anne E., and Diane P. Koenker. 2006. "Introduction." In *Turizm: The Russian and East European Tourist under Capitalism and Socialism,* edited by Anne E. Gorsuch and Diane P. Koenker, 1–14. Ithaca, NY: Cornell University Press.

Grant, Bruce. 2001. "New Moscow Monuments, or, States of Innocence." *American Ethnologist* 28(2): 332–62.

Gregg, Richard. 1977. "The Nature of Nature and the Nature of Eugene in the Bronze Horseman." *Slavic and East European Journal* 21(2): 167–79.

Grossman, Joan Delaney. 2003. "Briusov and the Healing Art: Northern Nature in 'Na granitakh.'" *Russian Review* 62(1): 110–31.

Halweil, Brian. N.d. "The Rise of Food Democracy." UN Chronicle Online Edition. Available at www.un.org/Pubs/chronicle/2005/issue1/0105p7.html (accessed November 11, 2005).

Haney, Lynne A. 2002. *Inventing the Needy: Gender and the Politics of Welfare in Hungary.* Berkeley: University of California Press.

Hann, Chris. 1996. "Introduction: Political Society and Civil Anthropology." In *Civil Society: Challenging Western Models,* edited by Chris Hann and Elizabeth Dunn, 1–26. London: Routledge.

———. 2003. "Introduction: Decollectivisation and the Moral Economy." In *The Postsocialist Agrarian Question: Property Relations and the Rural Condition,* edited by Chris Hann and the "Property Relations" Group, 1–46. Münster, Germany: Lit Verlag.

Hann, Chris, and Elizabeth Dunn, eds. 1996. *Civil Society: Challenging Western Models.* London: Routledge.

Hann, Chris, et al. 2007. "Anthropology's Multiple Temporalities and Its Future in Central and Eastern Europe: A Debate." Working Paper 90, Max Planck Institute, Halle/Saale, Germany.

Harper, Krista. 2006. *Wild Capitalism: Environmental Activists and Post-Socialist Ecology in Hungary.* New York: Columbia University Press.

Harvey, David. 1989. *The Condition of Postmodernity.* Oxford: Blackwell Publishers.

Hervouet, Ronan. 2003. "Dachas and Vegetable Gardens in Belarus: Economic and Subjective Stakes of an 'Ordinary Passion.'" *Anthropology of East Europe Review* 21(1). Available at http://condor.depaul.edu/%7Errotenbe/aeer/aeer21 _1.html (accessed May 16, 2006).

———. 2007. "Datchas et mémoires familiales en Biélorussie." *Ethnologie francaise* 37(3): 533–40.

Herzfeld, Michael. 1991. *A Place in History: Social and Monumental Time in a Cretan Town.* Princeton, NJ: Princeton University Press.

———. 1997. *Cultural Intimacy: Social Poetics in the Nation-State.* New York: Routledge.

———. 2006. "Spatial Cleansing: Monumental Vacuity and the Idea of the West." *Journal of Material Culture* 11(1/2): 127–49.

Humphrey, Caroline. 1995. "Creating a Culture of Disillusionment: Consumption in Moscow, a Chronicle of Changing Times." In *Worlds Apart: Modernity through the Prism of the Local,* edited by Daniel Miller, 43–68. London: Routledge.

———. 1998. "The Villas of the 'New Russians': A Sketch of Consumption and Cultural Identity in Post-Soviet Landscapes." *Focaal* 30–31: 85–106.

———. 2002. *The Unmaking of Soviet Life: Everyday Economies after Socialism.* Ithaca, NY: Cornell University Press.

Imbruce, Valerie. 2006. "From the Bottom Up: The Global Expansion of Chinese Vegetable Trade for New York City Markets." In *Fast Food/Slow Food: The Cultural Economy of the Global Food System,* edited by Richard Wilk, 163–79. Lanham, MD: Altamira Press.

Inda, Jonathan Xavier, and Renato Rosaldo. 2002. "Introduction: A World in Motion." In *The Anthropology of Globalization: A Reader,* edited by Jonathan Xavier Inda and Renato Rosaldo, 1–34. Malden, MA: Blackwell Publishers.

Ioffe, Grigory, and Tatyana Nefedova. 1998. "Environs of Russian Cities: A Case Study of Moscow." *Europe-Asia Studies* 50(8): 1325–56.

Jung, Yuson. 2005. "Shifting Perceptions of Standardized Food in Postsocialist Urban Bulgaria." Paper presented at the American Association for the Advancement of Slavic Studies meetings, Salt Lake City, UT, November

———. 2006. "Consumer Lament: An Ethnographic Study on Consumption, Needs, and Everyday Complaints in Postsocialist Bulgaria." PhD diss., Harvard University.

———. 2009. "From Canned Foods to Canny Consumers: Cultural Competence in the Age of Mechanical Production." In *Food and Everyday Life in the Postsocialist World,* edited by Melissa L. Caldwell, 29–56. Bloomington: Indiana University Press.

Kalachev, Sergei. 2004. "Zariadis' zdorov'em!" *Sad svoimi rukami* (6): 47–49.

Kaltoft, Pernille. 1999. "Values about Nature in Organic Farming Practice and Knowledge." *Sociologia Ruralis* 39(1): 39–53.

Kiseleva, Galina. 2005. "Kto pomozhet krest'ianinu?" *Tverskie Vedemosti* 5(1510): 3.

Kivelson, Valerie. 2006. *Cartographies of Tsardom: The Land and Its Meanings in Seventeenth-Century Russia.* Ithaca, NY: Cornell University Press.

Klumbytė, Neringa. 2009. "The Geopolitics of Taste: The 'Euro' and 'Soviet' Sausage Industries in Lithuania." In *Food and Everyday Life in the Postsocialist World,* edited by Melissa L. Caldwell, 130–53. Bloomington: Indiana University Press.

Koenker, Diane P. 2006. "The Proletarian Tourist in the 1930s: Between Mass Excursion and Mass Escape." In *Turizm: The Russian and East European Tourist under Capitalism and Socialism,* edited by Anne E. Gorsuch and Diane P. Koenker, 119–40. Ithaca, NY: Cornell University Press.

Kormina, Jeanne. 2010. "*Avtobusniki:* Russian Orthodox Pilgrims' Longing for Authenticity." In *Eastern Christians in Anthropological Perspective,* edited by Chris Hann and Hermann Goltz, 267–86. Berkeley: University of California Press.

Koshar, Rudy. 2002. "Seeing, Traveling, and Consuming: An Introduction." In *Histories of Leisure,* edited by Rudy Koshar, 1–24. Oxford: Berg.

Kotkin, Stephen. 1995. *Magnetic Mountain: Stalinism as a Civilization.* Berkeley: University of California Press.

Kovaleva, Nataliia, and Ivan Kovalev. 2004. "Gde 'lezhit' voda?" *Sad svoimi rukami* (6): 11–13.

Kramer, Andrew E. 2008. "Russia's Lazy Collective Farms Are a Hot Capitalist Property." *New York Times,* August 31.

Ladd, Brian. 1997. *The Ghosts of Berlin.* Chicago: University of Chicago Press.

Latour, Bruno. 1993. *We Have Never Been Modern.* Translated by Catherine Porter. Harlow, England: Longman.

Lawson, Laura J. 2005. *City Bountiful: A Century of Community Gardening in America.* Berkeley: University of California Press.

Layton, Susan. 2006. "Russian Military Tourism: The Crisis of the Crimean War Period." In *Turizm: The Russian and East European Tourist under Capitalism and Socialism,* edited by Anne E. Gorsuch and Diane P. Koenker, 43–63. Ithaca, NY: Cornell University Press.

LeBlanc, Ronald D. 1997. "Tolstoy's Way of No Flesh: Abstinence, Vegetarianism, and Christian Physiology." In *Food in Russian History and Culture,* edited by Musya Glants and Joyce Toomre, 80–102. Bloomington: Indiana University Press.

Ledeneva, Alena V. 1998. *Russia's Economy of Favours: Blat, Networking and Informal Exchange.* Cambridge: Cambridge University Press.

Leitch, Alison. 2003. "Slow Food and the Politics of Pork Fat: Italian Food and European Identity." *Ethnos* 68(4): 437–62.

Lemon, Alaina. 2000. "Talking Transit and Spectating Transition: The Moscow Metro." In *Altering States: Ethnographies of Transition in East Central Europe and the Former Soviet Union,* edited by Daphne Berdahl, Matti Bunzl, and Martha Lampland, 14–39. Ann Arbor: University of Michigan Press.

Likhachev, D. C. 1998. *Poeziia Sadov: K semantike sadovo-parkovykh stilei. Sad kak tekst.* Moscow: Soglasie and Tipografiia "Novosti."

Löfgren, Orvar. 1987. "Rational and Sensitive: Changing Attitudes to Time, Nature and the Home." In Jonas Frykman and Orvar Löfgren, *Culture Builders: A Historical Anthropology of Middle-Class Life,* translated by Alan Crozier, 11–153. New Brunswick, NJ: Rutgers University Press.

Loginov, Sergei. 2005. "Smert' russkoi derevni." *Veche Tveri,* April 19, 52(3634): 7.

Longhurst, Robyn. 2006. "Plots, Plants and Paradoxes: Contemporary Domestic Gardens in Aotearoa/New Zealand." *Social and Cultural Geography* 7(4): 581–93.

Lounsbery, Anne. 2005. "'No, this is not the provinces!' Provincialism, Authenticity, and Russianness in Gogol's Day." *Russian Review* 64: 259–80.

Lovell, Stephen. 2002. "Soviet Exurbia: Dachas in Postwar Russia." In *Socialist Spaces: Sites of Everyday Life in the Eastern Bloc,* edited by David Crowley and Susan E. Reid, 105–21. Oxford: Berg.

———. 2003. *Summerfolk: A History of the Dacha, 1710–2000.* Ithaca, NY: Cornell University Press.

Malinowski, Bronislaw. 1961. *Argonauts of the Western Pacific.* New York: E. P. Dutton.

Malpas, Anna. 2008. "Court Ruling Affects Few Dachas." *St. Petersburg Times,* June 6, 1379(43).

Mandel, Ruth. 2002. "Seeding Civil Society." In *Postsocialism: Ideals, Ideologies and Practices in Eurasia,* edited by C. M. Hann, 279–96. London: Routledge.

Markova, Tat'iana. 2005. "Rot v chernike—eto khorosho!" *Tverskaia Zhizn'* 140 (25,751): 6.

Mart'ianova, Liudmila. 2005. "Komy okhraniat' les?" *Tverskie Vedemosti* 4(1509): 3.

Maurer, Eva. 2006. "*Al'pinizm* as Mass Sport and Elite Recreation: Soviet Mountaineering Camps under Stalin." In *Turizm: The Russian and East European Tourist under Capitalism and Socialism,* edited by Anne E. Gorsuch and Diane P. Koenker, 141–62. Ithaca, NY: Cornell University Press.

McCannon, John. 2000. "In Search of Primeval Russia: Stylistic Evolution in the Landscapes of Nicholas Roerich, 1897–1914." *Ecumene* 7(3): 271–97.

McFaul, Michael. 1999–2000. "Getting Russia Right." *Foreign Policy* 117: 58–73.

McReynolds, Louise. 2003. *Russia at Play: Leisure Activities at the End of the Tsarist Era.* Ithaca, NY: Cornell University Press.

———. 2006. "The Prerevolutionary Russian Tourist: Commercialization in the Nineteenth Century." In *Turizm: The Russian and East European Tourist under Capitalism and Socialism,* edited by Anne E. Gorsuch and Diane P. Koenker, 17–42. Ithaca, NY: Cornell University Press.

Medvednik, Rita. 2004. "Pitanie bez toksinov." *Zdorov'e ot prirody* (June): 88–95.

Mincyte, Diana. 2009. "Self-Made Women: Informal Dairy Markets in Europeanizing Lithuania." In *Food and Everyday Life in the Postsocialist World,* edited by Melissa L. Caldwell, 78–100. Bloomington: Indiana University Press.

Mitrokhin, Nikolai. 2004. *Russkaia Pravoslavnaia Tserkov': Sovremennoe sostoianie i aktual'nye problemy.* Moscow: Novoe Literaturnoe Obozrenie.

Monastyrskaya, Nelli. 2005. "Ex-Premier Is Being Pushed into Opposition." *Moskovskiye Novosti,* July 15–21, 27: 6. Condensed and reprinted in *The Current Digest of the Post-Soviet Press,* August 10, 2005, 57(28).

Moon, David. 1996. "Estimating the Peasant Population of Late Imperial Russia from the 1897 Census: A Research Note." *Europe-Asia Studies* 48(1): 141–53.

Morozov, Sergei. 1998. "Ikh Ediat, A Oni Gliadiat . . ." *Gurman,* August–September: 1–14.

Nesterova, Nadezhda. 2001. "Ten' katastrophy nad tverskimi lesami." *Tverskie Vedemosti* 28(1162): 3.

Nevile, Jennifer. 1999. "Dance and the Garden: Moving and Static Choreography in Renaissance Europe." *Renaissance Quarterly* 52(3): 805–36.

Newlin, Thomas. 1996. "The Return of the Russian Odysseus: Pastoral Dreams and Rude Awakenings." *Russian Review* 55(3): 448–74.

Nivat, Georges. 2003. "The Russian Landscape in Myth." *Russian Studies in Literature* 39(2): 51–70.

Ogden, J. Alexander. 2005. "The Woods of Childhood: Forest and Fairy Tale in Pavel Zasodimskii's Nature Writing." *Russian Review* 64(2): 281–98.

Orlovskii, Stanislav. 2005. "Dachei po ambitsiiam." *Versiia,* August 8–14 (5): 6.

Ortar, Nathalie. 2005. "Les Multiples Usages de la Datcha des Jardins Collectifs." *Anthropologie et Sociétés* 29(2): 169–85.

———. 2007. "Villagers and *Dachniki* in Post-Soviet Russia: A Complex Relation." In *Reflecting Transformation in Post-socialist Rural Areas,* edited by Maarit Heinonen, Jouko Nikula, Inna Kopoteva, and Leo Granberg. Cambridge: Cambridge Scholars Publishing.

Orwin, Donna. 1999. "The Return to Nature: Tolstoyan Echoes in *The Idiot.*" *Russian Review* 58(1): 87–102.

Oushakine, Serguei. 2000a. "In the State of Post-Soviet Aphasia: Symbolic Development in Contemporary Russia." *Europe-Asia Studies* 52(6): 991–1016.

———. 2000b. "The Quantity of Style: Imaginary Consumption in the New Russia." *Theory, Culture and Society* 17(5): 97–120.

Pallot, Judith. 2000. "Imagining the Rational Landscape in Late Imperial Russia." *Journal of Historical Geography* 26(2): 273–91.

Pankin, Aleksei. 2005a. "The Dacha Theory of History." *Moscow Times,* July 18, no. 3210.

———. 2005b. "Istoriia v dachakh." *Izvestiia* July 15, 121(26,922): 4.

Parker, Stanley. 1983. *Leisure and Work.* London: George Allen & Unwin.

Parkins, Wendy. 2004. "Out of Time: Fast Subjects and Slow Living." *Time and Society* 13(2/3): 363–82.

Patico, Jennifer. 2001. "Globalization in the Postsocialist Marketplace: Consumer Readings of Difference and Development in Urban Russia." *Kroeber Anthropological Society Papers* 86: 1127–42.

———. 2005. "To Be Happy in a Mercedes: Tropes of Value and Ambivalent Visions of Marketization." *American Ethnologist* 32(3): 479–96.

———. 2008. *Consumption and Social Change in a Post-Soviet Middle Class.* Stanford, CA: Stanford University Press and the Woodrow Wilson Center Press.

Paxson, Margaret. 2005. *Solovyovo: The Story of Memory in a Russian Village.* Bloomington: Indiana University Press and the Woodrow Wilson Center Press.

Perrotta, Louise. 2002. "Rural Identities in Transition: Partible Persons and Partial Peasants in Post-Soviet Russia." In *Post-Socialist Peasant? Rural and Urban Constructions of Identity in Eastern Europe, East Asia and the Former Soviet Union,* edited by Pamela Leonard and Deema Kaneff, 117–35. New York: Palgrave.

Pesmen, Dale. 2000. *Russia and Soul: An Exploration.* Ithaca, NY: Cornell University Press.

Petrini, Carlo. 2001a. *Slow Food: The Case for Taste.* Translated by William McCuaig. New York: Columbia University Press.

———. 2001b. *Slow Food: Collected Thoughts on Taste, Tradition, and the Honest Pleasures of Food,* edited by Carlo Petrini, with Ben Watson and Slow Food Editore. White River Junction, VT: Chelsea Green Publishing.

Petryna, Adriana. 2002. *Life Exposed: Biological Citizens after Chernobyl.* Princeton, NJ: Princeton University Press.

Phillips, Sarah Drue. 2002. "Half-lives and Healthy Bodies: Discourses on 'Contaminated' Food and Healing in Post-Chernobyl Ukraine." *Food and Foodways* 10: 27–53.

Postnikov, Alexei V. 2000. "Outline of the History of Russian Cartography." In *Regions: A Prism to View the Slavic-Eurasian World. Towards a Discipline of "Regionality,"* edited by Kimitaka Matsuzato, 1–49. Sapporo, Japan: Slavic Research Center, Hokkaido University.

Putnam, Robert D. 2000. *Bowling Alone: The Collapse and Revival of American Community.* New York: Simon and Schuster.

Putney, Christopher R. 2003. "Nikolai Gogol's 'Old-World Landowners': A Parable of Acedia." *Slavic and East European Journal* 47(1): 1–23.

Raffles, Hugh. 2002. *In Amazonia: A Natural History.* Princeton, NJ: Princeton University Press.

Rausing, Sigrid. 2002. "Re-constructing the 'Normal': Identity and the Consumption of Western Goods in Estonia." In *Markets and Moralities: Ethnographies of Postsocialism,* edited by Ruth Mandel and Caroline Humphrey, 127–42. Oxford: Berg.

Reid, Susan E. 2002. "Khrushchev's Children's Paradise: The Pioneer Palace, Moscow, 1958–1962." In *Socialist Spaces: Sites of Everyday Life in the Eastern Bloc,* edited by David Crowley and Susan E. Reid, 141–79. Oxford: Berg.

Reisinger, William M., Arthur H. Miller, and Vicki L. Hesli. 1995. "Public Behavior and Political Change in Post-Soviet States." *Journal of Politics* 57(4): 941–70.

Reynolds, Richard. 2008. "Stand By Your Beds." *The Guardian,* April 25. Available at www.guardian.co.uk/environment/2008/apr/25/activists.conservation (accessed April 28, 2008).

Richards, David. 1990. "Sunday View: Sunday at the Dacha with Rooster." *New York Times,* November 4.

Richardson, Tanya. 2008. *Kaleidoscopic Odessa: History and Place in Contemporary Ukraine.* Toronto: University of Toronto Press.

Ries, Nancy. 1997. *Russian Talk: Culture and Conversation during Perestroika.* Ithaca, NY: Cornell University Press.

———. 2002. "'Honest Bandits' and 'Warped People': Russian Narratives about Money, Corruption, and Moral Decay." In *Ethnography in Unstable Places:*

Everyday Lives in Contexts of Dramatic Political Change, edited by Carol J. Greenhouse, Elizabeth Mertz, and Kay B. Warren. Durham, NC: Duke University Press.

Ritzer, George. 2004. *The Globalization of Nothing.* Thousand Oaks, CA: Pine Forge Press.

Roosevelt, Priscilla R. 1990. "Tatiana's Garden: Noble Sensibilities and Estate Park Design in the Romantic Era." *Slavic Review* 49(3): 335–49.

———. 1995. *Life on the Russian Country Estate: A Social and Cultural History.* New Haven, CT: Yale University Press.

Rosenberg, Tina. 1996. *The Haunted Land: Facing Europe's Ghosts after Communism.* New York: Vintage.

Rosin, R. Thomas. 2001. "From Garden Suburb to Olde City Ward: A Longitudinal Study of Social Process and Incremental Architecture in Jaipur, India." *Journal of Material Culture* 6(2): 165–92.

Rotenberg, Robert. 1995. *Landscape and Power in Vienna.* Baltimore, MD: Johns Hopkins University Press.

Rothstein, Halina, and Robert A. Rothstein. 1997. "The Beginnings of Soviet Culinary Arts." In *Food in Russian History and Culture,* edited by Musya Glants and Joyce Toomre, 177–94. Bloomington: Indiana University Press.

Sachs, Jeffrey D. 2005. *The End of Poverty: Economic Possibilities for Our Time.* New York: Penguin Books.

Salmon, Shawn. 2006. "Marketing Socialism: Inturist in the Late 1950s and Early 1960s." In *Turizm: The Russian and East European Tourist under Capitalism and Socialism,* edited by Anne E. Gorsuch and Diane P. Koenker, 186–204. Ithaca, NY: Cornell University Press.

Sampson, Steven. 1995. "All Is Possible, Nothing Is Certain: The Horizons of Transition in a Romanian Village." In *East European Communities: The Struggle for Balance in Turbulent Times,* edited by David Kideckel, 159–76. Boulder, CO: Westview Press.

Sassen, Saskia. 1991. *The Global City.* Princeton, NJ: Princeton University Press.

Schama, Simon. 1995. *Landscape and Memory.* New York: Vintage Books.

Schönle, Andreas. 2000. "Gogol, the Picturesque, and the Desire for the People: A Reading of 'Rome.'" *Russian Review* 59(4): 597–613.

Schwartz, Katrina Z.S. 2006. *Nature and National Identity after Communism: Globalizing the Ethnoscape.* Pittsburgh, PA: University of Pittsburgh Press.

Shevchenko, Olga. 2002a. "'Between the Holes': Emerging Identities and Hybrid Patterns of Consumption in Post-Socialist Russia." *Europe-Asia Studies* 54(6): 841–66.

———. 2002b. "'In Case of Emergency': Consumption, Security, and the Meaning of Durables in a Transforming Society." *Journal of Consumer Culture* 2(2): 147–70.

Shlapentokh, Vladimir. 1989. *Public and Private Life of the Soviet People: Changing Values in Post-Stalin Russia.* New York: Oxford University Press.

Shvidkovsky, Dmitry. 1996. "A Grandmother's Garden for the Heir to the Imperial Throne." *Garden History* 24(1): 107–13.

Skliarova, Irina. 2005. "Volchii billet v les." *Veche Tveri* 75(3657): 4.

Skultans, Vieda. 1998. *The Testimony of Lives: Narrative and Memory in Post-Soviet Latvia.* London: Routledge.

Smith, Jeff. 2003. "From *Hazi* to Hyper Market: Discourses on Time, Money, and Food in Hungary." *Anthropology of East Europe Review* 21(1): 179–88.

Soloukhin, Vladimir. 1988. *Scenes from Russian Life.* Translated by David Martin. London: Peter Owen Publishers.

———. 2006. *Kaplia Rosy.* Moscow: Russkii Mir'.

Ssorin-Chaikov, Nikolai V. 2003. *The Social Life of the State in Subarctic Siberia.* Stanford, CA: Stanford University Press.

Stanford, Lois. 2006. "The Role of Ideology in New Mexico's CSA (Community Supported Agriculture) Organizations: Conflicting Visions between Growers and Members." In *Fast Food/Slow Food: The Cultural Economy of the Global Food System,* edited by Richard Wilk, 181–200. Lanham, MD: Altamira Press.

Stangl, Paul. 2003. "The Soviet War Memorial in Treptow, Berlin." *Geographical Review* 93(2): 213–36.

Stebbins, Robert A. 2004. *Between Work and Leisure: The Common Ground of Two Separate Worlds.* New Brunswick, NJ: Transaction Publishers.

Stephen, Chris. 2005. "All Dash to the Dacha." *Irish Times,* August 23.

Stephenson, Svetlana. 2006. *Crossing the Line: Vagrancy, Homelessness and Social Displacement in Russia.* Aldershot, England: Ashgate.

Stewart, Kathleen C. 1996a. "An Occupied Place." In *Senses of Place,* edited by Steven Feld and Keith H. Basso, 137–65. Santa Fe, NM: School of American Research Press.

———. 1996b. *A Space on the Side of the Road: Cultural Poetics in an "Other" America.* Princeton, NJ: Princeton University Press.

Struyk, Raymond J., and Karen Angelici. 1996. "The Russian Dacha Phenomenon." *Housing Studies* 11(2): 233–50.

Sunderland, Willard. 2004. *Taming the Wild Field: Colonization and Empire in the Russian Steppe.* Ithaca, NY: Cornell University Press.

Thompson, Gary D., and Julia Kidwell. 1998. "Explaining the Choice of Organic Produce: Cosmetic Defects, Prices, and Consumer Preferences." *American Journal of Agricultural Economics* 80(2): 277–87.

Toohey, Nathan. 2007. "MushieHunting at the Market." *Moscow Times,* September 19. Available at www.moscowtimes.ru/stories/2007/09/19/026-print.html (accessed September 19, 2007).

Tsing, Anna Lowenhaupt. 1993. *In the Realm of the Diamond Queen: Marginality in an Out-of-the-Way Place.* Princeton, NJ: Princeton University Press.

———. 2005. *Friction: An Ethnography of Global Connection.* Princeton, NJ: Princeton University Press.

Tumarkin, Nina. 1994. *The Living and the Dead: The Rise and Fall of the Cult of World War II in Russia.* New York: Basic Books.

Van Atta, Don. 1993a. "Introduction." In *The "Farmer Threat": The Political Economy of Agrarian Reform in Post-Soviet Russia,* edited by Don Van Atta, 1–5. Boulder, CO: Westview Press.

———. 1993b. "The Return of Individual Farming in Russia." In *The "Farmer Threat": The Political Economy of Agrarian Reform in Post-Soviet Russia,* edited by Don Van Atta, 71–95. Boulder, CO: Westview Press.

Valentino, Russell S. 1996. "A Wolf in Arkadia: Generic Fields, Generic Counter-statement and the Resources of Pastoral in *Fathers and Sons*." *Russian Review* 55(3): 475–93.

Vari, Alexander. 2006. "From Friends of Nature to Tourist-Soldiers: Nation Building and Tourism in Hungary, 1873–1914." In *Turizm: The Russian and East European Tourist under Capitalism and Socialism,* edited by Anne E. Gorsuch and Diane P. Koenker, 64–81. Ithaca, NY: Cornell University Press.

Verdery, Katherine. 1996. *What Was Socialism and What Comes Next?* Princeton, NJ: Princeton University Press.

———. 1999. *The Political Lives of Dead Bodies: Reburial and Postsocialist Change.* New York: Columbia University Press.

———. 2002 "Whither Postsocialism?" In *Postsocialism: Ideals, Ideologies and Practices in Eurasia,* edited by C. M. Hann, 15–21. London: Routledge.

Vitebsky, Piers. 2002. "Withdrawing from the Land: Social and Spiritual Crisis in the Indigenous Russian Arctic." In *Postsocialism: Ideals, Ideologies and Practices in Eurasia,* edited by C. M. Hann, 180–95. London: Routledge.

Wädekin, Karl-Eugen. 1980. "Round-Table Discussion on Private Food Production and Marketing." *Radio Liberty Research Bulletin,* RFE/RL 449(80): 1–4.

Wedel, Janine R. 1998. *Collision and Collusion: The Strange Case of Western Aid to Eastern Europe, 1989–1998.* New York: St. Martin's Press.

Wegren, Stephen K. 1993. "Political Institutions and Agrarian Reform in Russia." In *The "Farmer Threat": The Political Economy of Agrarian Reform in Post-Soviet Russia,* edited by Don Van Atta, 121–47. Boulder, CO: Westview Press.

———. 1995. "Rural Migration and Agrarian Reform in Russia: A Research Note." *Europe-Asia Studies* 47(5): 877–88.

Weiner, Douglas. R. 2000 [1998]. *Models of Nature: Ecology, Conservation and Cultural Revolution in Soviet Russia.* Pittsburgh, PA: University of Pittsburgh Press.

Williams, Raymond. 1973. *The Country and the City.* New York: Oxford University Press.

Worobec, Christine D. 1995. *Peasant Russia: Family and Community in the Post-Emancipation Period.* DeKalb: Northern Illinois University Press.

Young, Cathy. 1989. *Growing Up in Moscow: Memories of a Soviet Girlhood.* New York: Ticknor & Fields.

Yuen, Belinda. 1996. "Creating the Garden City: The Singapore Experience." *Urban Studies* 33(6): 955–70.

Yurchak, Alexei. 2006. *Everything Was Forever, Until It Was No More: The Last Soviet Generation.* Princeton, NJ: Princeton University Press.

Zarger, Rebecca. 2008. "School Garden Pedagogies." *Anthropology News* 49(4): 8–9.

Zavisca, Jane. 2003. "Contesting Capitalism at the Post-Soviet Dacha: The Meaning of Food Cultivation for Urban Russians." *Slavic Review* 62(4): 786–810.

Index

Text
10/13 Sabon

DISPLAY
Sabon

COMPOSITOR
BookMatters, Berkeley

PRINTER AND BINDER
Maple-Vail Book Manufacturing Group

www.ingramcontent.com/pod-product-compliance
Lightning Source LLC
Chambersburg PA
CBHW020350270326
41926CB00007B/381